Mastering Algorithms with C

Mastering Algorithms with C

Harish Gupta

ANMOL PUBLICATIONS PVT. LTD.
NEW DELHI-110 002 (INDIA)

ANMOL PUBLICATIONS PVT. LTD.
Regd. Office: 4360/4, Ansari Road, Daryaganj,
New Delhi-110002 (India)
Tel.: 23278000, 23261597, 23286875, 23255577
Fax: 91-11-23280289
Email: anmolpub@gmail.com
Visit us at: www.anmolpublications.com

Branch Office: No. 1015, Ist Main Road, BSK IIIrd Stage
IIIrd Phase, IIIrd Block, Bangalore-560 085 (India)
Tel.: 080-41723429 • Fax: 080-26723604
Email: anmolpublicationsbangalore@gmail.com

Mastering Algorithms with C

First Edition, 2010

ISBN 978-81-261-4384-9

PRINTED IN INDIA

Printed at Mehra Offset Press, Delhi.

Contents

Preface

This book is intended to be a textbook which helps in study and teaching of Algorithms with C language and helps in mastering them. Its purpose is to assist the students and teacher to do the great work of every instructor in field of Computer Programming and in writing Algorithms. To this end, care has been taken to select and emphasize those facts and events, which illustrate the real character of the people, which shows the progressive development and explain the influence that exercised upon modern civilization.

The book has many aspects and interest in study of Computer Language and Algorithms Programming, which becomes intensified to the extent that unity is perceived. The attempt has been made, therefore, to keep before the mind of the Computer students the real sequence of events. The early stages of Computer evolutions presented according to what we believe to be the most plausible and scientific views. The students should of course understand that the study of Computer Algorithms and its related Programming tools, which are largely based upon the intelligence and inferences. For the purpose of encouraging the reading of this book, each chapter is supplemented by extra explanation, diagrams and illustrations.

Author

Chapter 1

Introduction

ALGORITHM

An algorithm is any set of detailed instructions which results in a predictable end-state from a known beginning. Algorithms are only as good as the instructions given, however, and the result will be incorrect if the algorithm is not properly defined....In mathematics, computing, linguistics, and related disciplines, an algorithm is a definite list of well-defined instructions for completing a task.

C- LANGUAGE

C is a relatively small language, but one which wears well. C's small, unambitious feature set is a real advantage: there's less to learn; there isn't excess baggage in the way when you don't need it. It can also be a disadvantage: since it doesn't do everything for you, there's a lot you have to do yourself.

C is sometimes referred to as a "high-level assembly language." Some people think that's an insult, but it's actually a deliberate and significant aspect of the language. If you have programmed in assembly language, you'll probably find C very natural and comfortable (although if you continue to focus too heavily on machine-level details, you'll probably end up with unnecessarily nonportable programs). If you haven't programmed in assembly language, you may be frustrated by C's lack of certain higher-level features. In either case, you should understand why C was designed this way: so that seemingly-simple constructions expressed in C would not expand to arbitrarily expensive (in time or space) machine language constructions when compiled. If you write a C programme simply and succinctly, it is likely to result in a succinct, efficient machine language executable. If you find that the executable programme resulting from a C programme is not efficient, it's probably because of something silly you did, not because of something the compiler did behind your back which you have no control over. In any case, there's no point in complaining about C's low-level flavour: C is what it is.

A programming language is a tool, and no tool can perform every task unaided. If you're building a house, and I'm teaching you how to use a hammer, and you ask how to assemble rafters and trusses into gables, that's a legitimate question, but the answer has fallen out of the realm of "How do I use a hammer?" and into "How do I build a house?". In the same way, we'll see that C does not have built-in features to perform every function that we might ever need to do while programming.

As mentioned above, C imposes relatively few built-in ways of doing things on the programmer. Some common tasks, such as manipulating strings, allocating memory, and doing input/output (I/O), are performed by calling on library functions. Other tasks which you might want to do, such as creating or listing directories, or interacting with a mouse, or displaying windows or other user-interface elements, or doing colour graphics, are not defined by the C language at all. You can do these things from a C programme, of course, but you will be calling on services which are peculiar to your programming environment (compiler, processor, and operating system) and which are not defined by the C standard. Since this course is about portable C programming, it will also be steering clear of facilities not provided in all C environments.

Another aspect of C that's worth mentioning here is that it is, to put it bluntly, a bit dangerous. C does not, in general, try hard to protect a programmer from mistakes. If you write a piece of code which will (through some oversight of yours) do something wildly different from what you intended it to do, up to and including deleting your data or trashing your disk, and if it is possible for the compiler to compile it, it generally will. You won't get warnings of the form "Do you really mean to...?" or "Are you sure you really want to...?". C is often compared to a sharp knife: it can do a surgically precise job on some exacting task you have in mind, but it can also do a surgically precise job of cutting off your finger. It's up to you to use it carefully.

This aspect of C is very widely criticized; it is also used (justifiably) to argue that C is not a good teaching language. C aficionados love this aspect of C because it means that C does not try to protect them from themselves: when they know what they're doing, even if it's risky or obscure, they can do it. Students of C hate this aspect of C because it often seems as if the language is some kind of a conspiracy specifically designed to lead them into booby traps. This is another aspect of the language which it's fairly pointless to complain about. If you take care and pay attention, you can avoid many of the pitfalls. These notes will point out many of the obvious (and not so obvious) trouble spots.

EXAMPLES

FIRST EXAMPLE

The best way to learn programming is to dive right in and start writing real programs. This way, concepts which would otherwise seem abstract make sense, and the positive feedback you get from getting even a small programme to work gives you a great incentive to improve it or write the next one.

Diving in with "real" programs right away has another advantage, if only pragmatic: if you're using a conventional compiler, you can't run a fragment of a programme and see what it does; nothing will run until you have a complete (if tiny or trivial) programme. You can't learn everything you'd need to write a complete programme all at once, so you'll have to take some things "on faith" and parrot them in your first programs before you begin to understand them. (You can't learn to programme just one expression or statement at a time any more than you can learn to speak a foreign language one word at a time. If all you know is a handful of words, you can't actually *say* anything: you also need to know something about the language's word order and grammar and sentence structure and declension of articles and verbs.)

Besides the occasional necessity to take things on faith, there is a more serious potential drawback of this "dive in and programme" approach: it's a small step from learning-by-doing to learning-by-trial-and-error, and when you learn programming by trial-and-error, you can very easily learn many errors. When you're not sure whether something will work, or you're not even sure what you could use that might work, and you try something, and it does work, you do *not* have any guarantee that what you tried worked for the right reason. You might just have "learned" something that works only by accident or only on your compiler, and it may be very hard to un-learn it later, when it stops working.

Therefore, whenever you're not sure of something, be very careful before you go off and try it "just to see if it will work." Of course, you can never be absolutely sure that something is going to work before you try it, otherwise we'd never have to try things. But you should have an expectation that something is going to work before you try it, and if you can't predict how to do something or whether something would work and find yourself having to determine it experimentally, make a note in your mind that whatever you've just learned (based on the outcome of the experiment) is suspect.

The first example programme is the first example programme in any language: print or display a simple string, and exit.

Here is "hello, world" programme:

```
#include <stdio.h>
main()
{
   printf("Hello, world!\n");
   return 0;
}
```

If you have a C compiler, the first thing to do is figure out how to type this programme in and compile it and run it and see where its output went.The first line is practically boilerplate; it will appear in almost all programs we write. It asks that some definitions having to do with the "Standard I/ O Library" be included in our programme; these definitions are needed if we are to call the library function printf correctly.

The second line says that we are defining a function named main. Most of the time, we can name our functions anything we want, but the function name main is special: it is the function that will be "called" first when our programme starts running. The empty pair of parentheses indicates that our main function accepts no*arguments*, that is, there isn't any information which needs to be passed in when the function is called. The braces { and } surround a list of statements in C. Here, they surround the list of statements making up the function main.

The line,

```
printf("Hello, world!\n");
```

is the first statement in the programme. It asks that the function printf be called; printf is a library function which prints formatted output. The parentheses surroundprintf's argument list: the information which is handed to it which it should act on. The semicolon at the end of the line terminates the statement.

Printf's name reflects the fact that C was first developed when Teletypes and other printing terminals were still in widespread use. Today, of course, video displays are far more common. printf's "prints" to the *standard output,* that is, to the default location for programme output to go. Nowadays, that's almost always a video screen or a window on that screen. If you do have a printer, you'll typically have to do something extra to get a programme to print to it.

Printf's first (and, in this case, only) argument is the string which it should print. The string, enclosed in double quotes "", consists of the words "Hello, world!" followed by a special sequence: \n. In strings, any two-character sequence beginning with the backslash \ represents a single special character. The sequence \nrepresents the "new line" character, which prints a carriage return or line feed or whatever it takes to end one line of output and move down to the next. (This programme only prints one line of output, but it's still important to terminate it.)

The second line in the main function is,

```
return 0;
```

In general, a function may return a value to its caller, and main is no exception. When main returns (that is, reaches its end and stops functioning), the programme is at its end, and the return value from main tells the operating system (or whatever invoked the programme that main is the main function of) whether it succeeded or not. By convention, a return value of 0 indicates success.

This programme may look so absolutely trivial that it seems as if it's not even worth typing it in and trying to run it, but doing so may be a big (and is certainly a vital) first hurdle. On an unfamiliar computer, it can be arbitrarily difficult to figure out how to enter a text file containing programme source, or how to compile and link it, or how to invoke it, or what happened after (if?) it ran. The most experienced C programmers immediately go back to this one, simple programme whenever they're trying out a new system or a new way of entering or building programs or a new way of printing output from within programs. As Kernighan and Ritchie say, everything else is comparatively easy.

How *you* compile and run this (or any) programme is a function of the compiler and operating system you're using. The first step is to type it in, exactly as shown; this may involve using a text editor to create a file containing the programme text. You'll have to give the file a name, and all C compilers require that files containing C source end with the extension .c. So you might place the programme text in a file called hello.c.

The second step is to compile the programme. (Strictly speaking, compilation consists of two steps, compilation proper followed by linking, but we can overlook this distinction at first, especially because the compiler often takes care of initiating the linking step automatically.) On many Unix systems, the command to compile a C programme from a source file hello.c is,

```
cc -o hello hello.c
```

You would type this command at the Unix shell prompt, and it requests that the cc (C compiler) programme be run, placing its output (i.e. the new executable programme it creates) in the file hello, and taking its input (i.e. the source code to be compiled) from the file hello.c.

The third step is to run (execute, invoke) the newly-built hello programme. Again on a Unix system, this is done simply by typing the program's name:

```
hello
```

Depending on how your system is set up (in particular, on whether the current directory is searched for executables, based on the PATH variable), you may have to type,

```
./hello
```

to indicate that the hello programme is in the current directory (as opposed to some "bin" directory full of executable programs, elsewhere).

You may also have your choice of C compilers. On many Unix machines, the cc command is an older compiler which does not recognize modern, ANSI Standard C syntax. An old compiler will accept the simple programs we'll be starting with, but it will not accept most of our later programs. If you find yourself getting baffling compilation errors on programs which you've typed in exactly as they're shown, it probably indicates that you're using an older compiler. On many machines, another compiler called acc or gcc is available, and you'll want to use it, instead.

One final caveat about Unix systems: don't name your test programs test, because there's already a standard command called test, and you and the command interpreter will get badly confused if you try to replace the system's test command with your own, not least because your own almost certainly does something completely different.

Under MS-DOS, the compilation procedure is quite similar. The name of the command you type will depend on your compiler (e.g. cl for the Microsoft C compiler,tc or bcc for Borland's Turbo C, etc.). You may have to manually perform the second, linking step, perhaps with a command named link or tlink. The executable file which the compiler/linker creates will have a name ending in .exe (or perhaps .com), but you can still invoke it by typing the base name (e.g. hello). See your compiler documentation for complete details; one of the manuals should contain a demonstration of how to enter, compile, and run a small programme that prints some simple output, just as we're trying to describe here.

In an integrated or "visual" progamming environment, such as those on the Macintosh or under various versions of Microsoft Windows, the steps you take to enter, compile, and run a programme are somewhat different (and, theoretically, simpler). Typically, there is a way to open a new source window, type source code into it, give it a file name, and add it to the programme (or "project") you're building. If necessary, there will be a way to specify what other source files (or "modules") make up the programme.

Then, there's a button or menu selection which compiles and runs the programme, all from within the programming environment. In a PC-compatible environment, you may have to choose between creating DOS programs or Windows programs.

If you have troubles pertaining to the printf function, try specifying a target environment of MS-DOS. Supposedly, some compilers which are targeted at Windows environments won't let you call printf, because until you call some fancier functions to request that a window be created, there's no window for printf to print to. Again, check the introductory or tutorial manual that came with the programming package; it should walk you through the steps necessary to get your first programme running.

SECOND EXAMPLE

Our second example is of little more practical use than the first, but it introduces a few more programming language elements:

```
#include <stdio.h>
/* print a few numbers, to illustrate a simple
```

```
loop */
main()
{
int i;
for(i = 0; i < 10; i = i + 1)
   printf("i is %d\n", i);
return 0;
}
```

As before, the line #include <stdio.h> is boilerplate which is necessary since we're calling the printf function, and main() and the pair of braces {} indicate and delineate the function named main we're (again) writing.

The first new line is the line

```
/* print a few numbers, to illustrate a simple
loop */
```

which is a *comment*. Anything between the characters /* and */ is ignored by the compiler, but may be useful to a person trying to read and understand the programme. You can add comments anywhere you want to in the programme, to document what the programme is, what it does, who wrote it, how it works, what the various functions are for and how *they* work, what the various variables are for, etc.

The second new line, down within the function main, is

```
int i;
```

which *declares* that our function will use a variable named i. The variable's type is int, which is a plain integer.

Next, we set up a *loop*:

```
for(i = 0; i < 10; i = i + 1)
```

The keyword for indicates that we are setting up a "for loop." A for loop is controlled by three expressions, enclosed in parentheses and separated by semicolons. These expressions say that, in this case, the loop starts by setting i to 0, that it continues as long as i is less than 10, and that after each iteration of the loop, i should be incremented by 1 (that is, have 1 added to its value).

Finally, we have a call to the printf function, as before, but with several differences. First, the call to printf is within the *body* of the for loop. This means that control flow does not pass once through the printf call, but instead that the call is performed as many times as are dictated by the for loop. In this case, printfwill be called several times: once when i is 0, once when i is 1, once when i is 2, and so on until i is 9, for a total of 10 times.

A second difference in the printf call is that the string to be printed, "i is %d", contains a per cent sign. When ever printf sees a per cent sign, it indicates thatprintf is not supposed to print the exact text of the string, but is instead supposed to read another one of its arguments to decide what to print. The letter after the per cent sign tells it what type of argument to expect and how to print it. In this case, the letter d indicates that printf is to expect an int, and to print it in decimal. Finally, we see that printf is in fact being called with another argument, for a total of two, separated by commas. The second argument is the variable i, which is in fact an int, as required by %d. The effect of all of this is that each time it is called, printf will print a line containing the current value of the variable i:

```
i is 0
i is 1
i is 2
...
```

After several trips through the loop, i will eventually equal 9. After that trip through the loop, the third control expression i = i + 1 will increment its value to 10. The condition i < 10 is no longer true, so no more trips through the loop are taken. Instead, control flow jumps down to the statement following the for loop, which is the return statement. The main function returns, and the programme is finished.

PROGRAMME STRUCTURE

We'll have more to say later about programme structure, but for now let's observe a few basics. A programme consists of one or more functions; it may also contain global variables. (Our two example programs so far have contained one function apiece, and no global variables.) At the top of a source file are typically a few boilerplate lines such as #include

<stdio.h>, followed by the definitions (i.e. code) for the functions. (It's also possible to split up the several functions making up a larger programme into several source files, as we'll see in a later chapter.)

Each function is further composed of *declarations* and *statements*, in that order. When a sequence of statements should act as one (for example, when they should all serve together as the body of a loop) they can be enclosed in braces (just as for the outer body of the entire function).

The simplest kind of statement is an *expression statement*, which is an expression (presumably performing some useful operation) followed by a semicolon. Expressions are further composed of *operators*, *objects*(variables), and *constants*.

C source code consists of several *lexical elements*. Some are words, such as for, return, main, and i, which are either *keywords* of the language (for, return) or *identifiers* (names) we've chosen for our own functions and variables (main, i). There are *constants* such as 1 and 10 which introduce new values into the programme.

There are *operators* such as =, +, and >, which manipulate variables and values. There are other punctuation characters (often called *delimiters*), such as parentheses and squiggly braces {}, which indicate how the other elements of the programme are grouped. Finally, all of the preceding elements can be separated by*whitespace*: spaces, tabs, and the "carriage returns" between lines.

The source code for a C programme is, for the most part, "free form." This means that the compiler does not care how the code is arranged: how it is broken into lines, how the lines are indented, or whether whitespace is used between things like variable names and other punctuation.

Lines like #include <stdio.h> are an exception; they must appear alone on their own lines, generally unbroken. Only lines beginning with # are affected by this rule; we'll see other examples later. You can use whitespace, indentation, and appropriate line breaks to make your programs more readable for yourself and other people (even though the compiler doesn't care). You can place explanatory *comments* anywhere in your programme—any text between the characters /* and */ is ignored by the compiler. (In fact, the compiler pretends that all it saw was whitespace.) Though comments are ignored by the compiler, well-chosen comments can make a programme *much* easier to read.

The usage of whitespace is our first *style* issue. It's typical to leave a blank line between different parts of the programme, to leave a space on either side of operators such as + and =, and to *indent* the bodies of loops and other control flow constructs.

Typically, we arrange the indentation so that the subsidiary statements controlled by a loop statement (the "loop body," such as the printf call in our second example programme) are all aligned with each other and placed one tab stop (or some consistent number of spaces) to the right of the controlling statement.

This indentation (like all whitespace) is not required by the compiler, but it makes programs*much* easier to read. (However, it can also be misleading, if used incorrectly or in the face of inadvertent mistakes.

The compiler will decide what "the body of the loop" is based on its own rules, not the indentation, so if the indentation does not match the compiler's interpretation, confusion is inevitable.)

To drive home the point that the compiler doesn't care about indentation, line breaks, or other whitespace, here are a few (extreme) examples:

The fragments,

```
for(i = 0; i < 10; i = i + 1)
printf("%d\n", i);
```

and

```
for(i = 0; i < 10; i = i + 1) printf("%d\n",
i);
```

and

```
for(i=0;i<10;i=i+1)printf("%d\n",i);
```

and

```
for(i = 0; i < 10; i = i + 1)
printf("%d\n", i);
```

```
and
for    (   i
=  0   ;
i  <  10
;  i   =
i   +  1
)  printf  (
"%d\n" ,    i
)   ;
and
for
(i=0;
i<10;i=
i+1)printf
("%d\n", i);
```

are all treated exactly the same way by the compiler. Some programmers argue forever over the best set of "rules" for indentation and other aspects of programming style, calling to mind the old philosopher's debates about the number of angels that could dance on the head of a pin.

Style issues (such as how a programme is laid out) *are* important, but they're not something to be too dogmatic about, and there are also other, deeper style issues besides mere layout and typography:

Although C compilers do not care about how a programme looks, proper indentation and spacing are critical in making programs easy for people to read. We recommend writing only one statement per line, and using blanks around operators to clarify grouping.

The position of braces is less important, although people hold passionate beliefs. We have chosen one of several popular styles. Pick a style that suits you, then use it consistently.

There is some value in having a reasonably standard style (or a few standard styles) for code layout. Please don't take the above advice to "pick a style that suits you" as an invitation to invent your own brand-new style.

If (perhaps after you've been programming in C for a while) you have specific objections to specific facets of existing styles, you're welcome to modify them, but if you don't have any particular leanings, you're probably best off copying an existing style at first. (If you want to place your own stamp of originality on the programs that you write, there are better avenues for your creativity than inventing a bizarre layout; you might instead try to make the logic easier to follow, or the user interface easier to use, or the code freer of bugs.)

Chapter 2

Study of Data Types and Operators

VARIABLE TYPES

The *type* of a variable determines what kinds of values it may take on. An *operator* computes new values out of old ones. An *expression* consists of variables, constants, and operators combined to perform some useful computation. In this chapter, we'll learn about C's basic types, how to write constants and declare variables of these types, and what the basic operators are.

There are several implications to remember:

- The "set of values" is finite. C's int type can not represent *all* of the integers; its float type can not represent *all* floating-point numbers.
- When you're using an object (that is, a variable) of some type, you may have to remember what values it can take on and what operations you can perform on it. For example, there are several operators which play with the binary (bit-level) representation of integers, but these operators are not meaningful for and may not be applied to floating-point operands.
- When declaring a new variable and picking a type for it, you have to keep in mind the values and operations you'll be needing.

TYPES

There are only a few basic data types in C. The first ones we'll be encountering and using are:

- Char a character
- Int an integer, in the range -32,767 to 32,767
- Long int a larger integer (up to +-2,147,483,647)
- Float a floating-point number
- Double a floating-point number, with more precision and perhaps greater range than float

If you can look at this list of basic types and say to yourself, "Oh, how simple, there are only a few types, I won't have to worry much about choosing among them," you'll have an easy time with declarations. Some masochists wish that the type system were more complicated so that they could specify more things about each variable, but those of us who would rather not have to specify these extra things each time are glad that we don't have to.

The ranges listed above for types int and long int are the guaranteed minimum ranges. On some systems, either of these types (or, indeed, any C type) may be able to hold larger values, but a programme that depends on extended ranges will not be as portable.

Some programmers become obsessed with knowing exactly what the sizes of data objects will be in various situations, and go on to write programs which depend on these exact sizes.

Determining or controlling the size of an object is occasionally important, but most of the time we can sidestep size issues and let the compiler do most of the worrying. From the ranges listed above, we can determine that type int must be at least 16 bits, and that type long int must be at least 32 bits. But neither of these sizes is exact; many systens have 32-bit ints, and some systems have 64-bit long ints.

You might wonder how the computer stores characters. The answer involves a *character set,* which is simply a mapping between some set of characters and some set of small numeric codes. Most machines today use the ASCII character set, in which the letter A is represented by the code 65, the ampersand & is represented by the code 38, the digit 1 is represented by the code 49, the space character is represented by the code 32, etc. (Most of the time, of course, you have *no* need to know or even worry about these particular code values; they're automatically translated into the right shapes on the screen or printer when characters are printed out, and they're automatically generated when you type characters on the keyboard.

Eventually, though, we'll appreciate, and even take some control over, exactly when these translations—from characters to their numeric codes—are performed.) Character codes are usually small—the largest code value in ASCII is 126, which is the ~ (tilde or circumflex) character. Characters usually fit in a byte, which is usually 8 bits. In C, type char is defined as occupying one byte, so it is usually 8 bits.

Most of the simple variables in most programs are of types int, long int, or double. Typically, we'll use int anddouble for most purposes, and long int any time we need to hold integer values greater than 32,767. As we'll see, even when we're manipulating individual characters, we'll usually use an int variable, for reasons to be discussed later. Therefore, we'll rarely use individual variables of type char; although we'll use plenty of arrays of char.

CONSTANTS

A *constant* is just an immediate, absolute value found in an expression. The simplest constants are decimal integers, e.g. 0,1, 2, 123 .

Occasionally it is useful to specify constants in base 8 or base 16 (octal or hexadecimal); this is done by prefixing an extra 0 (zero) for octal, or 0 × for hexadecimal: the constants 100, 0144, and 0 × 64 all represent the same number. (If you're not using these non-decimal constants, just remember not to use any leading zeroes. If you accidentally write 0123 intending to get one hundred and twenty three, you'll get 83 instead, which is 123 base 8.)

We write constants in decimal, octal, or hexadecimal for our convenience, not the compiler's. The compiler doesn't care; it always converts everything into binary internally, anyway. (There is, however, no good way to specify constants in source code in binary.)

A constant can be forced to be of type long int by suffixing it with the letter L (in upper or lower case, although upper case is strongly recommended, because a lower case l looks too much like the digit 1).

A constant that contains a decimal point or the letter e (or both) is a floating-point constant: 3.14, 10..01, 123e4, 123.456e7 . The e indicates multiplication by a power of 10; 123.456e7 is 123.456 times 10 to the 7th, or 1,234,560,000. (Floating-point constants are of type double by default.)

We also have constants for specifying characters and strings. (Make sure you understand the difference between a character and a string: a character is exactly one character; a string is a set of zero or more characters; a string containing one character is distinct from a lone character.) A character constant is simply a single character between single quotes:'A', '.', '%'. The numeric value of a character constant is, naturally enough, that character's value in the machine's character set. (In ASCII, for example, 'A' has the value 65.)

A *string* is represented in C as a sequence or array of characters. A string constant is a sequence of zero or more characters enclosed in double quotes: "apple","hello, world", "this is a test".

Within character and string constants, the backslash character \ is special, and is used to represent characters not easily typed on the keyboard or for various reasons not easily typed in constants.

The most common of these "character escapes" are:

```
\n a "newline" character
\b a backspace
\r a carriage return (without a line feed)
\' a single quote (e.g. in a character constant)
\" a double quote (e.g. in a string constant)
\\ a single backslash
```

For example, "he said \"hi\"" is a string constant which contains two double quotes, and '\'' is a character constant consisting of a (single) single quote. Notice once again that the character constant 'A' is very different from the string constant "A".

DECLARATIONS

Informally, a *variable* (also called an *object*) is a place you can store a value. So that you can refer to it unambiguously, a variable needs a name. You can think of the variables in your programme as a set of boxes or cubbyholes, each with a label giving its name; you might imagine that storing a value "in" a variable consists of writing the value on a slip of paper and placing it in the cubbyhole.

A *declaration* tells the compiler the name and type of a variable you'll be using in your programme. In its simplest form, a declaration consists of the type, the name of the variable, and a terminating semicolon:

```
char c;
int i;
float f;
```

You can also declare several variables of the same type in one declaration, separating them with commas:

```
int i1, i2;
```

Later we'll see that declarations may also contain *in*itializers, qualifiers and storage classes, and that we can declare arrays,functions, pointers, and other kinds of data structures.

The placement of declarations is significant. You can't place them just anywhere (i.e. they cannot be interspersed with the other statements in your programme). They must either be placed at the beginning of a function, or at the beginning of a brace-enclosed block of statements (which we'll learn about in the next chapter), or outside of any function. Furthermore, the placement of a declaration, as well as its storage class, controls several things about its *visibility* and *lifetime,* You may wonder *why* variables must be declared before use.

There are two reasons:

- It makes things somewhat easier on the compiler; it knows right away what kind of storage to allocate and what code to emit to store and manipulate each variable; it doesn't have to try to intuit the programmer's intentions.

- It forces a bit of useful discipline on the programmer: you cannot introduce variables willy-nilly; you must think about them enough to pick appropriate types for them. (The compiler's error messages to you, telling you that you apparently forgot to declare a variable, are as often helpful as they are a nuisance: they're helpful when they tell you that you misspelled a variable, or forgot to think about exactly how you were going to use it.)

Although there are a few places where declarations can be omitted (in which case the compiler will assume an implicit declaration), making use of these removes the advantages of reason 2 above, so I recommend always declaring everything explicitly.

Most of the time, I recommend writing one declaration per line. For the most part, the compiler doesn't care what order declarations are in.

You can order the declarations alphabetically, or in the order that they're used, or to put related declarations next to each other. Collecting all variables of the same type together on one line essentially orders declarations by type, which isn't a very useful order (it's only slightly more useful than random order).

A declaration for a variable can also contain an initial value. This *initializer* consists of an equals sign and an expression, which is usually a single constant:

```
int i = 1;
int i1 = 10, i2 = 20;
```

VARIABLE NAMES

Within limits, you can give your variables and functions any names you want. These names (the formal term is "identifiers") consist of letters, numbers, and underscores. For our purposes, names must begin with a letter.

Theoretically, names can be as long as you want, but extremely long ones get tedious to type after a while, and the compiler is not required to keep track of extremely long ones perfectly. (What this means is that if you were to name a variable, say,supercalafragalisticespialidocious, the compiler might get lazy and pretend that you'd named it super calafragalisticespialidocio, such that if you later misspelled itsupercalafragalisticespialidociouz, the compiler wouldn't catch your mistake.

Nor would the compiler necessarily be able to tell the difference if for some perverse reason you *deliberately* declared a second variable namedsupercalafragalisticespialidociouz.)

The capitalization of names in C is significant: the variable names variable, Variable, and VARIABLE (as well as silly combinations like variAble) are all distinct.

A final restriction on names is that you may not use *keywords* (the words such as int and for which are part of the syntax of the language) as the names of variables or functions (or as identifiers of any kind).

ARITHMETIC OPERATORS

The basic operators for performing arithmetic are the same in many computer languages:

```
+  addition
-  subtraction
*  multiplication
/  division
%  modulus (remainder)
```

The - operator can be used in two ways: to subtract two numbers (as in a - b), or to negate one number (as in -a + bor a + -b). When applied to integers, the division operator / discards any remainder, so 1/ 2 is 0 and 7/ 4 is 1. But when either operand is a floating-point quantity (type float or double), the division operator yields a floating-point result, with a potentially nonzero fractional part. So 1/ 2.0 is 0.5, and 7.0/ 4.0 is 1.75.

The *modulus* operator % gives you the remainder when two integers are divided: 1 % 2 is 1; 7 % 4 is 3.

An additional arithmetic operation you might be wondering about is exponentiation. Some languages have an exponentiation operator (typically ^ or **), but C doesn't. (To square or cube a number, just multiply it by itself.)

Multiplication, division, and modulus all have higher *precedence* than addition and subtraction. The term "precedence" refers to how "tightly" operators bind to their operands (that is, to the things they operate on). In mathematics, multiplication has higher precedence than addition, so 1 + 2 * 3 is 7, not 9. In other words, 1 + 2 * 3 is equivalent to1 + (2 * 3). C is the same way.

All of these operators "group" from left to right, which means that when two or more of them have the same precedence and participate next to each other in an expression, the evaluation conceptually proceeds from left to right.

For example, 1 - 2 - 3 is equivalent to (1 - 2) - 3 and gives -4, not +2. ("Grouping" is sometimes called *associativity*, although the term is used somewhat differently in programming than it is in mathematics. Not all C operators group from left to right; a few group from right to left.)

Whenever the default precedence or associativity doesn't give you the grouping you want, you can always use explicit parentheses.

For example, if you wanted to add 1 to 2 and then multiply the result by 3, you could write (1 + 2) * 3. By the way, the word "arithmetic" as used in the title of this section is an adjective, not a noun, and it's pronounced differently than the noun: the accent is on the third syllable.

ASSIGNMENT OPERATORS

The assignment operator = assigns a value to a variable.

For example,

```
x = 1
```

sets x to 1, and

```
a = b
```

sets a to whatever b's value is. The expression

```
i = i + 1
```

is, as we've mentioned elsewhere, the standard programming idiom for increasing a variable's value by 1: this expression takes i's old value, adds 1 to it, and stores it back into i. (C provides several "shortcut" operators for modifying variables in this and similar ways, which we'll meet later.)

We've called the = sign the "assignment operator" and referred to "assignment expressions" because, in fact, = *is* an operator just like + or -. C does not have "assignment statements"; instead, an assignment like a = b is an expression and can be used wherever any expression can appear. Since it's an expression, the assignment a = b has a value, namely, the same value that's assigned to a. This value can then be used in a larger expression; for example, we might write

```
c = a = b
which is equivalent to
c = (a = b)
```

and assigns b's value to both a and c. (The assignment operator, therefore, groups from right to left.).

It's usually a matter of style whether you initialize a variable with an initializer in its declaration or with an assignment expression near where you first use it. That is, there's no particular difference between,

```
int a = 10;
and
int a;
/* later... */
a = 10;
```

FUNCTION CALLS

We'll have much more to say about functions in a later chapter, but for now let's just look at how they're called.You call a function by mentioning its name followed by a pair of parentheses. If the function takes any arguments, you place the arguments between the parentheses, separated by commas.

These are all function calls:

```
printf("Hello, world!\n")
printf("%d\n", i)
sqrt(144.)
getchar()
```

The arguments to a function can be arbitrary expressions. Therefore, you don't have to say things like,

int sum = a + b + c;

printf("sum = %d\n", sum);

if you don't want to; you can instead collapse it to,

```
printf("sum = %d\n", a + b + c);
```

Many functions return values, and when they do, you can embed calls to these functions within larger expressions:

```
c = sqrt(a * a + b * b)
x = r * cos(theta)
i = f1(f2(j))
```

The first expression squares a and b, computes the square root of the sum of the squares, and assigns the result to c. (In other words, it computes a * a + b * b, passes that number to the sqrt function, and assigns sqrt's return value toc.) The second expression passes the value of the variable theta to the cos (cosine) function, multiplies the result by r, and assigns the result to x. The third expression passes the value of the variable j to the function f2, passes the return value of f2 immediately to the function f1, and finally assigns f1's return value to the variable i.

Chapter 3

Statements and Control Flow

CONCEPT

Statements are the "steps" of a programme. Most statements compute and assign values or call functions, but we will eventually meet several other kinds of statements as well. By default, statements are executed in sequence, one after another.

We can, however, modify that sequence by using *control flow constructs* which arrange that a statement or group of statements is executed only if some condition is true or false, or executed over and over again to form a *loop*. (A somewhat different kind of control flow happens when we call a function: execution of the caller is suspended while the called function proceeds. My definitions of the terms *statement* and *control flow* are somewhat circular. A statement is an element within a programme which you can apply control flow to; control flow is how you specify the order in which the statements in your programme are executed. (A weaker definition of a statement might be "a part of your programme that does something," but this definition could as easily be applied to expressions or functions.)

EXPRESSION STATEMENTS

Most of the statements in a C programme are *expression statements*. An expression statement is simply an expression followed by a semicolon.

The lines,

```
i = 0;
```

```
i = i + 1;
and
printf("Hello, world!\n");
```

are all expression statements. (In some languages, such as Pascal, the semicolon separates statements, such that the last statement is not followed by a semicolon. In C, however, the semicolon is a statement terminator; all simple statements are followed by semicolons. The semicolon is also used for a few other things in C; we've already seen that it terminates declarations, too.)

Expression statements do all of the real work in a C programme. Whenever you need to compute new values for variables, you'll typically use expression statements (and they'll typically contain assignment operators). Whenever you want your programme to do something visible, in the real world, you'll typically call a function (as part of an expression statement).

We've already seen the most basic example: calling the function printf to print text to the screen. But anything else you might do—read or write a disk file, talk to a modem or printer, draw pictures on the screen—will also involve function calls. (Furthermore, the functions you call to do these things are usually different depending on which operating system you're using.

The C language does not define them, so we won't be talking about or using them much.) Expressions and expression statements can be arbitrarily complicated. They don't have to consist of exactly one simple function call, or of one simple assignment to a variable. For one thing, many functions return values, and the values they return can then be used by other parts of the expression. For example, C provides a sqrt (square root) function, which we might use to compute the hypotenuse of a right triangle like this:

```
c = sqrt(a*a + b*b);
```

To be useful, an expression statement must do something; it must have some lasting effect on the state of the programme. (Formally, a useful statement must have at least one *side effect*.) The first two sample expression statements in this section (above) assign new values to the variable i, and the third one calls printf to print something out, and these are good examples of statements that do something useful.

To make the distinction clear, we may note that degenerate constructions such as,

```
0;
i;
or
i + 1;
```

are syntactically valid statements—they consist of an expression followed by a semicolon—but in each case, they compute a value without doing anything with it, so the computed value is discarded, and the statement is useless. But if the "degenerate" statements in this paragraph don't make much sense to you, don't worry; it's because they, frankly, don't make much sense.)

It's also possible for a single expression to have multiple side effects, but it's easy for such an expression to be (a) confusing or (b) undefined. For now, we'll only be looking at expressions (and, therefore, statements) which do one well-defined thing at a time.

IF STATEMENTS

The simplest way to modify the control flow of a programme is with an if statement, which in its simplest form looks like this:

```
if(x > max)
max = x;
```

Even if you didn't know any C, it would probably be pretty obvious that what happens here is that if x is greater than max,x gets assigned to max. (We'd use code like this to keep track of the maximum value of x we'd seen—for each new x, we'd compare it to the old maximum value max, and if the new value was greater, we'd update max.)

More generally, we can say that the syntax of an if statement is:

```
if(expression)
statement
```

where *expression* is any expression and *statement* is any statement.

What if you have a series of statements, all of which should be executed together or not at all depending on whether some condition is true?

The answer is that you enclose them in braces:

```
if(expression)
{
statement<sub>1</sub>
statement<sub>2</sub>
statement<sub>3</sub>
}
```

As a general rule, anywhere the syntax of C calls for a statement, you may write a series of statements enclosed by braces. (You do not need to, and should not, put a semicolon after the closing brace, because the series of statements enclosed by braces is not itself a simple expression statement.)

An if statement may also optionally contain a second statement, the "else clause," which is to be executed if the condition is not met.

Here is an example:

```
if(n > 0)
average = sum/ n;
else  {
printf("can't compute average\n");
average = 0;
}
```

The first statement or block of statements is executed if the condition *is* true, and the second statement or block of statements (following the keyword else) is executed if the condition is *not* true. In this example, we can compute a meaningful average only if n is greater than 0; otherwise, we print a message saying that we cannot compute the average.

The general syntax of an if statement is therefore:

```
if(expression)
statement<sub>1</sub>
else
statement<sub>2</sub>
```

where both *statement₁* and *statement₂* may be lists of statements enclosed in braces .

It's also possible to nest one if statement inside another. (For that matter, it's in general possible to nest any kind of statement or control flow construct within another.) For example, here is a little piece of code which decides roughly which quadrant of the compass you're walking into, based on an x value which is positive if you're walking east, and a y value which is positive if you're walking north:

```
if(x > 0)
{
if(y > 0)
printf("Northeast.\n");
else   printf("Southeast.\n");
}
else {
if(y > 0)
printf("Northwest.\n");
else   printf("Southwest.\n");
}
```

When you have one if statement (or loop) nested inside another, it's a very good idea to use explicit braces {}, as shown, to make it clear (both to you and to the compiler) how they're nested and which else goes with which if. It's also a good idea to indent the various levels, also as shown, to make the code more readable to humans.

Why do both? You use indentation to make the code visually more readable to yourself and other humans, but the compiler doesn't pay attention to the indentation (since all whitespace is essentially equivalent and is essentially ignored). Therefore, you also have to make sure that the punctuation is right.

Here is an example of another common arrangement of if and else. Suppose we have a variable grade containing a student's numeric grade, and we want to print out the corresponding letter grade.

Here is code that would do the job:

```
if(grade >= 90)
```

```
printf("A");
else if(grade >= 80)
printf("B");
else if(grade >= 70)
   printf("C");
   else if(grade >= 60)
   printf("D");
   else     printf("F");
```

What happens here is that exactly one of the five printf calls is executed, depending on which of the conditions is true. Each condition is tested in turn, and if one is true, the corresponding statement is executed, and the rest are skipped. If none of the conditions is true, we fall through to the last one, printing "F".

In the cascaded if/else/if/else/... chain, each else clause is another if statement. This may be more obvious at first if we reformat the example, including every set of braces and indenting each if statement relative to the previous one:

```
if(grade >= 90)
{
printf("A");
}
else  {
if(grade >= 80)
{
printf("B");
}
else  {
if(grade >= 70)
{
printf("C");
}
else   {
if(grade >= 60)
{
printf("D");
}
else   {
```

```
printf("F");
}
}
}
}
```

By examining the code this way, it should be obvious that exactly one of the printf calls is executed, and that whenever one of the conditions is found true, the remaining conditions do not need to be checked and none of the later statements within the chain will be executed.

But once you've convinced yourself of this and learned to recognize the idiom, it's generally preferable to arrange the statements as in the first example, without trying to indent each successive if statement one tabstop further out.

BOOLEAN EXPRESSIONS

An if statement like:

```
if(x > max)
max = x;
```

is perhaps deceptively simple. Conceptually, we say that it checks whether the condition x > max is "true" or "false". The mechanics underlying C's conception of "true" and "false," however, deserve some explanation. We need to understand how true and false values are represented, and how they are interpreted by statements like if.

As far as C is concerned, a true/false condition can be represented as an integer. (An integer can represent many values; here we care about only two values: "true" and "false." The study of mathematics involving only two values is called Boolean algebra, after George Boole, a mathematician who refined this study.) In C, "false" is represented by a value of 0 (zero), and "true" is represented by any value that is nonzero. Since there are many nonzero values (at least 65,534, for values of type int), when we have to pick a specific value for "true," we'll pick 1.

The *relational operators* such as <, <=, >, and >= are in fact operators, just like +, -, *, and /. The relational operators take two values, look at them, and "return" a value of 1 or 0 depending on whether the tested relation was true or false. The complete set of relational operators in C is:

```
<  less than
<= less than or equal
>  greater than
>= greater than or equal
== equal
!= not equal
```

For example, 1 < 2 is 1, 3 > 4 is 0, 5 == 5 is 1, and 6 = 6 is 0.

We've now encountered perhaps the most easy-to-stumble-on "gotcha!" in C: the equality-testing operator is ==, not a single =, which is assignment. If you accidentally write

```
if(a = 0)
```

and you probably will at some point; everybody makes this mistake , it will *not* test whether a is zero, as you probably intended. Instead, it will *assign* 0 to a, and then perform the "true" branch of the if statement if a is *non*zero. But a will have just been assigned the value 0, so the "true" branch will never be taken! (This could drive you crazy while debugging—you wanted to do something if a was 0, and after the test, a *is* 0, whether it was supposed to be or not, but the "true" branch is nevertheless not taken.)

The relational operators work with arbitrary numbers and generate true/false values. You can also combine true/false values by using the *Boolean operators,* which take true/false values as operands and compute new true/false values.

The three Boolean operators are:

```
&& and
|| or
!  not (takes one operand; "unary")
```

The && ("and") operator takes two true/false values and produces a true (1) result if both operands are true (that is, if the left-hand side is true and the right-hand side is true). The || ("or") operator takes two true/false values and produces a true (1) result if either operand is true.

The ("not") operator takes a single true/false value and negates it, turning false to true and true to false (0 to 1 and nonzero to 0).

For example, to test whether the variable i lies between 1 and 10, you might use

```
if(1 < i && i < 10)
...
```

Here we're expressing the relation "i is between 1 and 10" as "1 is less than i and i is less than 10."

It's important to understand why the more obvious expression,

```
if(1 < i < 10)   /* WRONG */
```

would not work. The expression 1 < i < 10 is parsed by the compiler analogously to 1 + i + 10. The expression 1 + i + 10 is parsed as (1 + i) + 10 and means "add 1 to i, and then add the result to 10." Similarly, the expression 1 < i < 10 is parsed as (1 < i) < 10 and means "see if 1 is less than i, and then see if the result is less than 10." But in this case, "the result" is 1 or 0, depending on whether i is greater than 1. Since both 0 and 1 are less than 10, the expression 1 < i < 10 would *always* be true in C, regardless of the value of i!

Relational and Boolean expressions are usually used in contexts such as an if statement, where something is to be done or not done depending on some condition. In these cases what's actually checked is whether the expression representing the condition has a zero or nonzero value. As long as the expression is a relational or Boolean expression, the interpretation is just what we want. For example, when we wrote

```
if(x > max)
```

the > operator produced a 1 if x was greater than max, and a 0 otherwise. The if statement interprets 0 as false and 1 (or any nonzero value) as true.

But what if the expression is not a relational or Boolean expression? As far as C is concerned, the controlling expression (of conditional statements like if) can in fact be *any* expression: it doesn't have to "look like" a Boolean expression; it doesn't have to contain relational or logical operators. All C looks at (when it's evaluating an if statement, or anywhere else where it needs a true/false value) is whether the expression evaluates to 0 or nonzero. For example, if you have a variable x, and you want to do something if x is nonzero, it's possible to write,

```
if(x)
statement
```

and the statement will be executed if x is nonzero (since nonzero means "true").

This possibility (that the controlling expression of an if statement doesn't have to "look like" a Boolean expression) is both useful and potentially confusing. It's useful when you have a variable or a function that is "conceptually Boolean," that is, one that you consider to hold a true or false (actually nonzero or zero) value.

For example, if you have a variableverbose which contains a nonzero value when your programme should run in verbose mode and zero when it should be quiet, you can write things like,

```
if(verbose)
printf("Starting first pass\n");
```

and this code is both legal and readable, besides which it does what you want. The standard library contains a functionisupper() which tests whether a character is an upper-case letter, so if c is a character, you might write,

```
if(isupper(c))
...
```

Both of these examples (verbose and isupper()) are useful and readable.

However, you will eventually come across code like:

```
if(n)
average = sum/ n;
```

where n is just a number. Here, the programmer wants to compute the average only if n is nonzero (otherwise, of course, the code would divide by 0), and the code works, because, in the context of the if statement, the trivial expression n is (as always) interpreted as "true" if it is nonzero, and "false" if it is zero.

"Coding shortcuts" like these can seem cryptic, but they're also quite common, so you'll need to be able to recognize them even if you don't choose to write them in your own code. Whenever you see code like,

```
if(x)
```
or
```
if(f())
```
where x or f() do not have obvious "Boolean" names, you can read them as "if x is nonzero" or "if f() returns nonzero."

WHILE LOOPS

Loops generally consist of two parts: one or more *control expressions* which (not surprisingly) control the execution of the loop, and the *body,* which is the statement or set of statements which is executed over and over.

The most basic *loop* in C is the while loop. A while loop has one control expression, and executes as long as that expression is true. This example repeatedly doubles the number 2 (2, 4, 8, 16...) and prints the resulting numbers as long as they are less than 1000:

```
int x = 2;
while(x < 1000)
{
printf("%d\n", x);
x = x * 2;
}
```

Once again, we've used braces {} to enclose the group of statements which are to be executed together as the body of the loop.

The general syntax of a while loop is:

```
while(expression)
statement
```

A while loop starts out like an if statement: if the condition expressed by the *expression* is true, the *statement* is executed. However, after executing the statement, the condition is tested again, and if it's still true, the statement is executed again. Presumably, the condition depends on some value which is changed in the body of the loop.

As long as the condition remains true, the body of the loop is executed over and over again. (If the condition is false right at the start, the body of the loop is not executed at all.)

As another example, if you wanted to print a number of

blank lines, with the variable n holding the number of blank lines to be printed, you might use code like this:

```
while(n > 0)
{
printf("\n");
n = n - 1;
}
```

After the loop finishes (when control "falls out" of it, due to the condition being false), n will have the value 0.

You use a while loop when you have a statement or group of statements which may have to be executed a number of times to complete their task. The controlling expression represents the condition "the loop is not done" or "there's more work to do." As long as the expression is true, the body of the loop is executed; presumably, it makes at least some progress at its task.

When the expression becomes false, the task is done, and the rest of the programme (beyond the loop) can proceed. When we think about a loop in this way, we can seen an additional important property: if the expression evaluates to "false" before the very first trip through the loop, we make *zero* trips through the loop.

In other words, if the task is already done (if there's no work to do) the body of the loop is not executed at all. (It's always a good idea to think about the "boundary conditions" in a piece of code, and to make sure that the code will work correctly when there is no work to do, or when there is a trivial task to do, such as sorting an array of one number. Experience has shown that bugs at boundary conditions are quite common.)

FOR LOOPS

Our second loop, which we've seen at least one example of already, is the for loop.

The first one we saw was:

```
for (i = 0; i < 10; i = i + 1)
printf("i is %d\n", i);
```

More generally, the syntax of a for loop is,

```
for(expr<sub>1</sub>; expr<sub>2</sub>;
expr<sub>3</sub>)
statement
```

Here we see that the for loop has three control expressions. As always, the *statement* can be a brace-enclosed block.

Many loops are set up to cause some variable to step through a range of values, or, more generally, to set up an initial condition and then modify some value to perform each succeeding loop as long as some condition is true.

The three expressions in a for loop encapsulate these conditions: *expr₁* sets up the initial condition, *expr₂* tests whether another trip through the loop should be taken, and *expr₃* increments or updates things after each trip through the loop and prior to the next one. In our first example, we had i = 0 as*expr₁*, i < 10 as *expr₂*, i = i + 1 as *expr₃*, and the call to printf as*statement*, the body of the loop. So the loop began by setting i to 0, proceeded as long as i was less than 10, printed outi's value during each trip through the loop, and added 1 to i between each trip through the loop. When the compiler sees a for loop, first, *expr₁* is evaluated. Then, *expr₂* is evaluated, and if it is true, the body of the loop (*statement*) is executed. Then, *expr₃* is evaluated to go to the next step, and*expr₂* is evaluated again, to see if there *is* a next step.

During the execution of a for loop, the sequence is:

```
expr<sub>1</sub>
expr<sub>2</sub>
statement
expr<sub>3</sub>
expr<sub>2</sub>
statement
expr<sub>3</sub>
...
expr<sub>2</sub>
statement
expr<sub>3</sub>
expr<sub>2</sub>
```

The first thing executed is *expr₁*. *expr₃* is evaluated after *every* trip through the loop. The last thing executed is always *expr₂*, because when *expr₂* evaluates false, the loop exits.

All three expressions of a for loop are optional. If you leave out *expr₁*, there simply is no initialization step, and the variable(s) used with the loop had better have been initialized already.

If you leave out *expr₂*, there is no test, and the default for the for loop is that another trip through the loop should be taken (such that unless you break out of it some other way, the loop runs forever). If you leave out *expr₃*, there is no increment step.

The semicolons separate the three controlling expressions of a for loop. (These semicolons, by the way, have nothing to do with statement terminators.) If you leave out one or more of the expressions, the semicolons remain. Therefore, one way of writing a deliberately infinite loop in C is

```
for(;;)
...
```

It's useful to compare C's for loop to the equivalent loops in other computer languages you might know.

The C loop,

```
for(i = x; i <= y; i = i + z)
```

is roughly equivalent to:

```
for I = X to Y step Z (BASIC)
do 10 i=x,y,z    (FORTRAN)
for i:= x to y  (Pascal)
```

In C (unlike FORTRAN), if the test condition is false before the first trip through the loop, the loop won't be traversed at all. In C (unlike Pascal), a loop control variable (in this case, i) is guaranteed to retain its final value after the loop completes, and it is also legal to modify the control variable within the loop, if you really want to. (When the loop terminates due to the test condition turning false, the value of the control variable after the loop will be the first value for which the condition failed, not the last value for which it succeeded.)

It's also worth noting that a for loop can be used in more

general ways than the simple, iterative examples we've seen so far. The "control variable" of a for loop does not have to be an integer, and it does not have to be incremented by an additive increment.

It could be "incremented" by a multiplicative factor (1, 2, 4, 8...) if that was what you needed, or it could be a floating-point variable, or it could be another type of variable which we haven't met yet which would step, not over numeric values, but over the elements of an array or other data structure.

Strictly speaking, a for loop doesn't have to have a "control variable" at all; the three expressions can be anything, although the loop will make the most sense if they are related and together form the expected initialize, test, increment sequence.

The powers-of-two example of the previous section does fit this pattern, so we could rewrite it like this:

```
int x;
for(x = 2; x < 1000; x = x * 2)
printf("%d\n", x);
```

There is no earth-shaking or fundamental difference between the while and for loops. In fact, given the general for loop

```
for(expr<sub>1</sub>; expr<sub>2</sub>;
expr<sub>3</sub>)
statement
```

you could usually rewrite it as a while loop, moving the initialize and increment expressions to statements before and within the loop:

```
expr<sub>1</sub>;
while(expr<sub>2</sub>)
{
statement
expr<sub>3</sub>;
}
```

Similarly, given the general while loop:

```
while(expr)
statement
```

you could rewrite it as a for loop:

```
for(; expr;)
        statement
```

Another contrast between the for and while loops is that although the test expression (*expr₂*) is optional in a for loop, it is required in a while loop. If you leave out the controlling expression of a while loop, the compiler will complain about a syntax error. (To write a deliberately infinite while loop, you have to supply an expression which is always nonzero. The most obvious one would simply be while(1) .)

If it's possible to rewrite a for loop as a while loop and vice versa, why do they both exist? Which one should you choose? In general, when you choose a for loop, its three expressions should all manipulate the same variable or data structure, using the initialize, test, increment pattern.

If they don't manipulate the same variable or don't follow that pattern, wedging them into a for loop buys nothing and a while loop would probably be clearer.

The reason that one loop or the other can be clearer is simply that, when you see a for loop, you *expect* to see an idiomatic initialize/test/increment of a single variable, and if the for loop you're looking at doesn't end up matching that pattern, you've been momentarily misled.

BREAK AND CONTINUE

Sometimes, due to an exceptional condition, you need to jump out of a loop early, that is, before the main controlling expression of the loop causes it to terminate normally. Other times, in an elaborate loop, you may want to jump back to the top of the loop (to test the controlling expression again, and perhaps begin a new trip through the loop) without playing out all the steps of the current loop.

The break and continue statements allow you to do these two things. (They are, in fact, essentially restricted forms of goto.). To put everything we've seen in this chapter together, as well as demonstrate the use of the break statement, here is a programme for printing prime numbers between 1 and 100:

```
#include <stdio.h>
```

```
#include <math.h>
main()
{
int i, j;
printf("%d\n", 2);
for(i = 3; i <= 100; i = i + 1)
{
for(j = 2; j < i; j = j + 1)
{
if(i % j == 0)
break;
if(j > sqrt(i))
{
printf("%d\n", i);
break;
}
}
}
return 0;
}
```

The outer loop steps the variable i through the numbers from 3 to 100; the code tests to see if each number has any divisors other than 1 and itself.

The trial divisor j loops from 2 up to i. j is a divisor of i if the remainder of i divided by jis 0, so the code uses C's "remainder" or "modulus" operator % to make this test. (Remember that i % j gives the remainder when i is divided by j.) If the programme finds a divisor, it uses break to break out of the inner loop, without printing anything. But if it notices that jhas risen higher than the square root of i, without its having found any divisors, then i must not have any divisors, so i is prime, and its value is printed.

Once we've determined that i is prime by noticing that j > sqrt(i), there's no need to try the other trial divisors, so we use a second break statement to break out of the loop in that case, too.

The simple algorithm and implementation we used here (like many simple prime number algorithms) does not work for 2, the only even prime number, so the programme "cheats" and prints out 2 no matter what, before going on to test the numbers from 3 to 100.

Many improvements to this simple programme are of course possible; you might experiment with it. (Did you notice that the "test" expression of the inner loop for(j = 2; j < i; j = j + 1) is in a sense unnecessary, because the loop always terminates early due to one of the two break statements?)

Chapter 4

Idea about Declarations and Initialization

ARRAYS

So far, we've been declaring simple variables: the declaration,

```
int i;
```

declares a single variable, named i, of type int. It is also possible to declare an *array* of several elements. The declaration

```
int a[10];
```

declares an array, named a, consisting of ten elements, each of type int. Simply speaking, an array is a variable that can hold more than one value. You specify which of the several values you're referring to at any given time by using a numeric*subscript*. (Arrays in programming are similar to vectors or matrices in mathematics.)

We can represent the array a above with a picture like this:

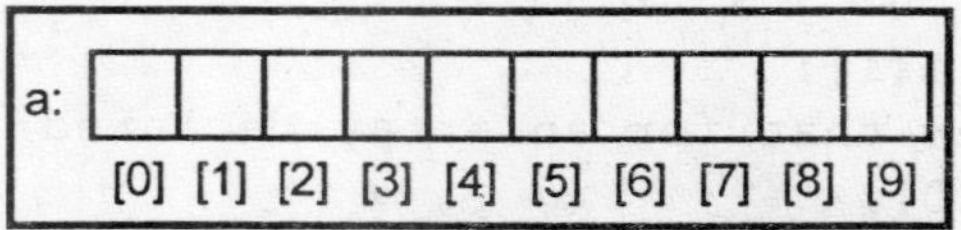

In C, arrays are *zero-based*: the ten elements of a 10-element array are numbered from 0 to 9. The subscript which specifies a single element of an array is simply an integer expression in square brackets. The first element of the array isa[0], the second element is a[1], etc. You can use these "array subscript expressions" anywhere you can use the name of a simple variable, for example:

```
a[0] = 10;
a[1] = 20;
a[2] = a[0] + a[1];
```

Notice that the subscripted array references (i.e. expressions such as a[0] and a[1]) can appear on either side of the assignment operator.

The subscript does not have to be a constant like 0 or 1; it can be any integral expression. For example, it's common to loop over all elements of an array:

```
int i;
for(i = 0; i < 10; i = i + 1)
a[i] = 0;
```

This loop sets all ten elements of the array a to 0.

Arrays are a real convenience for many problems, but there is not a lot that C will do with them for you automatically. In particular, you can neither set all elements of an array at once nor assign one array to another; both of the assignments,

```
a = 0; /* WRONG */
and
int b[10];
b = a; /* WRONG */
are illegal.
```

To set all of the elements of an array to some value, you must do so one by one, as in the loop example above. To copy the contents of one array to another, you must again do so one by one:

```
int b[10];
for(i = 0; i < 10; i = i + 1)
b[i] = a[i];
Remember that for an array declared
int a[10];
```

there is no element a[10]; the topmost element is a[9]. This is one reason that zero-based loops are also common in C.

Note that the for loop:

```
for(i = 0; i < 10; i = i + 1)
...
```

does just what you want in this case: it starts at 0, the number 10 suggests (correctly) that it goes through 10 iterations, but the less-than comparison means that the last trip through the loop has i set to 9. (The comparison i <= 9 would also work, but it would be less clear and therefore poorer style.)

In the little examples so far, we've always looped over all 10 elements of the sample array a. It's common, however, to use an array that's bigger than necessarily needed, and to use a second variable to keep track of how many elements of the array are currently in use.

For example, we might have an integer variable,

```
int na;    /* number of elements of a[] in use
           */
```

Then, when we wanted to do something with a (such as print it out), the loop would run from 0 to na, not 10 (or whatevera's size was):

```
for(i = 0; i < na; i = i + 1)
printf("%d\n", a[i]);
```

Naturally, we would have to ensure ensure that na's value was always less than or equal to the number of elements actually declared in a.

Arrays are not limited to type int; you can have arrays of char or double or any other type. Here is a slightly larger example of the use of arrays. Suppose we want to investigate the behaviour of rolling a pair of dice. The total roll can be anywhere from 2 to 12, and we want to count how often each roll comes up. We will use an array to keep track of the counts: a[2] will count how many times we've rolled 2, etc.

We'll simulate the roll of a die by calling C's random number generation function, rand(). Each time you call rand(), it returns a different, pseudo-random integer. The values that rand() returns typically span a large range, so we'll use C's*modulus* (or "remainder") operator % to produce random numbers in the range we want. The expression rand()% 6produces random numbers in the range 0 to 5, and rand()% 6 + 1 produces random numbers in the range 1 to 6.

Here is the programme:

```
#include <stdio.h>
#include <stdlib.h>
main()
```

```
{
int i;
int d1, d2;
int a[13]; /* uses [2..12] */
for(i = 2; i <= 12; i = i + 1)
a[i] = 0;
for(i = 0; i < 100; i = i + 1)
{
d1 = rand()% 6 + 1;
d2 = rand()% 6 + 1;
a[d1 + d2] = a[d1 + d2] + 1;
}
for(i = 2; i <= 12; i = i + 1)
printf("%d: %d\n", i, a[i]);
return 0;
}
```

We include the header <stdlib.h> because it contains the necessary declarations for the rand() function. We declare the array of size 13 so that its highest element will be a[12]. (We're wasting a[0] and a[1]; this is no great loss.) The variables d1 and d2 contain the rolls of the two individual dice; we add them together to decide which cell of the array to increment, in the line,

```
a[d1 + d2] = a[d1 + d2] + 1;
```

After 100 rolls, we print the array out. Typically (as craps players well know), we'll see mostly 7's, and relatively few 2's and 12's.

By the way, it turns out that using the % operator to reduce the range of the rand function is *not* always a good idea. We'll say more about this problem in an exercise.

ARRAY INITIALIZATION

Although it is not possible to assign to all elements of an array at once using an assignment expression, it is possible to initialize some or all elements of an array when the array is defined.

The syntax looks like this:

```
int a[10] = {0, 1, 2, 3, 4, 5, 6, 7, 8, 9};
```

The list of values, enclosed in braces {}, separated by commas, provides the initial values for successive elements of the array.

Under older, pre-ANSI C compilers, you could not always supply initializers for "local" arrays inside functions; you could only initialize "global" arrays, those outside of any function.

Those compilers are now rare, so you shouldn't have to worry about this distinction any more. We'll talk more about local and global variables later in this chapter.

If there are fewer initializers than elements in the array, the remaining elements are automatically initialized to 0.

For example,

```
int a[10] = {0, 1, 2, 3, 4, 5, 6};
```

would initialize a[7], a[8], and a[9] to 0. When an array definition includes an initializer, the array dimension may be omitted, and the compiler will infer the dimension from the number of initializers.

For example,

```
int b[] = {10, 11, 12, 13, 14};
```

would declare, define, and initialize an array b of 5 elements (i.e. just as if you'd typed int b[5]). Only the dimension is omitted; the brackets [] remain to indicate that b is in fact an array.

In the case of arrays of char, the initializer may be a string constant:

```
char s1[7] = "Hello,";
char s2[10] = "there,";
char s3[] = "world!";
```

As before, if the dimension is omitted, it is inferred from the size of the string initializer. (We haven't covered strings in detail yet—we'll do so in chapter 8—but it turns out that all strings in C are terminated by a special character with the value 0.

Therefore, the array s3 will be of size 7, and the explicitly-sized s1 does need to be of size at least 7. For s2, the last 4 characters in the array will all end up being this zero-value character.)

MULTIDIMENSIONAL ARRAYS

When we said that "Arrays are not limited to type int; you can have arrays of... any other type," we meant that more literally than you might have guessed.

If you have an "array of int," it means that you have an array each of whose elements is of type int. But you can have an array each of whose elements is of type *x*, where *x* is any type you choose.

In particular, you can have an array each of whose elements is another array! We can use these arrays of arrays for the same sorts of tasks as we'd use multidimensional arrays in other computer languages (or matrices in mathematics). Naturally, we are not limited to arrays of arrays, either; we could have an array of arrays of arrays, which would act like a 3-dimensional array, etc.

The declaration of an array of arrays looks like this:

```
int a2[5][7];
```

You have to read complicated declarations like these "inside out." What this one says is that a2 is an array of 5 somethings, and that each of the somethings is an array of 7 ints. More briefly, "a2 is an array of 5 arrays of 7 ints," or, "a2 is an array of array of int." In the declaration of a2, the brackets closest to the identifier a2 tell you what a2 first and foremost is.

That's how you know it's an array of 5 arrays of size 7, not the other way around. You can think of a2 as having 5 "rows" and 7 "columns," although this interpretation is not mandatory. (You could also treat the "first" or inner subscript as "x" and the second as "y." Unless you're doing something fancy, all you have to worry about is that the subscripts when you access the array match those that you used when you declared it, as in the examples below.) To illustrate the use of multidimensional arrays, we might fill in the elements of the above array a2 using this piece of code:

```
int i, j;
for(i = 0; i < 5; i = i + 1)
{
```

```
for(j = 0; j < 7; j = j + 1)
a2[i][j] = 10 * i + j;
}
```

This pair of nested loops sets a[1][2] to 12, a[4][1] to 41, etc. Since the first dimension of a2 is 5, the first subscripting index variable, i, runs from 0 to 4. Similarly, the second subscript varies from 0 to 6.

We could print a2 out (in a two-dimensional way, suggesting its structure) with a similar pair of nested loops:

```
for(i = 0; i < 5; i = i + 1)
{
for(j = 0; j < 7; j = j + 1)
printf("%d\t", a2[i][j]);
printf("\n");
}
```

The character \t in the printf string is the tab character. Just to see more clearly what's going on, we could make the "row" and "column" subscripts explicit by printing them, too:

```
for(j = 0; j < 7; j = j + 1)
printf("\t%d:", j);
printf("\n");
for(i = 0; i < 5; i = i +1)
{
printf("%d:", i);
for(j = 0; j < 7; j = j + 1)
printf("\t%d", a2[i][j]);
printf("\n");
}
```

This last fragment would print:

```
0: 1: 2: 3: 4: 5: 6:
0: 0 1 2 3 4 5 6
1: 10 11 12 13 14 15 16
2: 20 21 22 23 24 25 26
3: 30 31 32 33 34 35 36
4: 40 41 42 43 44 45 46
```

Finally, there's no reason we have to loop over the "rows" first and the "columns" second; depending on what we wanted to do, we could interchange the two loops, like this:

```
for(j = 0; j < 7; j = j + 1)
{
for(i = 0; i < 5; i = i + 1)
printf("%d\t", a2[i][j]);
printf("\n");
}
```

Notice that i is still the first subscript and it still runs from 0 to 4, and j is still the second subscript and it still runs from 0 to 6.

VISIBILITY

We haven't said so explicitly, but variables are channels of communication within a programme. You set a variable to a value at one point in a programme, and at another point (or points) you read the value out again. The two points may be in adjoining statements, or they may be in widely separated parts of the programme.

How long does a variable last? How widely separated can the setting and fetching parts of the programme be, and how long after a variable is set does it persist? Depending on the variable and how you're using it, you might want different answers to these questions.

The *visibility* of a variable determines how much of the rest of the programme can access that variable. You can arrange that a variable is visible only within one part of one function, or in one function, or in one source file, or anywhere in the programme. (We haven't really talked about source files yet; we'll be exploring them soon.)

Why would you want to limit the visibility of a variable? For maximum flexibility, wouldn't it be handy if all variables were potentially visible everywhere? As it happens, that arrangement would be *too* flexible: everywhere in the programme, you would have to keep track of the names of all the variables declared anywhere else in the programme, so that you didn't accidentally re-use one. Whenever a variable had the wrong value by mistake, you'd have to search the entire programme for the bug, because any statement in the entire programme could potentially have modified that variable. You would constantly be stepping all over yourself by using a common variable name like i in two parts of your programme, and having one snippet of code accidentally overwrite the values being used by another part of the code. The communication would be sort of like an old party line—you'd always be accidentally interrupting other conversations, or having your conversations interrupted.

To avoid this confusion, we generally give variables the narrowest or smallest visibility they need. A variable declared within the braces {} of a function is visible only within that function; variables declared within functions are called *local variables*. If another function somewhere else declares a local variable with the same name, it's a different variable entirely, and the two don't clash with each other.

On the other hand, a variable declared outside of any function is a *global variable*, and it is potentially visible anywhere within the programme. You use global variables when you *do* want the communications path to be able to travel to any part of the programme. When you declare a global variable, you will usually give it a longer, more descriptive name (not something generic like i) so that whenever you use it you will remember that it's the same variable everywhere. Another word for the visibility of variables is *scope*.

How long do variables last? By default, local variables (those declared within a function) have *automatic duration*: they spring into existence when the function is called, and they (and their values) disappear when the function returns. Global variables, on the other hand, have *static duration*: they last, and the values stored in them persist, for as long as the programme does. (Of course, the values can in general still be overwritten, so they don't necessarily persist forever.)

Finally, it is possible to split a function up into several source files, for easier maintenance. When several source files are combined into one programme (we'll be seeing how in the next chapter) the compiler must have a way of correlating the global variables which might be used to communicate between the several source files. Furthermore, if a global variable is going to be useful for communication, there must be exactly one of it: you wouldn't want one function in one source file to store a value in one global variable named globalvar, and then have another function in another source file read from a*different* global variable named globalvar.

Therefore, a global variable should have exactly one *defining instance,* in one place in one source file. If the same variable is to be used anywhere else (i.e. in some other source file or files), the variable is declared in those other file(s) with an *external declaration,* which is not a defining instance.

The external declaration says, "hey, compiler, here's the name and type of a global variable I'm going to use, but don't define it here, don't allocate space for it; it's one that's defined somewhere else, and I'm just referring to it here." If you accidentally have two distinct defining instances for a variable of the same name, the compiler (or the linker) will complain that it is "multiply defined."

It is also possible to have a variable which is global in the sense that it is declared outside of any function, but private to the one source file it's defined in. Such a variable is visible to the functions in that source file but not to any functions in any other source files, even if they try to issue a matching declaration.

You get any extra control you might need over visibility and lifetime, and you distinguish between defining instances and external declarations, by using *storage classes.* A storage class is an extra keyword at the beginning of a declaration which modifies the declaration in some way. Generally, the storage class (if any) is the first word in the declaration, preceding the type name. (Strictly speaking, this ordering has not traditionally been necessary, and you may see some code with the storage class, type name, and other parts of a declaration in an unusual order.)

We said that, by default, local variables had automatic duration. To give them static duration (so that, instead of coming and going as the function is called, they persist for as long as the function does), you precede their declaration with thestatic keyword:

```
static int i;
```

By default, a declaration of a global variable (especially if it specifies an initial value) is the defining instance. To make it an external declaration, of a variable which is defined somewhere else, you precede it with the keyword extern:

```
extern int j;
```

Finally, to arrange that a global variable is visible only within its containing source file, you precede it with the statickeyword:

```
static int k;
```

Notice that the static keyword can do two different things: it adjusts the duration of a local variable from automatic to static, or it adjusts the visibility of a global variable from truly global to private-to-the-file. To summarize, we've talked about two different attributes of a variable: visibility and duration. *These are orthogonal, as shown in this table*:

	duration:	
visibility:	automatic	static
local	normal local variables	static local variables
global	N/A	normal global variables

We can also distinguish between file-scope global variables and truly global variables, based on the presence or absence of the static keyword.

We can also distinguish between external declarations and defining instances of global variables, based on the presence or absence of the extern keyword.

DEFAULT INITIALIZATION

The duration of a variable (whether static or automatic) also affects its default initialization. If you do not explicitly initialize them, automatic-duration variables (that is, local, non-static ones) are not guaranteed to have any particular initial value; they will typically contain garbage.

It is therefore a fairly serious error to attempt to use the value of an automatic variable which has never been initialized or assigned to: the programme will either work incorrectly, or the garbage value may just happen to be "correct" such that the programme appears to work correctly! However, the particular value that the garbage takes on can vary depending literally on *anything*: other parts of the programme, which compiler was used, which hardware or operating system the programme is running on, the time of day, the phase of the moon.So you hardly want to say that a programme which uses an uninitialized variable "works"; it may seem to work, but it works for the wrong reason, and it may stop working tomorrow.

Static-duration variables (global and static local), on the other hand, are guaranteed to be initialized to 0 if you do not use an explicit initializer in the definition.

Once upon a time, there was another distinction between the initialization of automatic vs. static variables: you could initialize *aggregate* objects, such as arrays, only if they had static duration.

If your compiler complains when you try to initialize a local array, it's probably an old, pre-ANSI compiler. Modern, ANSI-compatible compilers remove this limitation, so it's no longer much of a concern.

EXAMPLES

Here is an example demonstrating almost everything we've seen so far:

```
int globalvar = 1;
extern int anotherglobalvar;
static int privatevar;
f()
{
int localvar;
int localvar2 = 2;
static int persistentvar;
}
```

Here we have six variables, three declared outside and three declared inside of the function f(). Globalvar is a global variable. The declaration we see is its defining instance (it happens also to include an initial value).globalvar can be used anywhere in this source file, and it could be used in other source files, too (as long as corresponding external declarations are issued in those other source files).

Anotherglobalvar is a second global variable. It is *not* defined here; the defining instance for it (and its initialization) is somewhere else.

Privatevar is a "private" global variable. It can be used anywhere within this source file, but functions in other source files cannot access it, even if they try to issue external declarations for it. (If other source files try to declare a global variable called "privatevar", they'll get their own; they won't be sharing this one.) Since it has static duration and receives no explicit initialization, privatevar will be initialized to 0.

Localvar is a local variable within the function f(). It can be accessed only within the function f(). (If any other part of the programme declares a variable named "localvar", that variable will be distinct from the one we're looking at here.)localvar is conceptually "created" each time f() is called, and disappears when f() returns.

Any value which was stored in localvar last time f() was running will be lost and will not be available next time f() is called. Furthermore, since it has no explicit initializer, the value of localvar will in general be garbage each time f() is called.

Localvar2 is also local, and everything that we said about localvar applies to it, except that since its declaration includes an explicit initializer, it will be initialized to 2 each time f() is called.

Finally, persistentvar is again local to f(), but it *does* maintain its value between calls to f(). It has static duration but no explicit initializer, so its initial value will be 0. The defining instances and external declarations we've been looking at so far have all been of simple variables. There are also defining instances and external declarations of functions, which we'll be looking at in the next chapter.

(Also, don't worry about static variables for now if they don't make sense to you; they're a relatively sophisticated concept, which you won't need to use at first.)

The term *declaration* is a general one which encompasses defining instances and external declarations; defining instances and external declarations are two different kinds of declarations. Furthermore, either kind of declaration suffices to inform the compiler of the name and type of a particular variable (or function). If you have the defining instance of a global variable in a source file, the rest of that source file can use that variable without having to issue any external declarations. It's only in source files where the defining instance hasn't been seen that you need external declarations.

You will sometimes hear a defining instance referred to simply as a "definition," and you will sometimes hear an external declaration referred to simply as a "declaration." These usages are mildly ambiguous, in that you can't tell out of context whether a "declaration" is a generic declaration (that might be a defining instance or an external declaration) or whether it's an external declaration that specifically is not a defining instance. (Similarly, there are other constructions that can be called "definitions" in C, namely the definitions of preprocessor macros, structures, and typedefs, none of which we've met.) In these notes, we'll try to make things clear by using the unambiguous terms *defining instance* and *external declaration*. Elsewhere, you may have to look at the context to determine how the terms "definition" and "declaration" are being used.

Chapter 5

Functions and Programme Structure

A function is a "black box" that we've locked part of our programme into. The idea behind a function is that it *compartmentalizes* part of the programme, and in particular, that the code within the function has some useful properties:

- It performs some well-defined task, which will be useful to other parts of the programme.
- It might be useful to other programs as well; that is, we might be able to reuse it (and without having to rewrite it).
- The rest of the programme doesn't have to know the details of how the function is implemented. This can make the rest of the programme easier to think about.
- The function performs its task *well.* It may be written to do a little more than is required by the first programme that calls it, with the anticipation that the calling programme (or some other programme) may later need the extra functionality or improved performance. (It's important that a finished function do its job well, otherwise there might be a reluctance to call it, and it therefore might not achieve the goal of reusability.)
- By placing the code to perform the useful task into a function, and simply calling the function in the other parts of the programme where the task must be performed, the rest of the programme becomes clearer: rather than having some large, complicated,

difficult-to-understand piece of code repeated wherever the task is being performed, we have a single simple function call, and the name of the function reminds us which task is being performed.

- Since the rest of the programme doesn't have to know the details of how the function is implemented, the rest of the programme doesn't care if the function is reimplemented later, in some different way. This means that one part of the programme can be rewritten, to improve performance or add a new feature without having to rewrite the rest of the programme.

Functions are probably the most important weapon in our battle against software complexity.

FUNCTION BASICS

So what defines a function? It has a *name* that you call it by, and a list of zero or more *arguments* or *parameters* that you hand to it for it to act on or to direct its work; it has a *body* containing the actual instructions (statements) for carrying out the task the function is supposed to perform; and it may give you back a *return value,* of a particular type.

Here is a very simple function, which accepts one argument, multiplies it by 2, and hands that value back:

```
int multbytwo(int x)
{
int retval;
retval = x * 2;
return retval;
}
```

On the first line we see the return type of the function (int), the name of the function (multbytwo), and a list of the function's arguments, enclosed in parentheses. Each argument has both a name and a type; multbytwo accepts one argument, of type int, named x. The name x is arbitrary, and is used only within the definition of multbytwo. The caller of this function only needs to know that a single argument of type int is expected; the caller does not need to know what name the function will use internally to refer to that argument. (In particular, the caller does not have to pass the value of a variable named x.)

Next we see, surrounded by the familiar braces, the body of the function itself. This function consists of one declaration (of a local variable retval) and two statements. The first statement is a conventional expression statement, which computes and assigns a value to retval, and the second statement is a return statement, which causes the function to return to its caller, and also specifies the value which the function returns to its caller.

The return statement can return the value of any expression, so we don't really need the local retval variable; the function could be collapsed to,

```
int multbytwo(int x)
{
return x * 2;
}
```

How do we call a function? We've been doing so informally since day one, but now we have a chance to call one that we've written, in full detail. Here is a tiny skeletal programme to call multby2:

```
#include <stdio.h>
extern int multbytwo(int);
int main()
{
int i, j;
i = 3;
j = multbytwo(i);
printf("%d\n", j);
return 0;
}
```

This looks much like our other test programs, with the exception of the new line,

```
extern int multbytwo(int);
```

This is an *external function prototype declaration*. It is an external declaration, in that it declares something which is defined somewhere else. (We've already seen the defining instance of the function multbytwo, but maybe the compiler hasn't seen it yet.) The function prototype declaration contains the three pieces of information about the function that a caller needs to know: the function's name, return type, and argument type(s).

Since we don't care what name the multbytwo function will use to refer to its first argument, we don't need to mention it. (On the other hand, if a function takes several arguments, giving them names in the prototype may make it easier to remember which is which, so names may optionally be used in function prototype declarations.) Finally, to remind us that this is an external declaration and not a defining instance, the prototype is preceded by the keyword extern.

The presence of the function prototype declaration lets the compiler know that we intend to call this function, multbytwo. The information in the prototype lets the compiler generate the correct code for calling the function, and also enables the compiler to check up on our code (by making sure, for example, that we pass the correct number of arguments to each function we call).

Down in the body of main, the action of the function call should be obvious: the line,

```
j = multbytwo(i);
```

calls multbytwo, passing it the value of i as its argument. When multbytwo returns, the return value is assigned to the variable j. (Notice that the value of main's local variable i will become the value of multbytwo's parameter x; this is absolutely not a problem, and is a normal sort of affair.)

This example is written out in "longhand," to make each step equivalent. The variable i isn't really needed, since we could just as well call,

```
j = multbytwo(3);
```

And the variable j isn't really needed, either, since we could just as well call,

```
printf("%d\n", multbytwo(3));
```

Here, the call to multbytwo is a subexpression which serves as the second argument to printf. The value returned bymultbytwo is passed immediately to printf. (Here, as in general, we see the flexibility and generality of expressions in C. An argument passed to a function may be an arbitrarily complex subexpression, and a function call is itself an expression which may be embedded as a subexpression within arbitrarily complicated surrounding expressions.)

We should say a little more about the mechanism by which an argument is passed down from a caller into a function.

Formally, C is *call by value*, which means that a function receives *copies* of the values of its arguments. We can illustrate this with an example. Suppose, in our implementation of multbytwo, we had gotten rid of the unnecessary retvalvariable like this:

```
int multbytwo(int x)
{
x = x * 2;
return x;
}
```

We might wonder, if we wrote it this way, what would happen to the value of the variable i when we called,

```
j = multbytwo(i);
```

When our implementation of multbytwo changes the value of x, does that change the value of i up in the caller? The answer is no. x receives a copy of i's value, so when we change x we don't change i.

However, there is an exception to this rule. When the argument you pass to a function is not a single variable, but is rather an array, the function does *not* receive a copy of the array, and it therefore *can* modify the array in the caller. The reason is that it might be too expensive to copy the entire array, and furthermore, it can be useful for the function to write into the caller's array, as a way of handing back more data than would fit in the function's single return value.

FUNCTION PROTOTYPES

In modern C programming, it is considered good practice to use prototype declarations for all functions that you call. As we mentioned, these prototypes help to ensure that the compiler can generate correct code for calling the functions, as well as allowing the compiler to catch certain mistakes you might make.

Strictly speaking, however, prototypes are optional. If you call a function for which the compiler has not seen a prototype, the compiler will do the best it can, assuming that you're calling the function correctly.

If prototypes are a good idea, and if we're going to get in the habit of writing function prototype declarations for functions we call that we've written (such as multbytwo), what happens for library functions such as printf? Where are their prototypes? The answer is in that boilerplate line,

```
#include <stdio.h>
```

we've been including at the top of all of our programs. stdio.h is conceptually a file full of external declarations and other information pertaining to the "Standard I/O" library functions, including printf. The #include directive (which we'll meet formally in a later chapter) arranges that all of the declarations within stdio.h are considered by the compiler, rather as if we'd typed them all in ourselves. Somewhere within these declarations is an external function prototype declaration forprintf, which satisfies the rule that there should be a prototype for each function we call.

For other standard library functions we call, there will be other "header files" to include.) Finally, one more thing about external function prototype declarations. We've said that the distinction between external declarations and defining instances of normal variables hinges on the presence or absence of the keyword extern.

The situation is a little bit different for functions. The "defining instance" of a function is the function, including its body (that is, the brace-enclosed list of declarations and statements implementing the function). An external declaration of a function, even without the keyword extern, looks nothing like a function declaration. Therefore, the keyword extern is optional in function prototype declarations.

If you wish, you can write,

```
int multbytwo(int);
```

and this is just as good an external function prototype declaration as

```
extern int multbytwo(int);
```

You may want to stay in the habit of using extern in all external declarations, including function declarations, since "extern = external declaration" is an easier rule to remember.

FUNCTION PHILOSOPHY

What makes a good function? The most important aspect of a good "building block" is that have a single, well-defined task to perform. When you find that a programme is hard to manage, it's often because it has not been designed and broken up into functions cleanly.

Two obvious reasons for moving code down into a function are because:

- It appeared in the main programme several times, such that by making it a function, it can be written just once, and the several places where it used to appear can be replaced with calls to the new function.
- The main programme was getting too big, so it could be made (presumably) smaller and more manageable by lopping part of it off and making it a function.

These two reasons are important, and they represent significant benefits of well-chosen functions, but they are not sufficient to automatically identify a good function. As we've been suggesting, a good function has at least these two additional attributes:

- It does just one well-defined task, and does it well.
- Its interface to the rest of the programme is clean and narrow.

Attribute 3 is just a restatement of two things we said above. Attribute 4 says that you shouldn't have to keep track of too many things when calling a function. If you know what a function is supposed to do, and if its task is simple and well-defined, there should be just a few pieces of information you have to give it to act upon, and one or just a few pieces of information which it returns to you when it's done. If you find yourself having to pass lots and lots of information to a function, or remember details of its internal implementation to make sure that it will work properly this time, it's often a sign that the function is not sufficiently well-defined. (A poorly-defined function may be an arbitrary chunk of code that was ripped out of a main programme that was getting too big, such that it essentially has to have access to all of that main function's local variables.)

The whole point of breaking a programme up into functions is so that you don't have to think about the entire programme at once; ideally, you can think about just one function a' a time. We say that a good function is a "black box," which is supposed to suggest that the "container" it's in is opaque—callers can't see inside it (and the function inside can't see out). When you call a function, you only have to know what it does, not how it does it.

When you're *writing* a function, you only have to know what it's supposed to do, and you don't have to know why or under what circumstances its caller will be calling it. (When designing a function, we should perhaps think about the callers just enough to ensure that the function we're designing will be easy to call, and that we aren't accidentally setting things up so that callers will have to think about any internal details.)

Some functions may be hard to write (if they have a hard job to do, or if it's hard to make them do it truly well), but that difficulty should be compartmentalized along with the function itself.

Once you've written a "hard" function, you should be able to sit back and relax and watch it do that hard work on call from the rest of your programme. It should be pleasant to notice (in the ideal case) how much easier the rest of the programme is to write, now that the hard work can be deferred to this workhorse function.

In fact, if a difficult-to-write function's interface is well-defined, you may be able to get away with writing a quick-and-dirty version of the function first, so that you can begin testing the rest of the programme, and then go back later and rewrite the function to do the hard parts. As long as the function's original interface anticipated the hard parts, you won't have to rewrite the rest of the programme when you fix the function. What I've been trying to say in the preceding few paragraphs is that functions are important for far more important reasons than just saving typing. Sometimes, we'll write a function which we only call once, just because breaking it out into a function makes things clearer and easier.

If you find that difficulties pervade a programme, that the hard parts can't be buried inside black-box functions and then forgotten about; if you find that there are hard parts which involve complicated interactions among multiple functions, then the programme probably needs redesigning. For the purposes of explanation, we've been seeming to talk so far only about "main programs" and the functions they call and the rationale behind moving some piece of code down out of a "main programme" into a function.

But in reality, there's obviously no need to restrict ourselves to a two-tier scheme. Any function we find ourself writing will often be appropriately written in terms of sub-functions, sub-sub-functions, etc. (Furthermore, the "main programme," main(), is itself just a function.)

SEPARATE COMPILATION LOGISTICS

When a programme consists of many functions, it can be convenient to split them up into several source files. Among other things, this means that when a change is made, only the source file containing the change has to be recompiled, not the whole programme.

The job of putting the pieces of a programme together and producing the final executable falls to a tool called the *linker*. (We may or may not need to invoke the linker explicitly; a compiler often invokes it automatically, as needed.) The linker looks through all of the pieces making up the programme, sorting out the external declarations and defining instances.

The compiler has noted the definitions made by each source file, as well as the declarations of things used by each source file but (presumably) defined elsewhere. For each thing (global variable or function) used but not defined by one piece of the programme, the linker looks for another piece which does define that thing. The logistics of writing a programme in several source files, and then compiling and linking all of the source files together, depend on the programming environment you're using. We'll cover two possibilities, depending on whether you're using a traditional command-line compiler or a newer integrated development environment (IDE) or other graphical user interface (GUI) compiler.

When using a command-line compiler, there are usually two main steps involved in building an executable programme from one or more source files.

First, each source file is compiled, resulting in an *object file* containing the machine instructions (generated by the compiler) corresponding to just the code in that source file.

Second, the various object files are *linked*together, with each other and with *libraries* containing code for functions which you did not write (such as printf), to produce a final, executable programme. Under Unix, the cc command can perform one or both steps. So far, we've been using extremely simple invocations of ccsuch as

```
cc -o hello hello.c
```

This invocation compiles a single source file, hello.c, links it, and places the executable in a file named hello.

Suppose we have a programme which we're trying to build from three separate source files, x.c, y.c, and z.c. We could compile all three of them, and link them together, all at once, with the command

```
cc -o myprog x.c y.c z.c
```

Alternatively, we could compile them separately: the -c option to cc tells it to compile only, but not to link. Instead of building an executable, it merely creates an object file, with a name ending in .o, for each source file compiled.

So the three commands:

```
cc -c x.c
cc -c y.c
cc -c y.c
```

would compile x.c, y.c, and z.c and create object files x.o, y.o, and z.o. Then, the three object files could be linked together using.

```
cc -o myprog x.o y.o z.o
```

When the cc command is given an .o file, it knows that it does not have to compile it (it's an object file, already compiled); it just sends it through to the link process. Above we mentioned that the second, linking step also involves pulling in library functions. Normally, the functions from the Standard C library are linked in automatically. Occasionally, you must request a library manually; one common situation under Unix is that the math functions tend to be in a separate math library, which is requested by using -lm on the command line. Since the libraries must typically be searched *after* your program's own object files are linked (so that the linker knows which library functions your programme uses), any -l option must appear *after* the names of your files on the command line.

For example, to link the object file mymath.o (previously compiled with cc -c mymath.c) together with the math library, you might use

```
cc -o mymathprog mymath.o -lm
```

The l in the -l option is the lower case ell, for library; it is *not* the digit 1. Everything we've said about cc also applies to most other Unix C compilers. (Many of you will be using gcc, the FSF's GNU C Compiler.).

There are command-line compilers for MS-DOS systems which work similarly. For example, the Microsoft C compiler comes with a CL ("compile and link") command, which works almost the same as Unix cc.

You can compile and link in one step:

```
cl hello.c
or you can compile only:
cl/c hello.c
```

creating an object file named hello.obj which you can link later. The preceding has all been about command-line compilers. If you're using some kind of integrated development environment, such as Borland's Turbo C or the Microsoft Programmer's Workbench or Visual C or Think C or Codewarrior, most of the mechanical details are taken care of for you. Typically you define a "project," and there's a way to specify the list of files which make up your project.

Chapter 6

Basic I/O

INTRODUCTION

One of the reasons that has prevented many programming languages from becoming widely used for 'real programming' is their poor support for I/O, a subject which has never seemed to excite language designers. C has avoided this problem, oddly enough, by having no I/O at all! The C language approach has always been to do I/O using library functions, which ensures that system designers can provide tailored I/O instead of being forced to change the language itself.

As C has evolved, a library package known as the 'Standard I/O Library' or stdio, has evolved with it and has proved to be both flexible and portable. This package has now become part of the Standard.

The old stdio package relied heavily on the UNIX model of file access, in particular the assumption that there is no distinction between unstructured binary files and files containing readable text.

Many operating systems do maintain a distinction between the two, and to ensure that C programs can be written portably to run on both types of file model, the stdio package has been modified. There are changes in this area which affect many existing programs, although strenuous efforts were taken to limit the amount of damage.

I/O MODEL

The I/O model does not distinguish between the types of physical devices supporting the I/O. Each source or sink of data is treated in the same way, and is viewed as a *stream* of bytes. Since the smallest object that can be represented in C is the character, access to a file is permitted at any character boundary.

Any number of characters can be read or written from a movable point, known as the *file position indicator*. The characters will be read, or written, in sequence from this point, and the position indicator moved accordingly.

The position indicator is initially set to the beginning of a file when it is opened, but can also be moved by means of positioning requests. Opening a file in append mode has an implementation defined effect on the stream's file position indicator.

The overall effect is to provide sequential reads or writes unless the stream was opened in append mode, or the file position indicator is explicitly moved.

There are two types of file, *text files* and *binary files*, which, within a programme, are manipulated as *text streams* and *binary* streams once they have been opened for I/O. The stdio package does not permit operations on the contents of files 'directly', but only by viewing them as streams.

TEXT STREAMS

The Standard specifies what is meant by the term *text stream*, which essentially considers a file to contain lines of text. A line is a sequence of zero or more characters terminated by a newline character. It is quite possible that the actual representation of lines in the external environment is different from this and there may be transformations of the data stream on the way in and out of the programme; a common requirement is to translate the '\n' line-terminator into the sequence '\r\n' on output, and do the reverse on input. Other translations may also be necessary.

Data read in from a text stream is guaranteed to compare equal to the data that was earlier written out to the file if the data consists only of complete lines of printable characters and the control characters horizontal-tab and newline, no newline character is immediately preceded by space characters and the last character is a newline. It is guaranteed that, if the last character written to a text file is a newline, it will read back as the same.

It is implementation defined whether the last line written to a text file must terminate with a newline character; this is because on some implementations text files and binary files are the same.

Some implementations may strip the leading space from lines consisting only of a space followed by a newline, or strip trailing spaces at the end of a line!

An implementation must support text files with lines containing at least 254 characters, including the terminating newline.Opening a text stream in update mode may result in a binary stream in some implementations. Writing on a text stream may cause some implementations to truncate the file at that point—any data beyond the last byte of the current write being discarded.

BINARY STREAMS

A binary stream is a sequence of characters that can be used to record a program's internal data, such as the contents of structures or arrays in binary form.

Data read in from a binary stream will always compare equal to data written out earlier to the same stream, under the same implementation. In some circumstances, an implementation-defined number of NUL characters may be appended to a binary stream.

THE STDIO.H HEADER FILE

To provide support for streams of the various kinds, a number of functions and macros exist. The <stdio.h> header file contains the various declarations necessary for the functions, together with the following macro and type declarations:

FILE

The type of an object used to contain stream control information. Users of stdio never need to know the contents of these objects, but simply manipulate pointers to them. It is not safe to copy these objects within the programme; sometimes their addresses may be 'magic'.

`fpos_t`

A type of object that can be used to record unique values of a stream's file position indicator.

`_IOFBF _IOLBF _IONBF`

Values used to control the buffering of a stream in conjunction with thesetvbuf function.

`BUFSIZ`

The size of the buffer used by the setbuf function. An integral constant expression whose value is at least 256.

`EOF`

A negative integral constant expression, indicating the end-of-file condition on a stream i.e. that there is no more input.

`FILENAME_MAX`

The maximum length which a filename can have, if there is a limit, or otherwise the recommended size of an array intended to hold a file name.

`FOPEN_MAX`

The minimum number of files that the implementation guarantees may be held open concurrently; at least eight are guaranteed. Note that three predefined streams exist and may need to be closed if a programme needs to open more than five files explicitly.

`L_tmpnam`

The maximum length of the string generated by tmpnam; an integral constant expression.

`SEEK_CUR SEEK_END SEEK_SET`

Integral constant expressions used to control the actions of fseek.

`TMP_MAX`

The minimum number of unique filenames generated by tmpnam; an integral constant expression with a value of at least 25.

`stdin stdout stderr`

Predefined objects of type (FILE *) referring to the standard input, output and error streams respectively. These streams are automatically open when a programme starts execution.

OPENING, CLOSING AND BUFFERING OF STREAMS

OPENING

A stream is connected to a file by means of the fopen, freopen or tmpfilefunctions. These functions will, if successful, return a pointer to a FILE object.

Three streams are available without any special action; they are normally all connected to the physical device associated with the executing programme: usually your terminal.

They are referred to by the names stdin, the *standard input,* stdout, the *standard output,* and stderr, the *standard error* streams. Normal keyboard input is from stdin, normal terminal output is to stdout, and error messages are directed to stderr.

The separation of error messages from normal output messages allows the stdout stream to be connected to something other than the terminal device, and still to have error messages appear on the screen in front of you, rather than to be redirected to this file. These files are only fully buffered if they do not refer to interactive devices.

As mentioned earlier, the file position indicator may or may not be movable, depending on the underlying device. It is not possible, for example, to move the file position indicator on stdin if that is connected to a terminal, as it usually is.

All non-temporary files must have a *filename,* which is a string. The rules for what constitutes valid filenames are implementation defined. Whether a file can be simultaneously open multiple times is also implementation defined. Opening a new file may involve creating the file. Creating an existing file causes its previous contents to be discarded.

CLOSING

Files are closed by explicitly calling fclose, exit or by

returning from main. Any buffered data is flushed. If a programme stops for some other reason, the status of files which it had open is undefined.

BUFFERING

There are three types of buffering:

`Unbuffered`

Minimum internal storage is used by stdio in an attempt to send or receive data as soon as possible.

`Line buffered`

Characters are processed on a line-by-line basis. This is commonly used in interactive environments, and internal buffers are flushed only when full or when a newline is processed.

`Fully buffered`

Internal buffers are only flushed when full. The buffering associated with a stream can always be flushed by using fflushexplicitly. Support for the various types of buffering is implementation defined, and can be controlled within these limits using setbuf and setvbuf.

DIRECT FILE MANIPULATION

A number of functions exist to operate on files directly.

```
#include <stdio.h>
int remove(const char *filename);
int rename(const char *old, const char *new);
char *tmpnam(char *s);
FILE *tmpfile(void);
```

`remove`

Causes a file to be removed. Subsequent attempts to open the file will fail, unless it is first created again. If the file is already open, the operation ofremove is implementation defined. The return value is zero for success, any other value for failure.

`rename`

Changes the name of the file identified by old to new. Subsequent attempts to open the original name will fail, unless another file is created with the old name. As with remove, rename returns zero for a successful operation, any other value indicating a failure.

If a file with the new name exists prior to calling rename, the behaviour is implementation defined. If rename fails for any reason, the original file is unaffected.

`tmpnam`

Generates a string that may be used as a filename and is guaranteed to be different from any existing filename. It may be called repeatedly, each time generating a new name. The constant TMP_MAX is used to specify how many times tmpnam may be called before it can no longer find a unique name.TMP_MAX will be at least 25.

If tmpnam is called more than this number of times, its behaviour is undefined by the Standard, but many implementations offer no practical limit.

If the argument s is set to NULL, then tmpnam uses an internal buffer to build the name, and returns a pointer to that. Subsequent calls may alter the same internal buffer. The argument may instead point to an array of at leastL_tmpnam characters, in which case the name will be filled into the supplied buffer.

Such a filename may then be created, and used as a temporary file. Since the name is generated by the function, it is unlikely to be very useful in any other context. Temporary files of this nature are not removed, except by direct calls to the remove function. They are most often used to pass temporary data between two separate programs.

`tmpfile`

Creates a temporary binary file, opened for update, and returns a pointer to the stream of that file. The file will be removed when the stream is closed. If no file could be opened, tmpfile returns a null pointer.

OPENING NAMED FILES

Named files are opened by a call to the fopen function, whose declaration is this:

```
#include <stdio.h>
FILE *fopen(const char *pathname, const char *mode);
```

The pathname argument is the name of the file to open, such as that returned fromtmpnam, or some programme-specific filename.

Files can be opened in a variety of *modes,* such as *read* mode for reading data,*write* mode for writing data, and so on. Note that if you only want to write data to a file, fopen will *create* the file if it does not already exist, or truncate it to zero length if it did exist.

The Standard list of modes is shown in Table, although implementations may permit extra modes by appending extra characters at the end of the modes.

Table. File Opening Modes

Mode	Type of file	Read	Write	Create	Truncate
"r"	text	yes	n–	n–	no
"rb"	binary	yes	n–	n–	no
"r+"	text	yes	yes	n–	no
"r+b"	binary	yes	yes	n–	no
"rb+"	binary	yes	yes	n–	no
"w"	text	n–	yes	yes	yes
"wb"	binary	n–	yes	yes	yes
"w+"	text	yes	yes	yes	yes
"w+b"	binary	yes	yes	yes	yes
"wb+"	binary	yes	yes	yes	yes
"a"	text	n–	yes	yes	no
"ab"	binary	n–	yes	yes	no
"a+"	text	yes	yes	yes	no

"a+b"	binary	n–	yes	yes	no
"ab+"	binary	n–	yes	yes	no

Beware that some implementations of binary files may pad the last record withNULL characters, so opening them with modes ab, ab+ or a+b could position the file pointer beyond the last data written.

If a file is opened in append mode, all writes will occur at the end of the file, regardless of attempts to move the file position indicator with fseek. The initial position fo the file position indicator will be implementation defined.

Attempts to open a file in read mode, indicated by an 'r' as the first character in the mode string, will fail if the file does not already exist or can't be read.

Files opened for update ('+' as the second or third character of mode) may be both read and written, but a read may not immediately follow a write, or a write follow a read, without an intervening call to one (or more) of fflush, fseek, fsetpos or rewind. The only exception is that a write may immediately follow a read if EOF was read.

It may also be possible in some implementations to omit the b in the binary modes, using the same modes for text and binary files. Streams opened by fopen are fully buffered only if they are not connected to an interactive device; this ensures that prompts and responses are handled properly.

If fopen fails to open a file, it returns a null pointer; otherwise, it returns a pointer to the object controlling the stream. The stdin, stdout and stderr objects are not necessarily modifiable and it may not be possible to use the value returned fromfopen for assignment to one of them. For this reason, freopen is provided.

FREOPEN

The freopen function is used to take an existing stream pointer and associate it with another named file:

```
#include <stdio.h>
FILE *freopen(const char *pathname,
```

```
const char *mode, FILE *stream);
```

The mode argument is the same as for fopen. The stream is closed first, and any errors from the close are ignored. On error, NULL is returned, otherwise the new value for stream is returned.

CLOSING FILES

An open file is closed using fclose:

```
#include <stdio.h>
int fclose(FILE *stream);
```

Any unwritten data buffered for stream is flushed out and any unread data is thrown away. If a buffer had been automatically allocated for the stream, it is freed. The file is then closed.

Zero is returned on success, EOF if any error occurs.

SETBUF, SETVBUF

These two functions are used to change the buffering strategy for an open stream:

```
#include <stdio.h>
int setvbuf(FILE *stream, char *buf,
int type, size_t size);
void setbuf(FILE *stream, char *buf);
```

They must be used *before* the file is either read from or written to. The typeargument defines how the stream will be buffered.

Table. Table Type of buffering

Value	Effect
_IONBF	Do not buffer I/O
_IOFBF	Fully buffer I/O
_IOLBF	Line buffer: flush buffer when full, when newline is written or when a read is requested.

The buf argument can be a null pointer, in which case an array is automatically allocated to hold the buffered data. Otherwise, the user can provide a buffer, but should ensure that its lifetime is at least as long as that of the stream: a common mistake is to use automatic storage allocated inside a compound statement; in correct usage it is usual to obtain the storage from malloc instead. The size of the buffer is specified by the size argument. A call of setbuf is exactly the same as a call of setvbuf with IOFBF for the typeargument, and BUFSIZ for the size argument. If buf is a null pointer, the value_IONBF is used for type instead.

No value is returned by setbuf, setvbuf returns zero on success, non-zero if invalid values are provided for type or size, or the request cannot be complied with.

FFLUSH

```
#include <stdio.h>
int fflush(FILE *stream);
```

If stream refers to a file opened for output or update, any unwritten data is 'written' out. Exactly what that means is a function of the host environment, and C cannot guarantee, for example, that data immediately reaches the surface of a disk which might be supporting the file.

If the stream is associated with a file opened for input or update, any preceding ungetc operation is forgotten. The most recent operation on the stream must have been an output operation; if not, the behaviour is undefined.

A call of fflush with an argument of zero flushes every output or update stream. Care is taken to avoid those streams that have not had an output as their last operation, thus avoiding the undefined behaviour mentioned above.

EOF is returned if an error occurs, otherwise zero.

PRINTF

Printf's name comes from print formatted. It generates output under the control of a *format string* (its first argument) which consists of literal characters to be printed and also special character sequences—*format specifiers*—which request that other arguments be fetched, formatted, and inserted into the string. Our very first programme was nothing more than a call to printf, printing a constant string:

```
printf("Hello, world!\n");
```

Our second programme also featured a call to printf:

```
printf("i is %d\n", i);
```

In that case, whenever printf "printed" the string "i is %d", it did not print it verbatim; it replaced the two characters%d with the value of the variable i.

There are quite a number of format specifiers for printf. *Here are the basic ones:*

%d	print an int argument in decimal
%ld	print a long int argument in decimal
%c	print a character
%s	print a string
%f	print a float or double argument
%e	same as %f, but use exponential notation
%g	use %e or %f, whichever is better
%–	print an int argument in octal (base 8)
%x	print an int argument in hexadecimal (base 16)
%%	print a single %

It is also possible to specify the width and precision of numbers and strings as they are inserted (somewhat like FORTRAN format statements); we'll present those details in a later chapter. (Very briefly, for those who are curious: a notation like %3d means to print an int in a field at least 3 spaces wide; a notation like %5.2f means to print a float ordouble in a field at least 5 spaces wide, with two places to the right of the decimal.)

To illustrate with a few more examples: the call:

```
printf("%c %d %f %e %s %d%%\n", '1', 2, 3.14,
56000000., "eight", 9);
```

would print

```
1 2 3.140000 5.600000e+07 eight 9%
```

The call,

```
printf("%d %o %x\n", 100, 100, 100);
```

would print

```
100 144 64
```

Successive calls to printf just build up the output a piece at a time, so the calls

```
printf("Hello, ");
printf("world!\n");
```

would also print Hello, world! (on one line of output). Earlier we learned that C represents characters internally as small integers corresponding to the characters' values in the machine's character set (typically ASCII).

This means that there isn't really much difference between a character and an integer in C; most of the difference is in whether we choose to interpret an integer as an integer or a character. printf is one place where we get to make that choice: %d prints an integer value as a string of digits representing its decimal value, while %c prints the character corresponding to a character set value. So the lines

```
char c = 'A';
int i = 97;
printf("c = %c, i = %d\n", c, i);
```

would print c as the character A and i as the number 97. But if, on the other hand, we called

```
printf("c = %d, i = %c\n", c, i);
```

we'd see the decimal value (printed by %d) of the character 'A', followed by the character (whatever it is) which happens to have the decimal value 97.

You have to be careful when calling printf. It has no way of knowing how many arguments you've passed it or what their types are other than by looking for the format specifiers in the format string. If there are more format specifiers (that is, more % signs) than there are arguments, or if the arguments have the wrong types for the format specifiers, printf can misbehave badly, often printing nonsense numbers or (even worse) numbers which mislead you into thinking that some other part of your programme is broken.

Because of some automatic conversion rules which we haven't covered yet, you have a small amount of latitude in the types of the expressions you pass as arguments to printf. The argument for %c may be of type char or int, and the argument for %d may be of type char or int. The string argument for %s may be a string constant, an array of characters, or a pointer to some characters (though we haven't really covered strings or pointers yet). Finally, the arguments corresponding to %e, %f, and %g may be of types float or double. But other combinations do *not* work reliably: %d will not print a long int or a float or a double; %ld will not print an int; %e, %f, and %g will not print an int.

CHARACTER INPUT AND OUTPUT

Unless a programme can read some input, it's hard to keep it from doing exactly the same thing every time it's run, and thus being rather boring after a while.

The most basic way of reading input is by calling the function getchar. getchar reads one character from the "standard input," which is usually the user's keyboard, but which can sometimes be redirected by the operating system. getcharreturns the character it reads, or, if there are no more characters available, the special value EOF. A companion function is putchar, which writes one character to the "standard output." (The standard output is, again not surprisingly, usually the user's screen, although it, too, can be redirected. printf, like putchar, prints to the standard output; in fact, you can imagine that printf calls putchar to actually print each of the characters it formats.) Using these two functions, we can write a very basic programme to copy the input, a character at a time, to the output:

```
#include <stdio.h>
/* copy input to output */
main()
{
int c;
c = getchar();
while(c != EOF)
{
putchar(c);
c = getchar();
}
return 0;
}
```

This code is straightforward, and I encourage you to type it in and try it out. It reads one character, and if it is not the EOFcode, enters a while loop, printing one character and reading another, as long as the character read is not EOF. This is a straightforward loop, although there's one mystery surrounding the declaration of the variable c: if it holds characters, why is it an int?

We said that a char variable could hold integers corresponding to character set values, and that an int could hold integers of more arbitrary values. Since most character sets contain a few hundred characters, an int variable can in general comfortably hold all char values, and then some. Therefore, there's nothing wrong with declaring c as an int. But in fact, it's important to do so, because getchar can return every character value,*plus* that special, non-character value EOF, indicating that there are no more characters. Type char is only guaranteed to be able to hold all the character values; it is *not* guaranteed to be able to hold this "no more characters" value without possibly mixing it up with some actual character value. Therefore, you should always remember to use an int for anything you assigngetchar's return value to.

When you run the character copying programme, and it begins copying its input (your typing) to its output (your screen), you may find yourself wondering how to stop it. It stops when it receives end-of-file (EOF), but how do you send EOF? The answer depends on what kind of computer you're using. On Unix and Unix-related systems, it's almost always control-D. On MS-DOS machines, it's control-Z followed by the RETURN key. Under Think C on the Macintosh, it's control-D, just like Unix. On other systems, you may have to do some research to learn how to send EOF.

(Note, too, that the character you type to generate an end-of-file condition from the keyboard is *not* the same as the special EOF value returned by getchar. The EOF value returned by getchar is a code indicating that the input system has detected an end-of-file condition, whether it's reading the keyboard or a file or a magnetic tape or a network connection or anything else. In a disk file, at least, there is not likely to be any character *in* the file corresponding to EOF; as far as your programme is concerned, EOF indicates the absence of any more characters to read.)

Another excellent thing to know when doing any kind of programming is how to terminate a runaway programme. If a programme is running forever waiting for input, you can usually stop it by sending it an end-of-file, as above, but if it's running forever *not* waiting for something, you'll have to take more drastic measures. Under Unix, control-C (or, occasionally, the DELETE key) will terminate the current programme, almost no matter what. Under MS-DOS, control-C or control-BREAK will sometimes terminate the current programme, but by default MS-DOS only checks for control-C when it's looking for input, so an infinite loop can be unkillable.

There's a DOS command,

```
break on
```

which tells DOS to look for control-C more often, and I recommend using this command if you're doing any programming. (If a programme is in a really tight infinite loop under MS-DOS, there can be no way of killing it short of rebooting.) On the Mac, try command-period or command-option-ESCAPE.

You'll type a character, and see it on the screen right away, and assume it's your programme working, but it's only your computer echoing every key you type, as it always does. When you hit RETURN, a full line of characters is made available to your programme. It then zips several times through its loop, reading and printing all the characters in the line in quick succession. In other words, when you run this programme, it will probably seem to copy the input a line at a time, rather than a character at a time.

You may wonder how a programme could instead read a character right away, without waiting for the user to hit RETURN. That's an excellent question, but unfortunately the answer is rather complicated, and beyond the scope of our discussion here. (Among other things, how to read a character right away is one of the things that's not defined by the C language, and it's not defined by any of the standard library functions, either.

Stylistically, the character-copying programme above can be said to have one minor flaw: it contains two calls to getchar, one which reads the first character and one which reads (by virtue of the fact that it's in the body of the loop) all the other characters.

This seems inelegant and perhaps unnecessary, and it can also be risky: if there were more things going on within the loop, and if we ever changed the way we read characters, it would be easy to change one of the getchar calls but forget to change the other one. Is there a way to rewrite the loop so that there is only one call to getchar, responsible for reading all the characters? Is there a way to read a character, test it for EOF, and assign it to the variable c, all at the same time?

There is. It relies on the fact that the assignment operator, =, is just another operator in C. An assignment is not (necessarily) a standalone statement; it is an expression, and it has a value (the value that's assigned to the variable on the left-hand side), and it can therefore participate in a larger, surrounding expression. Therefore, most C programmers would write the character-copying loop like this:

```
while((c = getchar()) != EOF)
putchar(c);
```

The function getchar is called, as before, and its return value is assigned to the variable c. Then the value is immediately compared against the value EOF. Finally, the true/false value of the comparison controls the whileloop: as long as the value is not EOF, the loop continues executing, but as soon as an EOF is received, no more trips through the loop are taken, and it exits. The net result is that the call to getchar happens inside the test at the top of the whileloop, and doesn't have to be repeated before the loop and within the loop (more on this in a bit).

Stated another way, the syntax of a while loop is always,

`while(`*`expression`*`)...`

A comparison (using the = operator) is of course an expression; the syntax is,

```
expression != expression
```

And an assignment is an expression; the syntax is,

```
expression = expression
```

What we're seeing is just another example of the fact that expressions can be combined with essentially limitless generality and therefore infinite variety. The left-hand side of the = operator (its first *expression*) is the (sub)expression c = getchar(), and the combined expression is the *expression* needed by the while loop.

The extra parentheses around,

```
(c = getchar())
```

are important, and are there because because the *precedence* of the = operator is higher than that of the = operator.

If we (incorrectly) wrote,

```
while(c = getchar() != EOF) /* WRONG */
```

the compiler would interpret it as,

```
while(c = (getchar() != EOF))
```

That is, it would assign the result of the = operator to the variable c, which is *not* what we want.

"Precedence" refers to the rules for which operators are applied to their operands in which order, that is, to the rules controlling the default grouping of expressions and subexpressions. For example, the multiplication operator * has higher precedence than the addition operator +, which means that the expression a + b * c is parsed as a + (b * c). We'll have more to say about precedence later.

The line,

```
while((c = getchar()) != EOF)
```

epitomizes the cryptic brevity which C is notorious for. You may find this terseness infuriating (and you're not alone!), and it can certainly be carried too far, but bear with me for a moment while I defend it.

The simple example we've been discussing illustrates the tradeoffs well.

We have four things to do:

- Call getchar,
- Assign its return value to a variable,
- Test the return value against EOF, and

- Process the character (in this case, print it out again).

We can't eliminate any of these steps. We have to assign getchar's value to a variable because we have to do two different things with it (test, and print). Therefore, compressing the assignment and test into the same line is the only good way of avoiding two distinct calls to getchar. You may not agree that the compressed idiom is better for being more compact or easier to read, but the fact that there is now only one call to getchar *is* a real virtue.

Don't think that you'll have to write compressed lines like,

```
while((c = getchar()) != EOF)
```

right away, or in order to be an "expert C programmer." But, for better or worse, most experienced C programmers do like to use these idioms (whether they're justified or not), so you'll need to be able to at least recognize and understand them when you're reading other peoples' code.

READING LINES

It's often convenient for a programme to process its input not a character at a time but rather a line at a time, that is, to read an entire line of input and then act on it all at once. The standard C library has a couple of functions for reading lines, but they have a few awkward features, so we're going to learn more about character input (and about writing functions in general) by writing our own function to read one line.

Here it is:

```
#include <stdio.h>
/* Read one line from standard input, */
/* copying it to line array (but no more than
max chars). */
/* Does not place terminating \n in line array.
*/
/* Returns line length, or 0 for empty line, or
EOF for end-of-file. */
int getline(char line[], int max)
{
int nch = 0;
int c;
```

```
max = max - 1;  /* leave room for '\0' */
while((c = getchar()) != EOF)
{
if(c == '\n')
break;
if(nch < max)
{
line[nch] = c;
nch = nch + 1;
}
}
if(c == EOF && nch == 0)
return EOF;
line[nch] = '\0';
return nch;
}
```

As the comment indicates, this function will read one line of input from the standard input, placing it into the line array. The size of the line array is given by the max argument; the function will never write more than max characters into line.

The main body of the function is a getchar loop, much as we used in the character-copying programme. In the body of this loop, however, we're storing the characters in an array. Also, we're only reading one line of characters, then stopping and returning.

First of all, the getline function accepts an array as a parameter. As we've said, array parameters are an exception to the rule that functions receive copies of their arguments—in the case of arrays, the function *does* have access to the actual array passed by the caller, and *can* modify it. Since the function is accessing the caller's array, not creating a new one to hold a copy, the function does not have to declare the argument array's size; it's set by the caller. However, so that we won't overflow the caller's array by reading too long a line into it, we allow the caller to pass along the size of the array, which we promise not to exceed.

Second, we see an example of the break statement. The top of the loop looks like our earlier character-copying loop—

it stops when it reaches EOF—but we only want this loop to read one line, so we also stop (that is, break out of the loop) when we see the \n character signifying end-of-line. An equivalent loop, without the break statement, would be,

```
while((c = getchar()) != EOF && c != '\n')
{
if(nch < max)
{
line[nch] = c;
nch = nch + 1;
}
}
```

We haven't learned about the internal representation of strings yet, but it turns out that strings in C are simply arrays of characters, which is why we are reading the line into an array of characters. The end of a string is marked by the special character, '\0'. To make sure that there's always room for that character, on our way in we subtract 1 from max, the argument that tells us how many characters we may place in the line array. When we're done reading the line, we store the end-of-string character '\0' at the end of the string we've just built in the line array.

Finally, there's one subtlety in the code which isn't too important for our purposes now but which you may wonder about: it's arranged to handle the possibility that a few characters (i.e. the apparent beginning of a line) are read, followed immediately by an EOF, without the usual \n end-of-line character.

In any case, the function returns the length (number of characters) of the line it read, not including the \n. (Therefore, it returns 0 for an empty line.) Like getchar, it returns EOF when there are no more lines to read. (It happens that EOF is a negative number, so it will never match the length of a line that getline has read.)

Here is an example of a test programme which calls getline, reading the input a line at a time and then printing each line back out:

```
#include <stdio.h>
```

```
extern int getline(char [], int);
main()
{
char line[256];
while(getline(line, 256) != EOF)
printf("you typed \"%s\"\n", line);
return 0;
}
```

The notation char [] in the function prototype for getline says that getline accepts as its first argument an array ofchar. When the programme calls getline, it is careful to pass along the actual size of the array. You might notice a potential problem: since the number 256 appears in two places, if we ever decide that 256 is too small, and that we want to be able to read longer lines, we could easily change one of the instances of 256, and forget to change the other one.

READING NUMBERS

The getline function of the previous section reads one line from the user, as a *string*. What if we want to read a number? One straightforward way is to read a string as before, and then immediately convert the string to a number. The standard C library contains a number of functions for doing this. The simplest to use are atoi(), which converts a string to an integer, and atof(), which converts a string to a floating-point number. (Both of these functions are declared in the header<stdlib.h>, so you should #include that header at the top of any file using these functions.

You could read an integer from the user like this:

```
#include <stdlib.h>
char line[256];
int n;
printf("Type an integer:\n");
getline(line, 256);
n = atoi(line);
```

Now the variable n contains the number typed by the user. (This assumes that the user *did* type a valid number, and thatgetline did not return EOF.)

Reading a floating-point number is similar:

```
#include <stdlib.h>
char line[256];
double x;
printf("Type a floating-point number:\n");
getline(line, 256);
x = atof(line);
```

atof is actually declared as returning type double, but you could also use it with a variable of type float, because in general, C automatically converts between float and double as needed.

Another way of reading in numbers, which you're likely to see in other books on C, involves the scanf function, but it has several problems, so we won't discuss it for now. (Superficially, scanf seems simple enough, which is why it's often used, especially in textbooks. The trouble is that to perform input reliably using scanf is not nearly as easy as it looks, especially when you're not sure what the user is going to type.)

FORMATTED I/O

There are a number of related functions used for formatted I/O, each one determining the format of the I/O from a *format string*. For output, the format string consists of plain text, which is output unchanged, and embedded *format specifications* which call for some special processing of one of the remaining arguments to the function. On input, the plain text must match what is seen in the input stream; the format specifications again specify what the meaning of remaining arguments is.

Each format specification is introduced by a % character, followed by the rest of the specification.

OUTPUT: THE PRINTF FAMILY

For those functions performing output, the format specification takes the following form, with optional parts enclosed in brackets:

```
%<flags><field width><precision><length>
conversion
```

The meaning of *flags, field width, precision, length,* and *conversion* are given below, although tersely. For more detail, it is worth looking at what the Standard says.

flags

Zero or more of the following:

-

Left justify the conversion within its field.

+

A signed conversion will always start with a plus or minus sign.

space

If the first character of a signed conversion is not a sign, insert a space.

Overridden by + if present:

#

Forces an alternative form of output. The first digit of an octal conversion will always be a 0; inserts 0X in front of a non-zero hexadecimal conversion; forces a decimal point in all floating point conversions even if one is not necessary; does not remove trailing zeros from g and G conversions.

0

Pad d, i, o, u, x, X, e, E, f, F and G conversions on the left with zeros up to the field width. Overidden by the - flag. If a precision is specified for the d, i, o, u, x or X conversions, the flag is ignored. The behaviour is undefined for other conversions.

field width

A decimal integer specifying the minimum output field width. This will be exceeded if necessary. If an asterisk is used here, the next argument is converted to an integer and used for the value of the field width; if the value is negative it is treated as a - flag followed by a positive field width.

Output that would be less than the field width is padded with spaces (zeros if the*field width* integer starts with a zero) to fit. The padding is on the left unless the left-adjustment flag is specified.

precision

This starts with a period '.'. It specifies the minimum

number of digits for d,i, o, u, x, or X conversions; the number of digits after the decimal point for e,E, f conversions; the maximum number of digits for g and G conversions; the number of characters to be printed from a string for s conversion.

The amount of padding overrides the field width. If an asterisk is used here, the next argument is converted to an integer and used for the value of the field width. If the value is negative, it is treated as if it were missing. If only the period is present, the precision is taken to be zero.

length

h preceding a specifier to print an integral type causes it to be treated as if it were a short. (Note that the various sorts of short are always promoted to one of the flavours of int when passed as an argument.) l works like h but applies to a long integral argument.

L is used to indicate that a long doubleargument is to be printed, and only applies to the floating-point specifiers. These are cause undefined behaviour if they are used with the 'wrong' type of conversion.

Conversion

Table Conversions

Specifier	Effect	Default precision
d	signed decimal	1
i	signed decimal	1
u	unsigned decimal	1
–	unsigned octal	1
x	unsigned hexadecimal (0–f)	1
X	unsigned hexadecimal (0–F)	1
	Precision specifies minimum number of digits, expanded with leading zeros if necessary. Printing a value of zero with zero precision outputs no characters.	
f	Print a double with *precision* digits	6

	(rounded) after the decimal point. To suppress the decimal point use a *precision* of explicitly zero. Otherwise, at least one digit appears in front of the point.	
e, E	Print a double in exponential format, rounded, with one digit before the decimal point, *precision* after it. A *precision* of zero suppresses the decimal point. There will be at least two digits in the exponent, which is printed as 1.23e15 in e format, or 1.23E15 inE format.	6
g,G	Use style f, or e (E with G) depending unspecified on the exponent. If the exponent is less than "4 or e"*precision,* f is not used. Trailing zeros are suppressed, a decimal point is only printed if there is a following digit.	
c	The int argument is converted to an unsigned char and the resultant character printed.	
s	Print a string up to *precision* infinite digits long. If *precision*is not specified, or is greater than the length of the string, the string must be NUL terminated.	
p	Display the value of a (void *) pointer in a system-dependent way.	
n	The argument must be a pointer to an integer. The number of characters output so far by this call will be written into the integer.	
%	A %	—

The functions that use these formats are described in Table 9.6. All need the inclusion of <stdio.h>. Their declarations are as shown.

```
#include <stdio.h>
int fprintf(FILE *stream, const char *format...);
int printf(const char *format...);
int sprintf(char *s, const char *format...);
#include <stdarg.h>/* as well as stdio.h */
int vfprintf(FILE *stream, const char *format,
va list arg);
int vprintf(const char *format, va list arg);
int vsprintf(char *s, const char *format, va
list arg);
```

Table Functions Performing Formatted Output

Name	Purpose
fprintf	General formatted output as described. Output is written to the file indicated by stream.
printf	Identical to fprintf with a first argument equal to stdout.
sprintf	Identical to fprintf except that the output is not written to a file, but written into the character array pointed to by s.
vfprintf	Formatted output as for fprintf, but with the variable argument list replaced by arg which must have been initialized by va_start.va_end is not called by this function.
vprintf	Identical to vfprintf with a first argument equal to stdout.
vsprintf	Formatted output as for sprintf, but with the variable argument list replaced by arg which must have been initialized by va_start.va_end is not called by this function.

All of the above functions return the number of characters output, or a negative value on error. The trailing null is *not* counted by sprintf and vsprintf.

Implementations must permit at least 509 characters to be produced by any single conversion.

INPUT SCANF

A number of functions exist analogous to the printf family,

but for the purposes of input instead. The most immediate difference between the two families is that thescanf group needs to be passed *pointers* to their arguments, so that the values read can be assigned to the proper destinations. Forgetting to pass a pointer is a very common error, and one which the compiler cannot detect—the variable argument list prevents it.

The format string is used to control interpretation of a stream of input data, which generally contains values to be assigned to the objects pointed to by the remaining arguments to scanf.

The contents of the format string may contain:

white space

This causes the input stream to be read up to the next non-white-space character.

ordinary character

Anything except white-space or % characters. The next character in the input stream must match this character.

`conversion specification`

This is a % character, followed by an optional * character (which suppresses the conversion), followed by an optional nonzero decimal integer specifying the maximum field width, an optional h, l or L to control the length of the conversion and finally a non-optional conversion specifier. Note that use ofh, l, or L will affect the type of pointer which must be used.

Except for the specifiers c, n and [, a field of input is a sequence of non-space characters starting at the first non-space character in the input. It terminates at the first conflicting character or when the input field width is reached.

The result is put into wherever the corresponding argument points, unless the assignment is suppressed using the * mentioned already.

The following conversion specifiers may be used:

d i o u x

Convert a signed integer, a signed integer in a form acceptable to strtol, an octal integer, an unsigned integer and a hexadecimal integer respectively.

e f g

Convert a float (*not* a double).

s

Read a string, and add a null at the end. The string is terminated by whitespace on input (which is not read as part of the string).

[

Read a string. A list of characters, called the *scan set* follows the [. A]delimits the list. Characters are read until (but not including) the first character which is ***not*** in the scan set. If the first character in the list is a circumflex ^, then the scan set includes any character not in the list.

If the initial sequence is [^] or [], the] is not a delimiter, but part of the list and another] will be needed to end the list. If there is a minus sign (-) in the list, it must be either the first or the last character; otherwise the meaning is implementation defined.

c

Read a single character; white space is significant here. To read the first non-white space character, use %1s. A field width indicates that an array of characters is to be read.

p

Read a (void *) pointer previously written out using the %p of one of theprintfs.

%

A % is expected in the input, no assignment is made.

n

Return as an integer the number of characters read by this call so far. The size specifiers have the effect shown in Table.

Table. Size Specifiers

Specifier	Modifies	Converts
l	d i o u x	long int
h	d i o u x	short int
l	e f	double
L	e f	long double

The functions are described below, with the following declarations:

```
#include <stdio.h>
int fscanf(FILE *stream, const char *format...);
int sscanf(const char *s, const char *format...);
int scanf(const char *format...);
```

Fscanf takes its input from the designated stream, scanf is identical to fscanfwith a first argument of stdin, and sscanf takes its input from the designated character array.

Chapter 7

Operators and Strings

ASSIGNMENT OPERATORS

The first and more general way is that any time you have the pattern

```
v = v op e
```

where *v* is any variable (or anything like a[i]), *op* is any of the binary arithmetic operators we've seen so far, and *e* is any expression, you can replace it with the simplified

```
v op= e
```

For example, you can replace the expressions:

```
i = i + 1
j = j - 10
k = k * (n + 1)
a[i] = a[i]/ b
```

with,

```
i += 1
j -= 10
k *= n + 1
a[i]/= b
```

In an example in a previous chapter, we used the assignment

```
a[d1 + d2] = a[d1 + d2] + 1;
```

to count the rolls of a pair of dice. Using +=, we could simplify this expression to,

```
a[d1 + d2] += 1;
```

As these examples show, you can use the "op=" form with any of the arithmetic operators (and with several other operators that we haven't seen yet). The expression, *e*, does not have to be the constant 1; it can be any expression. You don't always need as many explicit parentheses when using the *op*= operators: the expression

```
k *= n + 1
```

is interpreted as,

```
k = k * (n + 1)
```

INCREMENT AND DECREMENT OPERATORS

The assignment operators of the previous section let us replace *v* = *v op e* with *v op*= *e*, so that we didn't have to mention*v* twice. In the most common cases, namely when we're adding or subtracting the constant 1 (that is, when *op* is + or - and*e* is 1), C provides another set of shortcuts: the *autoincrement* and *autodecrement* operators. In their simplest forms, they look like this:

```
++i    add 1 to i
—j subtract 1 from j
```

These correspond to the slightly longer i += 1 and j -= 1, respectively, and also to the fully "longhand" forms i = i + 1 and j = j - 1.

The ++ and — operators apply to one operand (they're *unary* operators). The expression ++i adds 1 to i, and stores the incremented result back in i. This means that these operators don't just compute new values; they also modify the value of some variable. (They share this property—modifying some variable—with the assignment operators; we can say that these operators all have *side effects*. That is, they have some effect, on the side, other than just computing a new value.)

The incremented (or decremented) result is also made available to the rest of the expression, so an expression like

```
k = 2 * ++i
```

means "add one to i, store the result back in i, multiply it by 2, and store *that* result in k." (This is a pretty meaningless expression; our actual uses of ++ later will make more sense.)

Both the ++ and — operators have an unusual property: they can be used in two ways, depending on whether they are written to the left or the right of the variable they're operating on. In either case, they increment or decrement the variable they're operating on; the difference concerns whether it's the old or the new value that's "returned" to the surrounding expression. The *prefix* form ++i increments i and returns the incremented value. The *postfix* form i++ increments i, but returns the *prior*, non-incremented value. Rewriting our previous example slightly, the expression,

```
k = 2 * i++
```

means "take i's old value and multiply it by 2, increment i, store the result of the multiplication in k."

The distinction between the prefix and postfix forms of ++ and — will probably seem strained at first, but it will make more sense once we begin using these operators in more realistic situations.

For example, our getline function of the previous chapter used the statements,

```
line[nch] = c;
nch = nch + 1;
```

as the body of its inner loop. Using the ++ operator, we could simplify this to,

```
line[nch++] = c;
```

We wanted to increment nch *after* deciding which element of the line array to store into, so the postfix form nch++ is appropriate.

Notice that it only makes sense to apply the ++ and — operators to variables (or to other "containers," such as a[i]).

It would be meaningless to say something like,

```
1++
or
(2+3)++
```

The ++ operator doesn't just mean "add one"; it means "add one *to a variable*" or "make a variable's value one more than it was before." But (1+2) is not a variable, it's an expression; so there's no place for ++ to store the incremented result.

Another unfortunate example is,

```
i = i++;
```

which some confused programmers sometimes write, presumably because they want to be extra sure that i is incremented by 1. But i++ all by itself is sufficient to increment i by 1; the extra (explicit) assignment to i is unnecessary and in fact counterproductive, meaningless, and incorrect. If you want to increment i (that is, add one to it, and store the result back in i), either use

```
i = i + 1;
or
i += 1;
or
++i;
or
i++;
```

Don't try to use some bizarre combination. Did it matter whether we used ++i or i++ in this last example? Remember, the difference between the two forms is what value (either the old or the new) is passed on to the surrounding expression. If there is no surrounding expression, if the++i or i++ appears all by itself, to increment i and do nothing else, you can use either form; it makes no difference.

Two ways that an expression can appear "all by itself," with "no surrounding expression," are when it is an expression statement terminated by a semicolon, as above, or when it is one of the controlling expressions of a for loop.

For example, both the loops,

```
for(i = 0; i < 10; ++i)
printf("%d\n", i);
and
for(i = 0; i < 10; i++)
printf("%d\n", i);
```

will behave exactly the same way and produce exactly the same results. (In real code, postfix increment is probably more common, though prefix definitely has its uses, too.)

In the preceding section, we simplified the expression:

```
a[d1 + d2] = a[d1 + d2] + 1;
```

from a previous chapter down to,

```
a[d1 + d2] += 1;
```

Using ++, we could simplify it still further to,

```
a[d1 + d2]++;
```

```
or
++a[d1 + d2];
```

(Again, in this case, both are equivalent.)

ORDER OF EVALUATION

When you start using the ++ and — operators in larger expressions, you end up with expressions which do several things at once, i.e., they modify several different variables at more or less the same time. When you write such an expression, you must be careful not to have the expression "pull the rug out from under itself" by assigning two different values to the same variable, or by assigning a new value to a variable at the same time that another part of the expression is trying to use the value of that variable.

Actually, we had already started writing expressions which did several things at once even before we met the ++ and —operators.

The expression,

```
(c = getchar()) != EOF
```

assigns getchar's return value to c, *and* compares it to EOF. The ++ and — operators make it much easier to cram a lot into a small expression: the example,

```
line[nch++] = c;
```

from the previous section assigned c to line[nch], *and* incremented nch. We'll eventually meet expressions which do*three* things at once, such as,

```
a[i++] = b[j++];
```

which assigns b[j] to a[i], and increments i, *and* increments j.

If you're not careful, though, it's easy for this sort of thing to get out of hand. Can you figure out exactly what the expressionm,

```
a[i++] = b[i++]; /* WRONG */
```

should do? I can't, and here's the important part: *neither can the compiler*. We know that the definition of postfix ++ is that the former value, before the increment, is what goes on to participate in the rest of the expression, but the expressiona[i++] = b[i++] contains *two* ++ operators. Which of them happens first? Does this expression assign the old ith element of b to the new ith element of a, or vice versa? No one knows.

When the order of evaluation matters but is not well-defined (that is, when we can't say for sure which order the compiler will evaluate the various dependent parts in) we say that the meaning of the expression is *undefined*, and if we're smart we won't write the expression in the first place. (Why would anyone ever write an "undefined" expression? Because sometimes, the compiler happens to evaluate it in the order a programmer wanted, and the programmer assumes that since it works, it must be okay.)

For example, suppose we carelessly wrote this loop:

```
int i, a[10];
i = 0;
while(i < 10)
a[i] = i++;          /* WRONG */
```

It looks like we're trying to set a[0] to 0, a[1] to 1, etc. But what if the increment i++ happens before the compiler decides which cell of the array a to store the (unincremented) result in? We might end up setting a[1] to 0, a[2] to 1, etc., instead. Since, in this case, we can't be sure which order things would happen in, we simply shouldn't write code like this. In this case, what we're doing matches the pattern of a for loop, anyway, which would be a better choice:

```
for(i = 0; i < 10; i++)
a[i] = i;
```

Now that the increment i++ isn't crammed into the same expression that's setting a[i], the code is perfectly well-defined, and is guaranteed to do what we want. In general, you should be wary of ever trying to second-guess the order an expression will be evaluated in, with two exceptions:

- You can obviously assume that precedence will dictate the order in which binary operators are applied. This typically says more than just what order things happens in, but also what the expression actually *means*. (In other words, the precedence of * over + says more than that the multiplication "happens first" in 1 + 2 * 3; it says that the answer is 7, not 9.)

- Although we haven't mentioned it yet, it is guaranteed that the logical operators && and || are evaluated left-to-right, and that the right-hand side is not evaluated at all if the left-hand side determines the outcome.
- To look at one more example, it might seem that the code

```
int i = 7;
printf("%d\n", i++ * i++);
```

would have to print 56, because no matter which order the increments happen in, 7*8 is 8*7 is 56. But ++ just says that the increment happens later, not that it happens immediately, so this code could print 49 (if the compiler chose to perform the multiplication first, and both increments later). And, it turns out that ambiguous expressions like this are such a bad idea that the ANSI C Standard does not require compilers to do anything reasonable with them at all. Theoretically, the above code could end up printing 42, or 8923409342, or 0, or crashing your computer.

Programmers sometimes mistakenly imagine that they can write an expression which tries to do too much at once and then predict exactly how it will behave based on "order of evaluation." For example, we know that multiplication has higher*precedence* than addition, which means that in the expression

```
i + j * k
```

j will be multiplied by k, and then i will be added to the result. Informally, we often say that the multiplication happens "before" the addition. That's true in this case, but it doesn't say as much as we might think about a more complicated expression, such as

```
i++ + j++ * k++
```

In this case, besides the addition and multiplication, i, j, and k are all being incremented. We can *not* say which of them will be incremented first; it's the compiler's choice. (In particular, it is *not* necessarily the case that j++ or k++ will happen first; the compiler might choose to save i's value somewhere and increment i first, even though it will have to keep the old value around until after it has done the multiplication.)

In the preceding example, it probably doesn't matter which variable is incremented first. It's not too hard, though, to write an expression where it does matter. In fact, we've seen one already: the ambiguous assignment a[i++] = b[i++]. We still don't know which i++ happens first.

We can *not* assume, based on the right-to-left behaviour of the = operator, that the right-hand i++ will happen first.) But if we had to know what a[i++] = b[i++] really did, we'd have to know whichi++ happened first.

Finally, note that parentheses don't dictate overall evaluation order any more than precedence does. Parentheses override precedence and say which operands go with which operators, and they therefore affect the overall meaning of an expression, but they don't say anything about the order of subexpressions or side effects. We could not "fix" the evaluation order of any of the expressions we've been discussing by adding parentheses.

If we wrote,

```
i++ + (j++ * k++)
```

we still wouldn't know which of the increments would happen first. (The parentheses would force the multiplication to happen before the addition, but precedence already would have forced that, anyway.) If we wrote,

```
(i++) * (i++)
```

the parentheses wouldn't force the increments to happen before the multiplication or in any well-defined order; this parenthesized version would be just as undefined as i++ * i++ was.

There's a line from Kernighan & Ritchie, which I am fond of quoting when discussing these issues:

The moral is that writing code that depends on order of evaluation is a bad programming practice in any language. Naturally, it is necessary to know what things to avoid, but if you don't know *how* they are done on various machines, you won't be tempted to take advantage of a particular implementation.

If you don't know *how* they are done on various machines, that innocence may help to protect you.

I actually prefer the first edition wording. Many textbooks encourage you to write small programs to find out how your compiler implements some of these ambiguous expressions, but it's just one step from writing a small programme to find out, to writing a real programme which makes use of what you've just learned. But you *don't* want to write programs that work only under one particular compiler, that take advantage of the way that one compiler (but perhaps no other) happens to implement the undefined expressions.

It's fine to be curious about what goes on "under the hood," and many of you will be curious enough about what's going on with these "forbidden" expressions that you'll want to investigate them, but please keep very firmly in mind that, for real programs, the very easiest way of dealing with ambiguous, undefined expressions (which one compiler interprets one way and another interprets another way and a third crashes on) is not to write them in the first place.

STRING

In fact, C's only truly built-in string-handling is that it allows us to use *string constants* (also called *string literals*) in our code. Whenever we write a string, enclosed in double quotes, C automatically creates an array of characters for us, containing that string, terminated by the \0 character. For example, we can declare and define an array of characters, and initialize it with a string constant:

```
char string[] = "Hello, world!";
```

In this case, we can leave out the dimension of the array, since the compiler can compute it for us based on the size of the initializer (14, including the terminating \0). This is the only case where the compiler sizes a string array for us, however; in other cases, it will be necessary that *we* decide how big the arrays and other data structures we use to hold strings are.

To do anything else with strings, we must typically call functions. The C library contains a few basic string manipulation functions, and to learn more about strings, we'll be looking at how these functions might be implemented.

Since C never lets us assign entire arrays, we use the strcpy function to copy one string to another:

```
#include <string.h>
char string1[] = "Hello, world!";
char string2[20];
strcpy(string2, string1);
```

The destination string is strcpy's first argument, so that a call to strcpy mimics an assignment expression (with the destination on the left-hand side).

Notice that we had to allocate string2 big enough to hold the string that would be copied to it. Also, at the top of any source file where we're using the standard library's string-handling functions (such as strcpy) we must include the line

```
#include <string.h>
```

which contains external declarations for these functions.

Since C won't let us compare entire arrays, either, we must call a function to do that, too. The standard library's strcmp function compares two strings, and returns 0 if they are identical, or a negative number if the first string is alphabetically "less than" the second string, or a positive number if the first string is "greater."

Roughly speaking, what it means for one string to be "less than" another is that it would come first in a dictionary or telephone book, although there are a few anomalies.

Here is an example:

```
char string3[] = "this is";
char string4[] = "a test";
if(strcmp(string3, string4) == 0)
printf("strings are equal\n");
else   printf("strings are different\n");
```

This code fragment will print "strings are different". Notice that strcmp does *not* return a Boolean, true/false, zero/nonzero answer, so it's not a good idea to write something like,

```
if(strcmp(string3, string4))
...
```

because it will behave backwards from what you might reasonably expect. (Nevertheless, if you start reading other people's code, you're likely to come across conditionals like if(strcmp(a, b)) or even if(!strcmp(a, b)).

The first does something if the strings are unequal; the second does something if they're equal. You can read these more easily if you pretend for a moment that strcmp's name were strdiff, instead.)

Another standard library function is strcat, which concatenates strings. It does *not* concatenate two strings together and give you a third, new string; what it really does is append one string onto the end of another.

If it gave you a new string, it would have to allocate memory for it somewhere, and the standard library string functions generally never do that for you automatically.

Here's an example:

```
char string5[20] = "Hello, ";
char string6[] = "world!";
printf("%s\n", string5);
strcat(string5, string6);
printf("%s\n", string5);
```

The first call to printf prints "Hello, ", and the second one prints "Hello, world!", indicating that the contents of string6 have been tacked on to the end ofstring5. Notice that we declared string5 with extra space, to make room for the appended characters.

If you have a string and you want to know its length (perhaps so that you can check whether it will fit in some other array you've allocated for it), you can callstrlen, which returns the length of the string (i.e. the number of characters in it), not including the \0:

```
char string7[] = "abc";
int len = strlen(string7);
printf("%d\n", len);
```

Finally, you can print strings out with printf using the %s format specifier, as we've been doing in these examples already (e.g. printf("%s\n", string5);). Since a string is just an array of characters, all of the string-handling functions we've just seen can be written quite simply, using no techniques more complicated than the ones we already know. In fact, it's quite instructive to look at how these functions might be implemented.

Here is a version of strcpy:

```
mystrcpy(char dest[], char src[])
{
int i = 0;
while(src[i] != '\0')
{
dest[i] = src[i];
i++;
}
dest[i] = '\0';
}
```

We've called it mystrcpy instead of strcpy so that it won't clash with the version that's already in the standard library. Its operation is simple: it looks at characters in the src string one at a time, and as long as they're not \0, assigns them, one by one, to the corresponding positions in the dest string. When it's done, it terminates the dest string by appending a \0. (After exiting the while loop, i is guaranteed to have a value one greater than the subscript of the last character in src.) For comparison, here's a way of writing the same code, using a for loop:

```
for(i = 0; src[i] != '\0'; i++)
dest[i] = src[i];
dest[i] = '\0';
```

Yet a third possibility is to move the test for the terminating \0 character out of the for loop header and into the body of the loop, using an explicit if and breakstatement, so that we can perform the test after the assignment and therefore use the assignment inside the loop to copy the \0 to dest, too:

```
for(i = 0;; i++)
{
```

```
dest[i] = src[i];
if(src[i] == '\0')
break;
}
```

Here is a version of strcmp:

```
mystrcmp(char str1[], char str2[])
{
int i = 0;
while(1)
{
if(str1[i] != str2[i])
return str1[i] - str2[i];
if(str1[i] == '\0' || str2[i] == '\0')
return 0;
i++;
}
}
```

Characters are compared one at a time. If two characters in one position differ, the strings are different, and we are supposed to return a value less than zero if the first string (str1) is alphabetically less than the second string. Since characters in C are represented by their numeric character set values, and since most reasonable character sets assign values to characters in alphabetical order, we can simply subtract the two differing characters from each other: the expression str1[i] - str2[i] will yield a negative result if the i'th character of str1 is less than the corresponding character in str2.

As it turns out, this will behave a bit strangely when comparing upper- and lower-case letters, but it's the traditional approach, which the standard versions of strcmp tend to use.) If the characters are the same, we continue around the loop, *unless* the characters we just compared were (both) \0, in which case we've reached the end of both strings, and they were both equal.

Notice that we used what may at first appear to be an infinite loop—the controlling expression is the constant 1, which is always true. What actually happens is that the loop runs until one of the two return statements breaks out of it (and the entire function). Note also that when one string is longer than the other, the first test will notice this (because one string will contain a real character at the [i] location, while the other will contain \0, and these are not equal) and the return value will be computed by subtracting the real character's value from 0, or vice versa. (Thus the shorter string will be treated as "less than" the longer.)

Finally, here is a version of strlen:

```
int mystrlen(char str[])
{
int i;
for(i = 0; str[i] != '\0'; i++)
{}
return i;
}
```

In this case, all we have to do is find the \0 that terminates the string, and it turns out that the three control expressions of the for loop do all the work; there's nothing left to do in the body. Therefore, we use an empty pair of braces {} as the loop body. Equivalently, we could use a *null statement*, which is simply a semicolon:

```
for(i = 0; str[i] != '\0'; i++)
;
```

Empty loop bodies can be a bit startling at first, but they're not unheard of. Everything we've looked at so far has come out of C's standard libraries. As one last example, let's write a substr function, for extracting a substring out of a larger string.

We might call it like this:

```
char string8[] = "this is a test";
char string9[10];
substr(string9, string8, 5, 4);
printf("%s\n", string9);
```

The idea is that we'll extract a substring of length 4, starting at character 5 (0-based) of string8, and copy the substring to string9.

Just as with strcpy, it's our responsibility to declare the destination string (string9) big enough. Here is an implementation of substr. Not surprisingly, it's quite similar to strcpy:

```
substr(char dest[], char src[], int offset, int len)
{
int i;
for(i = 0; i < len && src[offset + i] != '\0';
i++)
dest[i] = src[i + offset];
dest[i] = '\0';
}
```

If you compare this code to the code for mystrcpy, you'll see that the only differences are that characters are fetched from src[offset + i] instead of src[i], and that the loop stops when len characters have been copied (or when the src string runs out of characters, whichever comes first).

In this chapter, we've been careless about declaring the return types of the string functions, and (with the exception of mystrlen) they haven't returned values. The real string functions do return values, but they're of type "pointer to character," which we haven't discussed yet.

When working with strings, it's important to keep firmly in mind the differences between characters and strings. We must also occasionally remember the way characters are represented, and about the relation between character values and integers.

As we have had several occasions to mention, a character is represented internally as a small integer, with a value depending on the character set in use. For example, we might find that 'A' had the value 65, that 'a' had the value 97, and that '+' had the value 43. (These are, in fact, the values in the ASCII character set, which most computers use. However, you don't need to learn these values, because the vast majority of the time, you use character constants to refer to characters, and the compiler worries about the values for you. Using character constants in preference to raw numeric values also makes your programs more portable.)

As we may also have mentioned, there is a big difference between a character and a string, even a string which contains only one character (other than the \0). For example, 'A' is *not* the same as "A". To drive home this point, let's illustrate it with a few examples.

If you have a string:

```
char string[] = "hello, world!";
you can modify its first character by saying
string[0] = 'H';
```

Of course, there's nothing magic about the first character; you can modify any character in the string in this way. Be aware, though, that it is not always safe to modify strings in-place like this; we'll say more about the modifiability of strings in a later chapter on pointers. Since you're replacing a character, you want a character constant, 'H'. It would *not* be right to write

```
string[0] = "H"; /* WRONG */
```

because "H" is a string (an array of characters), not a single character. (The destination of the assignment, string[0], is a char, but the right-hand side is a string; these types don't match.)

On the other hand, when you need a string, you must use a string. To print a single newline, you could call,

```
printf("\n");
It would not be correct to call
printf('\n');    /* WRONG */
```

printf always wants a string as its first argument. (As one final example, putchar wants a single character, so putchar ('\n') would be correct, andputchar("\n") would be incorrect.)

We must also remember the difference between strings and integers. If we treat the character '1' as an integer, perhaps by saying,

```
int i = '1';
```

we will probably *not* get the value 1 in i; we'll get the value of the character '1' in the machine's character set. (In ASCII, it's 49.) When we do need to find the numeric value of a digit character (or to go the other way, to get the digit character with a particular value) we can make use of the fact that, in any character set used by C, the values for the digit characters, whatever they are, are contiguous. In other words, no matter what values '0' and '1' have, '1' - '0' will be 1 (and, obviously, '0' - '0' will be 0). So, for a variable c holding some digit character, the expression,

```
c - '0'
```

gives us its value. (Similarly, for an integer value i, i + '0' gives us the corresponding digit character, as long as 0 <= i <= 9.)

Just as the character '1' is not the integer 1, the string "123" is not the integer 123. When we have a string of digits, we can convert it to the corresponding integer by calling the standard function atoi:

```
char string[] = "123";
int i = atoi(string);
int j = atoi("456");
```

Chapter 8

Preprocessor

GENERAL UNDERSTANDING

Conceptually, the "preprocessor" is a translation phase that is applied to your source code before the compiler proper gets its hands on it. (Once upon a time, the preprocessor was a separate programme, much as the compiler and linker may still be separate programs today.) Generally, the preprocessor performs textual substitutions on your source code, in three sorts of ways:

- *File inclusion*: Inserting the contents of another file into your source file, as if you had typed it all in there.
- *Macro substitution*: Replacing instances of one piece of text with another.
- *Conditional compilation*: Arranging that, depending on various circumstances, certain parts of your source code are seen or not seen by the compiler at all.

The syntax of the preprocessor is different from the syntax of the rest of C in several respects. First of all, the preprocessor is "line based." Each of the preprocessor directives we're going to learn about (all of which begin with the # character) must begin at the beginning of a line, and each ends at the end of the line.

The rest of C treats line ends as just another whitespace character, and doesn't care how your programme text is arranged into lines.) Secondly, the preprocessor does not know about the structure of C—about functions, statements, or expressions. It is possible to play strange tricks with the preprocessor to turn something which does not look like C into C (or vice versa). It's also possible to run into problems when a preprocessor substitution does not do what you expected it to, because the preprocessor does not respect the structure of C statements and expressions (but you expected it to). For the simple uses of the preprocessor we'll be discussing, you shouldn't have any of these problems, but you'll want to be careful before doing anything tricky or outrageous with the preprocessor.

As it happens, playing tricky and outrageous games with the preprocessor is considered sporting in some circles, but it rapidly gets out of hand, and can lead to bewilderingly impenetrable programs.

WORKING

Although the preprocessor is probably going to be implemented as an integral part of an Standard C compiler, it can equally well be though of as a separate programme which transforms C source code containing preprocessor directives into source code with the directives removed.

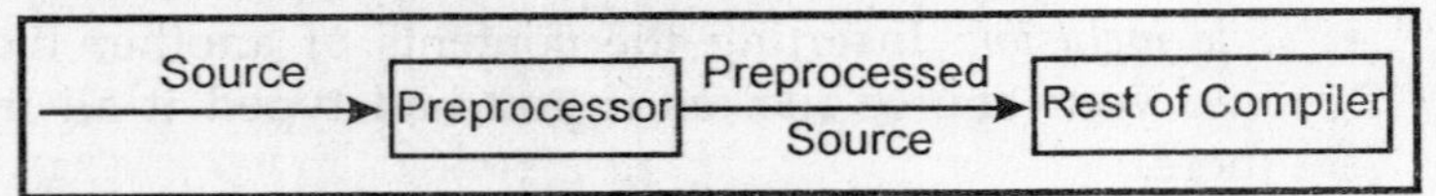

Fig. The Preprocessor

It's important to remember that the preprocessor is not working to the same rules as the rest of C. It works on a line-by-line basis, so the end of a line means something special to it. The rest of C thinks that end-of-line is little different from a space or tab character.

The preprocessor doesn't know about the scope rules of C. Preprocessor directives like #define take effect as soon as they are seen and remain in effect until the end of the file that contains them; the program's block structure is irrelevant. This is one of the reasons why it's a good idea to make sparing use of these directives.

The less you have in your programme that doesn't obey the 'normal' scope rules, the less likely you are to make mistakes. This is mainly what gives rise to our comments about the poor level of integration between the preprocessor and the rest of C. The Standard gives some complicated rules for the syntax of the preprocessor, especially with respect to *tokens*. To understand the operation of the preprocessor you need to know a little about them. The text that is being processed is not considered to be a uniform stream of characters, but is separated into tokens then processed piecemeal.

For a full definition of the process, it is best to refer to the Standard, but an informal description follows. Each of the terms used to head the list below is used later in descriptions of the rules.

- Header-name
  – '<' almost any character '>'
- Preprocessing-token
  – A header-name as above but only when the subject of #include,
  – Or an identifier which is any C identifier or keyword,
  – Or a constant which is any integral or floating constant,
  – Or a string-literal which is a normal C string,
  – Or an operator which is one of the C operators,
  – Or one of [] () {} *,: =;... # (punctuators)
  – Or any non-white-space character not covered by the list above.

The *'almost any character'* above means any character except '>' or newline.

FILE INCLUSION

A line of the form,

```
#include <filename.h>
or
#include "filename.h"
```

causes the contents of the file filename.h to be read, parsed, and compiled at that point. (After filename.h is processed, compilation continues on the line following the #include line.)

For example, suppose you got tired of retyping external function prototypes such as,

```
extern int getline(char [], int);
```

at the top of each source file. You could instead place the prototype in a header file, perhaps getline.h, and then simply place

```
#include "getline.h"
```

at the top of each source file where you called getline. (You might not find it worthwhile to create an entire header file for a single function, but if you had a package of several related function, it might be very useful to place all of their declarations in one header file.

As we may have mentioned, that's exactly what the Standard header files such as stdio.hare—collections of declarations (including external function prototype declarations) having to do with various sets of Standard library functions. When you use #include to read in a header file, you automatically get the prototypes and other declarations it contains, and you *should* use header files, precisely so that you will get the prototypes and other declarations they contain.

The difference between the <> and "" forms is where the preprocessor searches for filename.h. As a general rule, it searches for files enclosed in <> in central, standard directories, and it searches for files enclosed in "" in the "current directory," or the directory containing the source file that's doing the including. Therefore, "" is usually used for header files you've written, and <> is usually used for headers which are provided for you (which someone else has written).

The extension ".h", by the way, simply stands for "header," and reflects the fact that #include directives usually sit at the top (head) of your source files, and contain global declarations and definitions which you would otherwise put there. (That extension is not mandatory—you can theoretically name your own header files anything you wish—but .h is traditional, and recommended.)

As we've already begun to see, the reason for putting something in a header file, and then using #include to pull that header file into several different source files, is when the something (whatever it is) must be declared or defined consistently in all of the source files. If, instead of using a header file, you typed the something in to each of the source files directly, and the something ever changed, you'd have to edit all those source files, and if you missed one, your programme could fail in subtle (or serious) ways due to the mismatched declarations (i.e. due to the incompatibility between the new declaration in one source file and the old one in a source file you forgot to change). Placing common declarations and definitions into header files means that if they ever change, they only have to be changed in one place, which is a much more workable system.

What should you put in header files?

- External declarations of global variables and functions. We said that a global variable must have exactly one*defining instance,* but that it can have *external declarations* in many places. We said that it was a grave error to issue an external declaration in one place saying that a variable or function has one type, when the defining instance in some other place actually defines it with another type. (If the two places are two source files, separately compiled, the compiler will probably not even catch the discrepancy.) If you put the external declarations in a header file, however, and include the header wherever it's needed, the declarations are virtually guaranteed to be consistent. It's a good idea to include the header in the source file where the defining instance appears, too, so that the compiler can check that the declaration and definition match. (That is, if you ever change the type, you do still have to change it in two places: in the source file where the defining instance occurs, and in the header file where the external declaration appears. But at least you don't have to change it in an arbitrary number of places, and, if you've set things up correctly, the compiler can catch any remaining mistakes.)
- Preprocessor macro definitions (which we'll meet in the next section).

- Structure definitions (which we haven't seen yet).
- Typedef declarations (which we haven't seen yet).

However, there are a few things not to put in header files:

- Defining instances of global variables. If you put these in a header file, and include the header file in more than one source file, the variable will end up multiply defined.
- Function bodies (which are also defining instances). You don't want to put these in headers for the same reason—it's likely that you'll end up with multiple copies of the function and hence "multiply defined" errors. People sometimes put commonly-used functions in header files and then use #include to bring them (once) into each programme where they use that function, or use #include to bring together the several source files making up a programme, but both of these are poor ideas. It's much better to learn how to use your compiler or linker to combine together separately-compiled object files.

Since header files typically contain only external declarations, and should *not* contain function bodies, you have to understand just what does and doesn't happen when you #include a header file. The header file may provide the declarations for some functions, so that the compiler can generate correct code when you call them (and so that it can make sure that you're calling them correctly), but the header file does *not* give the compiler the functions themselves.

The actual functions will be combined into your programme at the end of compilation, by the part of the compiler called the *linker*. The linker may have to get the functions out of libraries, or you may have to tell the compiler/linker where to find them. In particular, if you are trying to use a third-party library containing some useful functions, the library will often come with a header file describing those functions. Using the library is therefore a two-step process: you must #include the header in the files where you call the library functions, *and* you must tell the linker to read in the functions from the library itself.

FILE INCLUSION

A line of the form,

```
#include <filename.h>
```

or

```
#include "filename.h"
```

causes the contents of the file filename.h to be read, parsed, and compiled at that point. (After filename.h is processed, compilation continues on the line following the #include line.) For example, suppose you got tired of retyping external function prototypes such as

```
extern int getline(char [], int);
```

at the top of each source file. You could instead place the prototype in a header file, perhaps getline.h, and then simply place

```
#include "getline.h"
```

at the top of each source file where you called getline. (You might not find it worthwhile to create an entire header file for a single function, but if you had a package of several related function, it might be very useful to place all of their declarations in one header file.) As we may have mentioned, that's exactly what the Standard header files such as stdio.hare—collections of declarations (including external function prototype declarations) having to do with various sets of Standard library functions. When you use #include to read in a header file, you automatically get the prototypes and other declarations it contains, and you *should* use header files, precisely so that you will get the prototypes and other declarations they contain.

The difference between the <> and "" forms is where the preprocessor searches for filename.h. As a general rule, it searches for files enclosed in <> in central, standard directories, and it searches for files enclosed in "" in the "current directory," or the directory containing the source file that's doing the including. Therefore, "" is usually used for header files you've written, and <> is usually used for headers which are provided for you (which someone else has written).

The extension ".h", by the way, simply stands for "header," and reflects the fact that #include directives usually sit at the top (head) of your source files, and contain global declarations and definitions which you would otherwise put there. (That extension is not mandatory—you can theoretically name your own header files anything you wish—but .h is traditional, and recommended.)

As we've already begun to see, the reason for putting something in a header file, and then using #include to pull that header file into several different source files, is when the something (whatever it is) must be declared or defined consistently in all of the source files.

If, instead of using a header file, you typed the something in to each of the source files directly, and the something ever changed, you'd have to edit all those source files, and if you missed one, your programme could fail in subtle (or serious) ways due to the mismatched declarations (i.e. due to the incompatibility between the new declaration in one source file and the old one in a source file you forgot to change). Placing common declarations and definitions into header files means that if they ever change, they only have to be changed in one place, which is a much more workable system.

What should you put in header files?

- External declarations of global variables and functions. We said that a global variable must have exactly one*defining instance*, but that it can have *external declarations* in many places. We said that it was a grave error to issue an external declaration in one place saying that a variable or function has one type, when the defining instance in some other place actually defines it with another type. (If the two places are two source files, separately compiled, the compiler will probably not even catch the discrepancy.) If you put the external declarations in a header file, however, and include the header wherever it's needed, the declarations are virtually guaranteed to be consistent. It's a good idea to include the header in the source file where the defining instance appears, too, so that the compiler can check that the declaration and definition match.

(That is, if you ever change the type, you do still have to change it in two places: in the source file where the defining instance occurs, and in the header file where the external declaration appears. But at least you don't have to change it in an arbitrary number of places, and, if you've set things up correctly, the compiler can catch any remaining mistakes.)

- Preprocessor macro definitions (which we'll meet in the next section).
- Structure definitions (which we haven't seen yet).
- Typedef declarations (which we haven't seen yet).

However, there are a few things not to put in header files:

- Defining instances of global variables. If you put these in a header file, and include the header file in more than one source file, the variable will end up multiply defined.
- Function bodies (which are also defining instances). You don't want to put these in headers for the same reason—it's likely that you'll end up with multiple copies of the function and hence "multiply defined" errors. People sometimes put commonly-used functions in header files and then use #include to bring them (once) into each programme where they use that function, or use #include to bring together the several source files making up a programme, but both of these are poor ideas. It's much better to learn how to use your compiler or linker to combine together separately-compiled object files.

Since header files typically contain only external declarations, and should *not* contain function bodies, you have to understand just what does and doesn't happen when you #include a header file. The header file may provide the declarations for some functions, so that the compiler can generate correct code when you call them (and so that it can make sure that you're calling them correctly), but the header file does *not* give the compiler the functions themselves. The actual functions will be combined into your programme at the end of compilation, by the part of the compiler called the *linker*. The linker may have to get the functions out of libraries, or you may have to tell the compiler/linker where to find them. In particular, if you are trying to use a third-party library containing some useful functions, the library will often come with a header file describing those functions. Using the library is therefore a two-step process: you must #include the header in the files where you call the library functions, *and* you must tell the linker to read in the functions from the library itself.

MACRO AND SUBSTITUTION

A preprocessor line of the form,

```
#define name text
```

defines a *macro* with the given name, having as its *value* the given replacement text. After that (for the rest of the current source file), wherever the preprocessor sees that name, it will replace it with the replacement text. The name follows the same rules as ordinary identifiers (it can contain only letters, digits, and underscores, and may not begin with a digit). Since macros behave quite differently from normal variables (or functions), it is customary to give them names which are all capital letters (or at least which begin with a capital letter). The replacement text can be absolutely anything—it's not restricted to numbers, or simple strings, or anything.

The most common use for macros is to propagate various constants around and to make them more self-documenting.

We say:

```
char line[100];
...
getline(line, 100);
```

but this is neither readable nor reliable; it's not necessarily obvious what all those 100's scattered around the programme are, and if we ever decide that 100 is too small for the size of the array to hold lines, we'll have to remember to change the number in two (or more) places. A much better solution is to use a macro:

```
#define MAXLINE 100
char line[MAXLINE];
```

```
...
getline(line, MAXLINE);
```

Now, if we ever want to change the size, we only have to do it in one place, and it's more obvious what the wordsMAXLINE sprinkled through the programme mean than the magic numbers 100 did.

Since the replacement text of a preprocessor macro can be anything, it can also be an expression, although you have to realise that, as always, the text is substituted (and perhaps evaluated) later. No evaluation is performed when the macro is defined.

For example, suppose that you write something like:

```
#define A 2
#define B 3
#define C A + B
```

this is a pretty meaningless example, but the situation does come up in practice). Then, later, suppose that you write

```
int x = C * 2;
```

If A, B, and C were ordinary variables, you'd expect x to end up with the value 10. But let's see what happens.

The preprocessor always substitutes text for macros exactly as you have written it. So it first substitites the replacement text for the macro C, resulting in

```
int x = A + B * 2;
```

Then it substitutes the macros A and B, resulting in,

```
int x = 2 + 3 * 2;
```

Only when the preprocessor is done doing all this substituting does the compiler get into the act. But when it evaluates that expression (using the normal precedence of multiplication over addition), it ends up initializing x with the value 8!

To guard against this sort of problem, it is always a good idea to include explicit parentheses in the definitions of macros which contain expressions. If we were to define the macro C as

```
#define C (A + B)
```

then the declaration of x would ultimately expand to

```
int x = (2 + 3) * 2;
```

and x would be initialized to 10, as we probably expected.

Notice that there does not have to be (and in fact there usually is *not*) a semicolon at the end of a #define line. (This is just one of the ways that the syntax of the preprocessor is different from the rest of C.)

If you type,

```
#define MAXLINE 100;   /* WRONG */
```

then when you later declare

```
char line[MAXLINE];
```

the preprocessor will expand it to

```
char line[100;]; /* WRONG */
```

which is a syntax error. This is what we mean when we say that the preprocessor doesn't know much of anything about the syntax of C—in this last example, the *value* or replacement text for the macro MAXLINE was the 4 characters 1 0 0; , and that's exactly what the preprocessor substituted (even though it didn't make any sense).

Simple macros like MAXLINE act sort of like little variables, whose values are constant (or constant expressions). It's also possible to have macros which look like little functions (that is, you invoke them with what looks like function call syntax, and they expand to replacement text which is a function of the actual arguments they are invoked with) but we won't be looking at these yet.

CONDITIONAL COMPILATION

The last preprocessor directive we're going to look at is #ifdef.

If you have the sequence,

```
#ifdef name
programme text
#else
more programme text
#endif
```

in your programme, the code that gets compiled depends on whether a preprocessor macro by that *name* is defined or not. If it is (that is, if there has been a #define line for a macro called *name*), then *"programme text"* is compiled and *"more programme text"* is ignored. If the macro is not defined, *"more programme text*" is compiled and "*programme text*" is ignored. This looks a lot like an if statement, but it behaves completely differently: an if statement controls which statements of your programme are executed at run time, but #ifdef controls which parts of your programme actually get compiled.

Just as for the if statement, the #else in an #ifdef is optional. There is a companion directive #ifndef, which compiles code if the macro is *not* defined (although the "#else clause" of an #ifndef directive will then be compiled if the macro*is* defined). There is also an #if directive which compiles code depending on whether a compile-time expression is true or false. (The expressions which are allowed in an #if directive are somewhat restricted, however, so we won't talk much about #if here.)

Conditional compilation is useful in two general classes of situations:

- You are trying to write a portable programme, but the way you do something is different depending on what compiler, operating system, or computer you're using. You place different versions of your code, one for each situation, between suitable #ifdef directives, and when you compile the progam in a particular environment, you arrange to have the macro names defined which select the variants you need in that environment. (For this reason, compilers usually have ways of letting you define macros from the invocation command line or in a configuration file, and many also predefine certain macro names related to the operating system, processor, or compiler in use. That way, you don't have to change the code to change the #define lines each time you compile it in a different environment.)

For example, in ANSI C, the function to delete a file is remove. On older Unix systems, however, the function was called unlink. So if filename is a variable containing the name of a file you want to delete, and if you want to be able to compile the programme under these older Unix systems, we write

```
#ifdef unix
unlink(filename);
#else
remove(filename);
#endif
```

Then, you could place the line,

```
#define unix
```

at the top of the file when compiling under an old Unix system. (Since all you're using the macro unix for is to control the #ifdef, you don't need to give it any replacement text at all. *Any* definition for a macro, even if the replacement text is empty, causes an #ifdef to succeed.)

In fact, in this example, you wouldn't even need to define the macro unix at all, because C compilers on old Unix systems tend to predefine it for you, precisely so you can make tests like these.

- You want to compile several different versions of your programme, with different features present in the different versions. You bracket the code for each feature with #ifdef directives, and (as for the previous case) arrange to have the right macros defined or not to build the version you want to build at any given time. This way, you can build the several different versions from the same source code. (One common example is whether you turn debugging statements on or off. You can bracket each debugging printout with #ifdef DEBUG and #endif, and then turn on debugging only when you need it.)

For example, you might use lines like this:

```
#ifdef DEBUG
printf("x is %d\n", x);
#endif
```

to print out the value of the variable x at some point in your programme to see if it's what you expect. To enable debugging printouts, you insert the line

```
#define DEBUG
```

at the top of the file, and to turn them off, you delete that line, but the debugging printouts quietly remain in your code, temporarily deactivated, but ready to reactivate if you find yourself needing them again later. (Also, instead of inserting and deleting the #define line, you might use a compiler flag such as -DDEBUG to define the macro DEBUGfrom the compiler invocatin line.)

Conditional compilation can be very handy, but it can also get out of hand. When large chunks of the programme are completely different depending on, say, what operating system the programme is being compiled for, it's often better to place the different versions in separate source files, and then only use one of the files (corresponding to one of the versions) to build the programme on any given system.

Also, if you are using an ANSI Standard compiler and you are writing ANSI-compatible code, you usually won't need so much conditional compilation, because the Standard specifies exactly how the compiler must do certain things, and exactly which library functions it much provide, so you don't have to work so hard to accommodate the old variations among compilers and libraries.

DIRECTIVES

Directives are always introduced by a line that starts with a # character, optionally preceded by white space characters (although it isn't common practice to indent the #). Table below is a list of the directives defined in the Standard.

Table. Preprocessor directives

Directive	Meaning
# include	include a source file
# define	define a macro
# undef	undefine a macro
# if	conditional compilation
# ifdef	conditional compilation
# ifndef	conditional compilation
# elif	conditional compilation
# else	conditional compilation

# endif	conditional compilation
# line	control error reporting
# error	force an error message
# pragma	used for implementation-dependent control
#	null directive; no effect

The meanings and use of these features are described in the following sections. Make a note that the # and the following keyword, if any, are individual items. They may be separated by white space.

DEFINE

There are two ways of defining *macros*, one of which looks like a function and one which does not.

Here is an example of each:

```
#define FMAC(a,b) a here, then b
#define NONFMAC some text here
```

Both definitions define a macro and some *replacement text*, which will be used to replace later occurrences of the macro name in the rest of the programme. After those definitions, they can be used as follows, with the effect of the macro replacement shown in comments:

```
NONFMAC
/* some text here */
FMAC(first text, some more)
/* first text here, then some more */
```

For the non-function macro, its name is simply replaced by its replacement text. The function macro is also replaced by its replacement text; wherever the replacement text contains an identifier which is the name of one of the macro's 'formal parameters', the actual text given as the argument is used in place of the identifier in the replacement text. The scope of the names of the formal parameters is limited to the body of the #define directive.

For both forms of macro, leading or trailing white space around the replacement text is discarded. A curious ambiguity arises with macros: how do you define a non-function macro whose replacement text happens to start with the opening parenthesis character (? The answer is simple. If the definition of the macro has a space in front of the (, then it isn't the definition of a function macro, but a simple replacement macro instead. When you *use* function-like macros, there's no equivalent restriction.

The Standard allows either type of macro to be redefined at any time, using another # define, provided that there isn't any attempt to change the type of the macro and that the tokens making up both the original definition and the redefinition are identical in number, ordering, spelling and use of white space. In this context all white space is considered equal, so this would be correct:

```
# define XXX abc/*comment*/def hij
# define XXX abc def hij
```

because comment is a form of white space. The token sequence for both cases (*w-s* stands for a white-space token) is:

```
# w-s define w-s XXX w-s abc w-s def w-s hij w-s
```

MACRO SUBSTITUTION

Where will occurrences of the macro name cause the replacement text to be substituted in its place? Practically anywhere in a programme that the identifier is recognized as a separate token, except as the identifier following the # of a preprocessor directive.

You can't do this:

```
#define define XXX
#define YYY ZZZ
```

and expect the second #define to be replaced by #XXX, causing an error. When the identifier associated with a non-function macro is seen, it is replaced by the macro replacement tokens, then *rescanned* (see later) for further replacements to make.

Function macros can be used like real functions; white space around the macro name, the argument list and so on, may include the newline character:

```
#define FMAC(a, b) printf("%s %s\n", a, b)
FMAC ("hello",
"sailor"
```

```
);
/* results in */
printf("%s %s\n", "hello", "sailor")
```

The 'arguments' of a function macro can be almost any arbitrary token sequence. Commas are used to separate the arguments from each other but can be hidden by enclosing them within parentheses, (and). Matched pairs of (and) inside the argument list balance each other out, so a) only ends the invocation of the macro if the corresponding (is the one that started the macro invocation.

```
#define CALL(a, b) a b
CALL(printf, ("%d %d %s\n",1, 24, "urgh"));
/* results in */
printf ("%d %d %s\n",1, 24, "urgh");
```

Note very carefully that the parentheses around the second argument to CALL were preserved in the replacement: they were not stripped from the text.

If you want to use macros like printt, taking a variable number of arguments, the Standard is no help to you. They are not supported. If any argument contains no preprocessor tokens then the behaviour is undefined. The same is true if the sequence of preprocessor tokens that forms the argument would otherwise have been another preprocessor directive:

```
#define CALL(a, b) a b
/* undefined behaviour in each case.... */
CALL(,hello)
CALL(xyz,
#define abc def)
```

In our opinion, the second of the erroneous uses of CALL should result in defined behaviour—anyone capable of writing that would clearly benefit from the attentions of a champion weightlifter wielding a heavy leather bullwhip.

When a function macro is being processed, the steps are as follows:

- All of its arguments are identified.
- Except in the cases listed in item 3 below, if any of the tokens in an argument are themselves candidates for macro replacement, the replacement is done until

no further replacement is possible. If this introduces commas into the argument list, there is no danger of the macro suddenly seeming to have a different number of arguments; the arguments are *only* determined in the step above.

- In the macro replacement text, identifiers naming one of the macro formal arguments are replaced by the (by now expanded) token sequence supplied as the actual argument. The replacement is suppressed only if the identifier is preceded by one of # or ##, or followed by ##.

STRINGIZING

There is special treatment for places in the macro replacement text where one of the macro formal parameters is found preceded by #. The token list for the actual argument has any leading or trailing white space discarded, then the # and the token list are turned into a single string literal.

Spaces between the tokens are treated as space characters in the string. To prevent 'unexpected' results, any "or \ characters within the new string literal are preceded by \.

This example demonstrates the feature:

```
#define MESSAGE(x) printf("Message: %s\n", #x)
MESSAGE (Text with "quotes");
/*
* Result is
* printf("Message: %s\n", "Text with
\"quotes\"");
*/
```

TOKEN PASTING

A ## operator may occur anywhere in the replacement text for a macro except at the beginning or end. If a parameter name of a function macro occurs in the replacement text preceded or followed by one of these operators, the actual token sequence for the corresponding macro argument is used to replace it. Then, for both function and non-function macros, the tokens surrounding the ## operator are joined together. If they don't form a valid token, the behaviour is undefined. Then rescanning occurs.

As an example of token pasting, here is a multi-stage operation, involving rescanning (which is described next).

```
#define REPLACE some replacement text
#define JOIN(a, b) a ## b
JOIN(REP, LACE)
becomes, after token pasting,
REPLACE
becomes, after rescanning
some replacement text
```

RESCANNING

Once the processing described above has occurred, the replacement text plus the following tokens of the source file is rescanned, looking for more macro names to replace. The one exception is that, within a macro's replacement text, the name of the macro itself is not expanded. Because macro replacement can be nested, it is possible for several macros to be in the process of being replaced at any one point: none of their names is a candidate for further replacement in the 'inner' levels of this process. This allows redefinition of existing functions as macros:

```
#define exit(x) exit((x)+1)
```

These macro names which were not replaced now become tokens which are immune from future replacement, even if later processing might have meant that they had become available for replacement. This prevents the danger of infinite recursion occurring in the preprocessor. The suppression of replacement is only if the macro name results directly from *replacement* text, not the other source text of the programme.

Here we mean:

```
#define m(x) m((x)+1)
/* so */
m(abc);
/* expands to */
m((abc)+1);
```

```
/*
* even though the m((abc)+1) above looks like a
macro,
* the rules say it is not to be re-replaced
*/
m(m(abc));
/*
* the outer m(starts a macro invocation,
* but the inner one is replaced first (as above)
* with m((abc)+1), which becomes the argument
to the outer call,
* giving us effectively
*/
m(m((abc+1));
/*
* which expands to
*/
m((m((abc+1))+1);
```

If that doesn't make your brain hurt, then go and read what the Standard says about it, which will.

NOTES

There is a subtle problem when using arguments to function macros.

```
/* warning - subtle problem in this example */
#define SQR(x) (x * x)
/*
* Wherever the formal parameters occur in
* the replacement text, they are replaced
* by the actual parameters to the macro.
*/
printf("sqr of %d is %d\n", 2, SQR(2));
```

The formal parameter of SQR is x; the actual argument is 2. The replacement text results in

```
printf("sqr of %d is %d\n", 2, (2 * 2));
```

The use of the parentheses should be noticed. The following example is likely to give trouble:

```
/* bad example */
```

```
#define DOUBLE(y) y+y
printf("twice %d is %d\n", 2, DOUBLE(2));
printf("six times %d is %d\n", 2, 3*DOUBLE(2));
```

The problem is that the last expression in the second printf is replaced by

```
3*2+2
```

which results in 8, not 12! The rule is that when using macros to build expressions, careful parenthesizing is necessary.

Here's another example:

```
SQR(3+4)
/* expands to */
(3+4 * 3+4)
/* oh dear, still wrong! */
```

so, when formal parameters occur in the replacement text, you should look carefully at them too. Correct versions of SQR and DOUBLE are these:

```
#define SQR(x) ((x)*(x))
#define DOUBLE(x) ((x)+(x))
```

Macros have a last little trick to surprise you with, as this shows.

```
#include <stdio.h>
#include <stdlib.h>
#define DOUBLE(x) ((x)+(x))
main(){
int a[20], *ip;
ip = a;
a[0] = 1;
a[1] = 2;
printf("%d\n", DOUBLE(*ip++));
exit(EXIT_SUCCESS);
}
```

Example: Why is this going to cause problems? Because the replacement text of the macro refers to *ip++ twice, so ip gets incremented twice. Macros should never be used with expressions that involve side effects, unless you check very carefully that they are safe.

Despite these warnings, they provide a very useful feature, and one which will be used a lot from now on.

UNDEF

The name of any #defined identifier can be forcibly forgotten by saying

```
#undef NAME
```

It isn't an error to #undef a name which isn't currently defined.

INCLUDE

This comes in two flavours:

```
#include <filename>
#include "filename"
```

both of which cause a new file to be read at the point where they occur. It's as if the single line containing the directive is replaced by the contents of the specified file. If that file contains erroneous statements, you can reasonably expect that the errors will be reported with a correct file name and line number.

It's the compiler writer's job to get that right. The Standard specifies that at least eight nested levels of # include must be supported.

The effect of using brackets <> or quotes " " around the filename is to change the places searched to find the specified file. The brackets cause a search of a number of implementation defined places, the quotes cause a search of somewhere associated with the original source file. Your implementation notes must tell you the specific details of what is meant by 'place'. If the form using quotes can't find the file, it tries again as if you had used brackets.

In general, brackets are used when you specify standard library header files, quotes are used for private header files—often specific to one programme only.

Although the Standard doesn't define what constitutes a valid file name, it does specify that there must be an implementation-defined unique way of translating file names of the form xxx.x (where x represents a 'letter'), into source file names. Distinctions of upper and lower case may be ignored and the implementation may choose only to use six significant characters before the '.' character.

You can also write this:

```
# define NAME <stdio.h>
# include NAME
to get the same effect as
# include <stdio.h>
```

but it's a rather roundabout way of doing it, and unfortunately it's subject to implementation defined rules about how the text between < and > is treated.

It's simpler if the replacement text for NAME comes out to be a string, for example,

```
#define NAME "stdio.h"
#include NAME
```

There is no problem with implementation defined behaviour here, but the paths searched are different, as explained above.

For the first case, what happens is that the token sequence which replaces NAME is (by the rules already given),

```
<
stdio
.
h
>
and for the second case
"stdio.h"
```

The second case is easy, since it's just a *string-literal* which is a legal token for a# include directive. It is implementation defined how the first case is treated, and whether or not the sequence of tokens forms a legal *header-name*.

Finally, the last character of a file which is being included must be a plain newline. Failure to include a file successfully is treated as an error.

PREDEFINED NAMES

The following names are predefined within the preprocessor:

__LINE__

The current source file line number, a decimal integer constant.

__FILE__

The 'name' of the current source code file, a string literal.

__DATE__

The current date, a string literal. The form is

Apr 21 1990

where the month name is as defined in the library function asctime and the first digit of the date is a space if the date is less than 10.

__TIME__

The time of the translation; again a string literal in the form produced by asctime, which has the form "hh:mm:ss".

__STDC__

The integer constant 1. This is used to test if the compiler is Standard-conforming, the intention being that it will have different values for different releases of the Standard.

A common way of using these predefined names is the following:

```
#define TEST(x) if(!(x))\
printf("test failed, line %d file %s\n",\
__LINE__, __FILE__)
/**/
TEST(a != 23);
/**/
```

Example: If the argument to TEST gives a false result, the message is printed, including the filename and line number in the message.

There's only one minor caveat: the use of the if statement can cause confusion in a case like this:

```
if(expression)
TEST(expr2);
else
statement_n;
```

The else will get associated with the hidden if generated by expanding the TESTmacro. This is most unlikely to happen in practice, but will be a thorough pain to track down if it ever does sneak up on you. It's good style to make the bodies of every control of flow statement compound anyway; then the problem goes away.

None of the names __LINE__, __FILE__, __DATE__, __TIME__, __STDC__ or defined may be used in #define or #undef directives.

The Standard specifies that any other reserved names will either start with an underscore followed by an upper case letter or another underscore, so you know that you are free to use any other names for your own purposes (but watch out for additional names reserved in Library header files that you may have included).

#LINE

This is used to set the value of the built in names __LINE__ and __FILE__. Why do this? Because a lot of tools nowadays actually generate C as their output. This directive allows them to control the current line number. It is of very limited interest to the 'ordinary' C programmer.

Its form is,

```
# line number optional-string-literal newline
```

The number sets the value of __LINE__, the string literal, if present, sets the value of __FILE__. In fact, the sequence of tokens following #line will be macro expanded. After expansion, they are expected to provide a valid directive of the right form.

CONDITIONAL COMPILATION

A number of the directives control conditional compilation, which allows certain portions of a programme to be selectively compiled or ignored depending upon specified conditions.

The directives concerned are: #if, #ifdef, #ifndef, #elif,#else, #endif together with the preprocessor unary operator defined.

The way that they are used is like this:

```
#ifdef NAME
/* compile these lines if NAME is defined */
#endif
#ifndef NAME
/* compile these lines if NAME is not defined
```

```
*/
#else
/* compile these lines if NAME is defined */
#endif
```

So, #ifdef and #endif can be used to test the definition or otherwise of a given macro name. Of course the #else can be used with #ifdef (and #if or #elif) too. There is no ambiguity about what a given #else binds to, because the use of#endif to delimit the scope of these directives eliminates any possible ambiguity. The Standard specifies that at least eight levels of nesting of conditional directives must be supported, but in practice there is not likely to be any real limit.

These directives are most commonly used to select small fragments of C that are machine specific (when it is not possible to make the whole programme completely machine independent), or sometimes to select different algorithms depending on the need to make trade-offs.

The #if and #elif constructs take a single integral constant expression as their arguments. Preprocessor integral constant expressions are the same as other integral constant expressions except that they must not contain cast operators. The token sequence that makes up the constant expression undergoes macro replacement, except that names prefixed by defined are not expanded. In this context, the expression defined NAME or defined (NAME) evaluates to 1 if NAMEis currently defined, 0 if it is not. Any other identifiers in the expression *including those that are C keywords* are replaced with the value 0. Then the expression is evaluated. The replacement even of keywords means that sizeof can't be used in these expressions to get the result that you would normally expect.

As with the other conditional statements in C, a resulting value of zero is used to represent 'false', anything else is 'true'.

The preprocessor always must use arithmetic with at least the ranges defined in the <limits.h> file and treats int expressions as long int and unsigned int as unsigned long int. Character constants do not necessarily have the same values as they do at execution time, so for highly portable programs, it's best to avoid using them in preprocessor expressions.

Overall, the rules mean that it is possible to get arithmetic results from the preprocessor which are different from the results at run time; although presumably only if the translation and execution are done on different machines.

Here's an example:

```
#include <limits.h>
#if ULONG_MAX+1 != 0
printf("Preprocessor: ULONG_MAX+1 != 0\n");
#endif
if(ULONG_MAX+1 != 0)
printf("Runtime: ULONG_MAX+1 != 0\n");
```

Example: It is conceivable that the preprocessor might perform arithmetic with a greater range than that used in the target environment. In that case, the preprocessor expression ULONG_MAX+1 might not 'overflow' to give the result of 0, whereas in the execution environment, it *must*.

The following skeleton example illustrates the use of such constants and also the 'conditional else', #elif.

```
#define NAME 100
#if ((NAME > 50) && (defined __STDC__))
/* do something */
#elif NAME > 25
/* do something else*/
#elif NAME > 10
/* do something else */
#else
/* last possibility */
#endif
```

A word of warning. These conditional compilation directives do not obey the same scope rules as the rest of C. They should be used sparingly, unless your programme is rapidly to become unreadable. It is impossible to read C when it is laced with these things every few lines. The urge to maim the author of a piece of code becomes very strong when you suddenly come across,

```
#else
}
#endif
```

with no #if or whatever immediately visible above. They should be treated like chilli sauce; essential at times, but more than a tiny sprinkle is too much.

#PRAGMA

This was the Standard Committee's way of 'opening the back door'. It allows implementation-defined things to take place. If the implementation was not expecting what you wrote (i.e. doesn't recognize it), it is ignored.

Here is a possible example:

```
#pragma byte_align
```

which could be used to tell the implementation that all structure members should be aligned on byte addresses - some processor architectures are able to cope with word-sized structure members aligned on byte addresses, but with a penalty in access speed being incurred.

It could, of course, mean anything else that the implementation chooses it to mean. If your implementation doesn't have any special meaning for this, then it will have no effect. It will ***not*** count as an error.

#ERROR

This directive is followed by one or more tokens at the end of the line. A diagnostic message is produced by the compiler, which includes those tokens, but no further detail is given in the Standard.

It might be used like this to abort a compilation on unsuitable hardware:

```
#include <limits.h>
#if CHAR_MIN > -128
#error character range smaller than required
#endif
```

which would be expected to produce some sort of meaningful compilation error and message.

Chapter 9

Pointers

POINTER OPERATIONS

The first things to do with pointers are to declare a pointer variable, set it to point somewhere, and finally manipulate the value that it points to. A simple pointer declaration looks like this:

```
int *ip;
```

This declaration looks like our earlier declarations, with one obvious difference: that asterisk. The asterisk means that ip, the variable we're declaring, is not of type int, but rather of type pointer-to-int. (Another way of looking at it is that *ip, which as we'll see is the value pointed to by ip, will be an int.)

We may think of setting a pointer variable to point to another variable as a two-step process: first we generate a pointer to that other variable, then we assign this new pointer to the pointer variable. We can say (but we have to be careful when we're saying it) that a pointer variable has a value, and that its value is "pointer to that other variable". This will make more sense when we see how to generate pointer values.

Pointers (that is, pointer values) are generated with the "address-of" operator &, which we can also think of as the "pointer-to" operator. We demonstrate this by declaring (and initializing) an int variable i, and then setting ip to point to it:

```
int i = 5;
ip = &i;
```

The assignment expression ip = &i; contains both parts of the "two-step process": &i generates a pointer to i, and the assignment operator assigns the new pointer to (that is, places it "in") the variable ip. Now ip "points to" i, which we can illustrate with this picture:

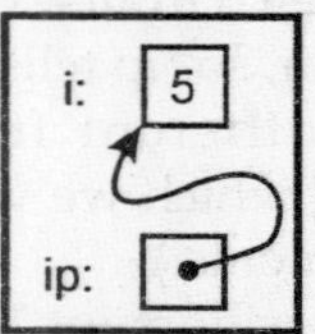

i is a variable of type int, so the value in its box is a number, 5. ip is a variable of type pointer-to-int, so the "value" in its box is an arrow pointing at another box. Referring once again back to the "two-step process" for setting a pointer variable: the & operator draws us the arrowhead pointing at i's box, and the assignment operator =, with the pointer variable ip on its left, anchors the other end of the arrow in ip's box.

We discover the value pointed to by a pointer using the "contents-of" operator, *. Placed in front of a pointer, the *operator accesses the value pointed to by that pointer. In other words, if ip is a pointer, then the expression *ip gives us whatever it is that's in the variable or location pointed to by ip. For example, we could write something like,

```
printf("%d\n", *ip);
```

which would print 5, since ip points to i, and i is (at the moment) 5.

You may wonder how the asterisk * can be the pointer contents-of operator when it is also the multiplication operator. There is no ambiguity here: it is the multiplication operator when it sits between two variables, and it is the contents-of operator when it sits in front of a single variable.

The situation is analogous to the minus sign: between two variables or expressions it's the subtraction operator, but in front of a single operator or expression it's the negation operator. Technical terms you may hear for these distinct roles are *unary* and *binary*: a *binary* operator applies to two operands, usually on either side of it, while a *unary* operator applies to a single operand. The contents-of operator * does not merely fetch values through pointers; it can also *set* values through pointers. We can write like

```
*ip = 7;
```

which means "set whatever ip points to to 7." Again, the * tells us to go to the location pointed to by ip, but this time, the location isn't the one to fetch from—we're on the left-hand sign of an assignment operator, so *ip tells us the location to store *to*. (The situation is no different from array subscripting expressions such as a[3] which we've already seen appearing on both sides of assignments.)

The result of the assignment *ip = 7 is that i's value is changed to 7, and the picture changes to:

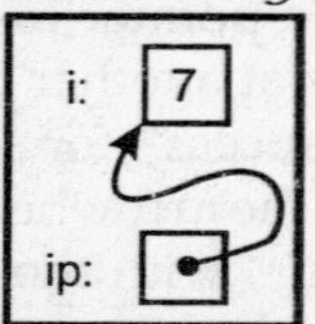

If we called printf("%d\n", *ip) again, it would now print 7. At this point, you may be wondering why we're going through this rigamarole—if we wanted to set i to 7, why didn't we do it directly? We'll begin to explore that next, but first let's notice the difference between changing a pointer (that is, changing what variable it points to) and changing the value at the location it points to. When we wrote *ip = 7, we changed the value pointed to by ip, but if we declare another variable j:

```
int j = 3;
```

and write

```
ip = &j;
```

we've changed ip itself. The picture now looks like this:

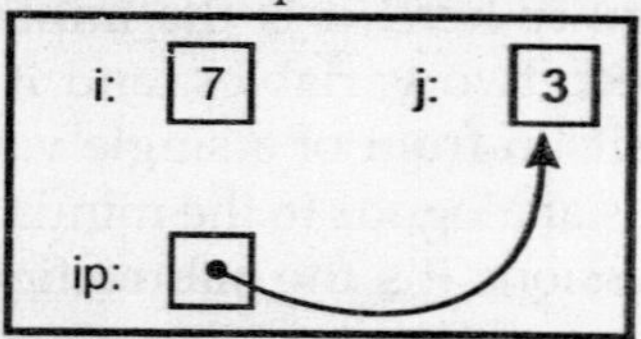

We have to be careful when we say that a pointer assignment changes "what the pointer points to." Our earlier assignment

```
*ip = 7;
```

changed the value pointed to by ip, but this more recent assignment,

```
ip = &j;
```

has changed what *variable* ip points to. It's true that "what ip points to" has changed, but this time, it has changed for a different reason. Neither i (which is still 7) nor j (which is still 3) has changed. (What has changed is ip's value.) If we again call,

```
printf("%d\n", *ip);
```

this time it will print 3.

We can also assign pointer values to other pointer variables.

If we declare a second pointer variable:

```
int *ip2;
```

then we can say

```
ip2 = ip;
```

Now ip2 points where ip does; we've essentially made a "copy" of the arrow:

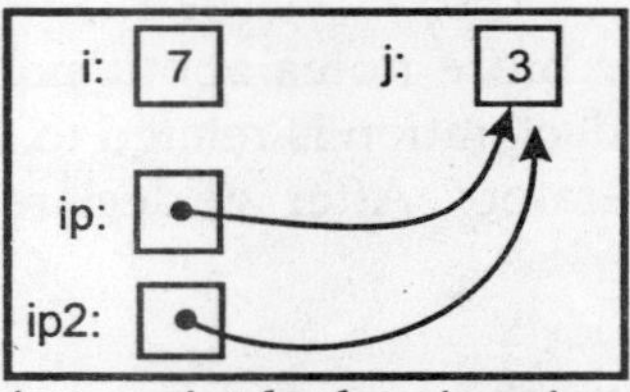

Now, if we set ip to point back to i again:

```
ip = &i;
```

the two arrows point to different places:

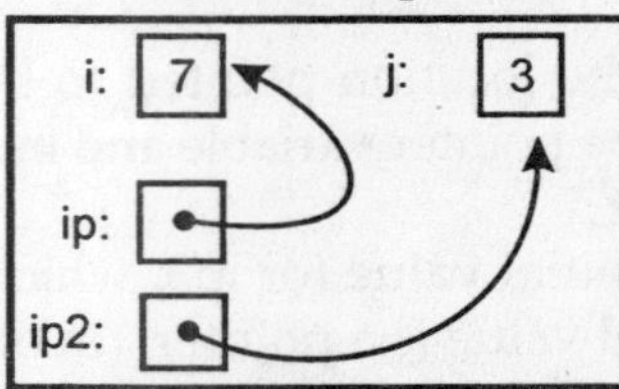

We can now see that the two assignments:

```
ip2 = ip;
```

and

```
*ip2 = *ip;
```

do two very different things. The first would make ip2 again point to where ip points (in other words, back to i again). The second would store, at the location pointed to by ip2, a copy of the value pointed to by ip; in other words (if ip andip2 still point to i and j respectively) it would set j to i's value, or 7.

It's important to keep very clear in your mind the distinction between *a pointer* and *what it points to*. The two are like apples and oranges (or perhaps oil and water); you can't mix them. You can't "set ip to 5" by writing something like,

```
ip = 5;     /* WRONG */
```

5 is an integer, but ip is a pointer. You probably wanted to "set *the value pointed to by* ip to 5," which you express by writing

```
*ip = 5;
```

Similarly, you can't "see what ip is" by writing,

```
printf("%d\n", ip);     /* WRONG */
```

Again, ip is a pointer-to-int, but %d expects an int. To print *what* ip *points to*, use,

```
printf("%d\n", *ip);
```

Finally, a few more notes about pointer declarations. The * in a pointer declaration is related to, but different from, the contents-of operator *. After we declare a pointer variable,

```
int *ip;
```

the expression,

```
ip = &i
```

sets what ip points to (that is, which location it points to), while the expression,

```
*ip = 5
```

sets the value of the location pointed to by ip. On the other hand, if we declare a pointer variable and include an initializer:

```
int *ip3 = &i;
```

we're setting the initial value for ip3, which is where ip3 will point, so that initial value is a pointer. (In other words, the *in the declaration int *ip3 = &i; is not the contents-of operator, it's the indicator that ip3 is a pointer.)

If you have a pointer declaration containing an initialization, and you ever have occasion to break it up into a simple declaration and a conventional assignment, do it like this:

```
int *ip3;
ip3 = &i;
```

Don't write,

```
int *ip3;
*ip3 = &i;
```

or you'll be trying to mix oil and water again.

Also, when we write,

```
int *ip;
```

although the asterisk affects ip's type, it goes with the identifier name ip, not with the type int on the left. To declare two pointers at once, the declaration looks like,

```
int *ip1, *ip2;
```

Some people write pointer declarations like this:

```
int* ip;
```

This works for one pointer, because C essentially ignores whitespace.

But if you ever write,

```
int* ip1, ip2;   /* PROBABLY WRONG */
```

it will declare one pointer-to-int ip1 and one *plain* int ip2, which is probably not what you meant.

What is all of this good for? If it was just for changing variables like i from 5 to 7, it would not be good for much. What it's good for, among other things, is when for various reasons we don't know exactly which variable we want to change, just like the bank didn't know exactly which club member it wanted to send the statement to.

POINTERS AND ARRAYS; POINTER ARITHMETIC

Pointers do not have to point to single variables. They can also point at the cells of an array. For example, we can write

```
int *ip;
int a[10];
ip = &a[3];
```

and we would end up with ip pointing at the fourth cell of the array a (remember, arrays are 0-based, so a[0] is the first cell).

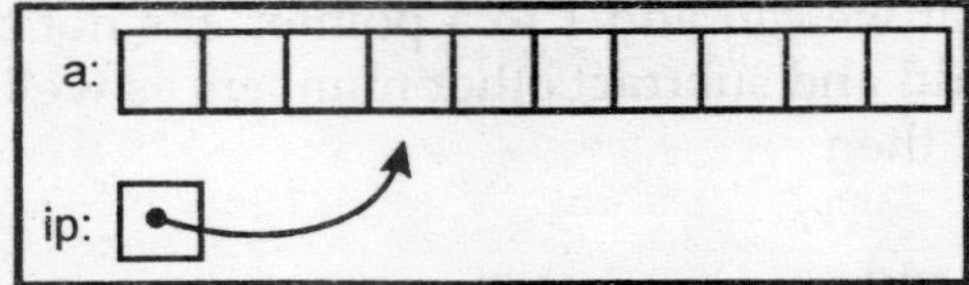

We could illustrate the situation like this:

We'd use this ip just like the one in the previous section: *ip gives us what ip points to, which in this case will be the value in a[3]. Once we have a pointer pointing into an array, we can start doing *pointer arithmetic*. Given that ip is a pointer to a[3], we can add 1 to ip:

```
ip + 1
```

What does it mean to add one to a pointer? In C, it gives a pointer to the cell one farther on, which in this case is a[4]. To make this clear, let's assign this new pointer to another pointer variable:

```
ip2 = ip + 1;
```

Now the picture looks like this:

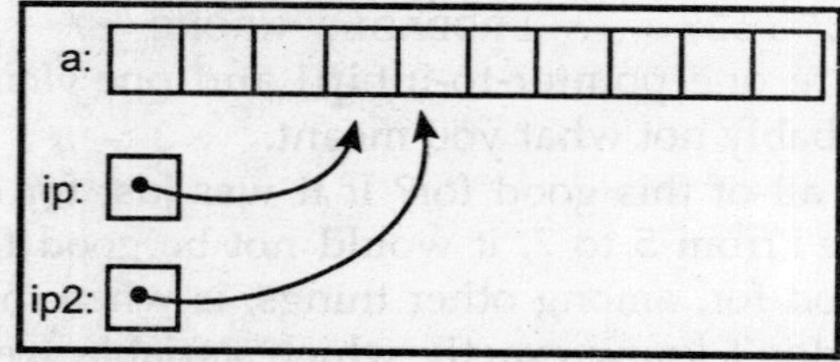

If we now do,

```
*ip2 = 4;
```

we've set a[4] to 4. But it's not necessary to assign a new pointer value to a pointer variable in order tc use it; we could also compute a new pointer value and use it immediately:

```
*(ip + 1) = 5;
```

In this last example, we've changed a[4] again, setting it to 5. The parentheses are needed because the unary "contents of" operator * has higher *precedence* (i.e., binds more tightly than) the addition operator. If we wrote *ip + 1, without the parentheses, we'd be fetching the value pointed to by ip, and adding 1 to that value. The expression *(ip + 1), on the other hand, accesses the value one past the one pointed to by ip.

Given that we can add 1 to a pointer, it's not surprising that we can add and subtract other numbers as well. If ip still points to a[3], then

```
*(ip + 3) = 7;
```

sets a[6] to 7, and,

```
*(ip - 2) = 4;
```

sets a[1] to 4.

Up above, we added 1 to ip and assigned the new pointer to ip2, but there's no reason we can't add one to a pointer, and change the same pointer:

```
ip = ip + 1;
```

Now ip points one past where it used to (to a[4], if we hadn't changed it in the meantime). The shortcuts we learned in a previous chapter all work for pointers, too: we could also increment a pointer using,

```
ip += 1;
```

or

```
ip++;
```

Of course, pointers are not limited to ints. It's quite common to use pointers to other types, especially char. Here is the innards of the mystrcmp function we saw in a previous chapter, rewritten to use pointers. (mystrcmp, you may recall, compares two strings, character by character.)

```
char *p1 = &str1[0], *p2 = &str2[0];
while(1)
{
if(*p1 != *p2)
return *p1 - *p2;
if(*p1 == '\0' || *p2 == '\0')
return 0;
p1++;
p2++;
}
```

The autoincrement operator ++ (like its companion, —) makes it easy to do two things at once. We've seen idioms likea[i++] which accesses a[i] and simultaneously increments i, leaving it referencing the next cell of the array a. We can do the same thing with pointers: an expression like *ip++ lets us access what ip points to, while simultaneously incrementing ip so that it points to the next element. The preincrement form works, too: *++ip increments ip, then accesses what it points to. Similarly, we can use notations like *ip— and *—ip.

As another example, here is the strcpy (string copy) loop

from a previous chapter, rewritten to use pointers:

```
char *dp = &dest[0], *sp = &src[0];
while(*sp != '\0')
*dp++ = *sp++;
*dp = '\0';
```

One question that comes up is whether the expression *p++ increments p or what it points to. The answer is that it increments p. To increment what p points to, you can use (*p)++.)

When you're doing pointer arithmetic, you have to remember how big the array the pointer points into is, so that you don't ever point outside it. If the array a has 10 elements, you can't access a[50] or a[-1] or even a[10] (remember, the valid subscripts for a 10-element array run from 0 to 9). Similarly, if a has 10 elements and ip points to a[3], you can't compute or access ip + 10 or ip - 5. (There is one special case: you can, in this case, compute, but not access, a pointer to the nonexistent element just beyond the end of the array, which in this case is &a[10].

POINTER SUBTRACTION AND COMPARISON

As we've seen, you can add an integer to a pointer to get a new pointer, pointing somewhere beyond the original (as long as it's in the same array).

For example, you might write,

```
ip2 = ip1 + 3;
```

Applying a little algebra, you might wonder whether,

```
ip2 - ip1 = 3
```

and the answer is, yes. When you subtract two pointers, as long as they point into the same array, the result is the number of elements separating them.

You can also ask (again, as long as they point into the same array) whether one pointer is greater or less than another: one pointer is "greater than" another if it points beyond where the other one points. You can also compare pointers for equality and inequality: two pointers are equal if they point to the same variable or to the same cell in an array, and are (obviously) unequal if they don't. (When testing for equality or inequality, the two pointers do not have to point into the same array.) One common use of pointer comparisons is when copying arrays using pointers. Here is a code fragment which copies 10 elements from array1 to array2, using pointers. It uses an end pointer, ep, to keep track of when it should stop copying.

```
int array1[10], array2[10];
int *ip1, *ip2 = &array2[0];
int *ep = &array1[10];
for(ip1 = &array1[0]; ip1 < ep; ip1++)
*ip2++ = *ip1;
```

As we mentioned, there is no element array1[10], but it is legal to compute a pointer to this (nonexistent) element, as long as we only use it in pointer comparisons like this (that is, as long as we never try to fetch or store the value that it points to.)

NULL POINTERS

We said that the value of a pointer variable is a pointer to some other variable. There is one other value a pointer may have: it may be set to a *null pointer*. A *null pointer* is a special pointer value that is known not to point anywhere. What this means that no other valid pointer, to any other variable or array cell or anything else, will ever compare equal to a null pointer.

The most straightforward way to "get" a null pointer in your programme is by using the predefined constant NULL, which is defined for you by several standard header files, including <stdio.h>, <stdlib.h>, and <string.h>. To initialize a pointer to a null pointer, you might use code like,

```
#include <stdio.h>
int *ip = NULL;
```

and to test it for a null pointer before inspecting the value pointed to you might use code like

```
if(ip != NULL)
printf("%d\n", *ip);
```

It is also possible to refer to the null pointer by using a constant 0, and you will see some code that sets null pointers by simply doing

```
int *ip = 0;
```

In fact, NULL is a preprocessor macro which typically has the value, or replacement text, 0.

Furthermore, since the definition of "true" in C is a value that is not equal to 0, you will see code that tests for non-null pointers with abbreviated code like,

```
if(ip)
printf("%d\n", *ip);
```

This has the same meaning as our previous example; if(ip) is equivalent to if(ip = 0) and to if(ip = NULL).

All of these uses are legal, and although I recommend that you use the constant NULL for clarity, you will come across the other forms, so you should be able to recognize them.

You can use a null pointer as a placeholder to remind yourself (or, more importantly, to help your programme remember) that a pointer variable does not point anywhere at the moment and that you should not use the "contents of" operator on it (that is, you should not try to inspect what it points to, since it doesn't point to anything). A function that returns pointer values can return a null pointer when it is unable to perform its task. (A null pointer used in this way is analogous to the EOFvalue that functions like getchar return.)

As an example, let us write our own version of the standard library function strstr, which looks for one string within another, returning a pointer to the string if it can, or a null pointer if it cannot. Here is the function, using the obvious brute-force algorithm: at every character of the input string, the code checks for a match there of the pattern string:

```
#include <stddef.h>
char *mystrstr(char input[], char pat[])
{
char *start, *p1, *p2;
for(start = &input[0]; *start != '\0'; start++)
{  /* for each position in input string... */
p1 = pat; /* prepare to check for pattern string
there */
p2 = start;
while(*p1 != '\0')
{
```

```
if(*p1 != *p2)   /* characters differ */
break;
p1++;
p2++;
}
if(*p1 == '\0') /* found match */
return start;
}
return NULL;
}
```

The start pointer steps over each character position in the input string. At each character, the inner loop checks for a match there, by using p1 to step over the pattern string (pat), and p2 to step over the input string (starting at start). We compare successive characters until either (a) we reach the end of the pattern string (*p1 == '\0'), or (b) we find two characters which differ. When we're done with the inner loop, if we reached the end of the pattern string (*p1 == '\0'), it means that all preceding characters matched, and we found a complete match for the pattern starting at start, so we return start. Otherwise, we go around the outer loop again, to try another starting position. If we run out of those (if*start == '\0'), without finding a match, we return a null pointer.

Notice that the function is declared as returning (and does in fact return) a pointer-to-char. We can use mystrstr (or its standard library counterpart strstr) to determine whether one string contains another:

```
if(mystrstr("Hello, world!", "lo") == NULL)
printf("no\n");
else  printf("yes\n");
```

In general, C does not initialize pointers to null for you, and it never tests pointers to see if they are null before using them. If one of the pointers in your programs points somewhere some of the time but not all of the time, an excellent convention to use is to set it to a null pointer when it doesn't point anywhere valid, and to test to see if it's a null pointer before using it. But you must use explicit code to set it to NULL, and to test it against NULL. (In other words, just setting an unused pointer variable to NULL doesn't guarantee safety; you also have to check for the null value before using the pointer.) On the other hand, if you know that a particular pointer variable is always valid, you don't have to insert a paranoid test against NULL before using it.

EQUIVALENCE' BETWEEN POINTERS AND ARRAYS

There are a number of similarities between arrays and pointers in C.

If you have an array,

```
int a[10];
```

you can refer to a[0], a[1], a[2], etc., or to a[i] where i is an int. If you declare a pointer variable ip and set it to point to the beginning of an array:

```
int *ip = &a[0];
```

you can refer to *ip, *(ip+1), *(ip+2), etc., or to *(ip+i) where i is an int.

There are also differences, of course. You cannot assign two arrays; the code

```
int a[10], b[10];
a = b; /* WRONG */
```

is illegal. As we've seen, though, you *can* assign two pointer variables:

```
int *ip1, *ip2;
ip1 = &a[0];
ip2 = ip1;
```

Pointer assignment is straightforward; the pointer on the left is simply made to point wherever the pointer on the right does. We haven't copied the data pointed to (there's still just one copy, in the same place); we've just made two pointers point to that one place.

The similarities between arrays and pointers end up being quite useful, and in fact C builds on the similarities, leading to what is called "the equivalence of arrays and pointers in C." When we speak of this "equivalence" we do not mean that arrays and pointers are the same thing (they are in fact quite different), but rather that they can be used in related ways, and that certain operations may be used between them. The first such operation is that it is possible to (apparently) assign an array to a pointer:

```
int a[10];
int *ip;
ip = a;
```

What can this mean? In that last assignment ip = a, aren't we mixing apples and oranges again? It turns out that we are not; C defines the result of this assignment to be that ip receives a pointer to the first element of a. In other words, it is as if you had written

```
ip = &a[0];
```

The second facet of the equivalence is that you can use the "array subscripting" notation [i] on pointers, too. If you write,

```
ip[3]
```

it is just as if you had written

```
*(ip + 3)
```

So when you have a pointer that points to a block of memory, such as an array or a part of an array, you can treat that pointer "as if" it *were* an array, using the convenient [i] notation. In other words, at the beginning of this section when we talked about *ip, *(ip+1), *(ip+2), and *(ip+i), we could have written ip[0], ip[1], ip[2], and ip[i]. As we'll see, this can be quite useful (or at least convenient).

The third facet of the equivalence (which is actually a more general version of the first one we mentioned) is that *whenever*you mention the name of an array in a context where the "value" of the array would be needed, C automatically generates a pointer to the first element of the array, as if you had written &array[0]. When you write something like,

```
int a[10];
int *ip;
ip = a + 3;
```

it is as if you had written,

```
ip = &a[0] + 3;
```

which (and you might like to convince yourself of this) gives the same result as if you had written,

```
ip = &a[3];
```

For example, if the character array,

char string[100];

contains some string, here is another way to find its length:

```
int len;
char *p;
for(p = string; *p != '\0'; p++)
;
len = p - string;
```

After the loop, p points to the '\0' terminating the string. The expression p - string is equivalent to p - &string[0], and gives the length of the string.

ARRAYS AND POINTERS AS FUNCTION ARGUMENTS

Earlier, we learned that functions in C receive copies of their arguments. (This means that C uses *call by value*; it means that a function can modify one of its arguments without modifying the value in the caller.) We didn't say so at the time, but when a function is called, the copies of the arguments are made as if by assignment. But since arrays can't be assigned, how can a function receive an array as an argument? The answer will explain why arrays are an apparent exception to the rule that functions cannot modify their arguments.

We've been regularly calling a function getline like this:

```
char line[100];
getline(line, 100);
```

with the intention that getline read the next line of input into the character array line. But in the previous paragraph, we learned that when we mention the name of an array in an expression, the compiler generates a pointer to its first element.

So the call above is as if we had written,

```
char line[100];
getline(&line[0], 100);
```

In other words, the getline function does *not* receive an array of char at all; it actually receives a pointer to char!

As we've seen throughout this chapter, it's

straightforward to manipulate the elements of an array using pointers, so there's no particular insurmountable difficulty if getline receives a pointer. One question remains, though: we had been defininggetline with its line parameter declared as an array:

```
int getline(char line[], int max)
{
...
}
```

We mentioned that we didn't have to specify a size for the line parameter, with the explanation that getline really used the array in its caller, where the actual size was specified. But that declaration certainly does look like an array—how can it work when getline actually receives a pointer?

The answer is that the C compiler does a little something behind your back. It knows that whenever you mention an array name in an expression, it (the compiler) generates a pointer to the array's first element. Therefore, it knows that a function can never actually receive an array as a parameter. Therefore, whenever it sees you defining a function that seems to accept an array as a parameter, the compiler quietly pretends that you had declared it as accepting a pointer, instead. The definition of getline above is compiled exactly as if it had been written,

```
int getline(char *line, int max)
{
...
}
```

Let's look at how getline might be written if we thought of its first parameter (argument) as a pointer, instead:

```
int getline(char *line, int max)
{
int nch = 0;
int c;
max = max - 1;  /* leave room for '\0' */
#ifndef FGETLINE
while((c = getchar()) != EOF)
#else
```

```
while((c = getc(fp)) != EOF)
#endif
{
if(c == '\n')
break;
if(nch < max)
{
*(line + nch) = c;
nch = nch + 1;
}
}
if(c == EOF && nch == 0)
return EOF;
*(line + nch) = '\0';
return nch;
}
```

But, as we've learned, we can also use "array subscript" notation with pointers, so we could rewrite the pointer version ofgetline like this:

```
int getline(char *line, int max)
{
int nch = 0;
int c;
max = max - 1;  /* leave room for '\0' */
#ifndef FGETLINE
while((c = getchar()) != EOF)
#else
while((c = getc(fp)) != EOF)
#endif
{
if(c == '\n')
break;
if(nch < max)
{
line[nch] = c;
nch = nch + 1;
}
}
```

```
if(c == EOF && nch == 0)
return EOF;
line[nch] = '\0';
return nch;
}
```

In other words, within the body of the function, it hardly matters whether we thought line was an array or a pointer, since we can use array subscripting notation with both arrays and pointers.

These games that the compiler is playing with arrays and pointers may seem bewildering at first, and it may seem faintly miraculous that everything comes out in the wash when you declare a function like getline that seems to accept an array. The equivalence in C between arrays and pointers can be confusing, but it *does* work and is one of the central features of C. If the games which the compiler plays (pretending that you declared a parameter as a pointer when you thought you declared it as an array) bother you, you can do two things:

- Continue to pretend that functions can receive arrays as parameters; declare and use them that way, but remember that unlike other arguments, a function can modify the copy in its caller of an argument that (seems to be) an array.
- Realise that arrays are always passed to functions as pointers, and always declare your functions as accepting pointers.

STRINGS

Because of the "equivalence" of arrays and pointers, it is extremely common to refer to and manipulate strings as character pointers, or char *'s. It is so common, in fact, that it is easy to forget that strings are arrays, and to imagine that they're represented by pointers. (Actually, in the case of strings, it may not even matter that much if the distinction gets a little blurred; there's certainly nothing wrong with referring to a character pointer, suitably initialized, as a "string.") Let's look at a few of the implications:

- Any function that manipulates a string will actually

accept it as a char * argument. The caller may pass an array containing a string, but the function will receive a pointer to the array's (string's) first element (character).

- The %s format in printf expects a character pointer.
- Although you have to use strcpy to copy a string from one array to another, you can use simple pointer assignment to assign a string to a pointer. The string being assigned might either be in an array or pointed to by another pointer. In other words, given
- char string[] = "Hello, world!";
- char *p1, *p2;

both

```
    p1 = string
```

and

```
    p2 = p1
```

are legal. (Remember, though, that when you assign a pointer, you're making a copy of the pointer but *not* of the data it points to. In the first example, p1 ends up pointing to the string in string. In the second example, p2 ends up pointing to the same string as p1. In any case, after a pointer assignment, if you ever change the string (or other data) pointed to, the change is "visible" to *both* pointers.

- Many programs manipulate strings exclusively using character pointers, never explicitly declaring any actual arrays. As long as these programs are careful to allocate appropriate memory for the strings, they're perfectly valid and correct.

When you start working heavily with strings, however, you have to be aware of one subtle fact.

When you initialize a character array with a string constant:

```
char string[] = "Hello, world!";
```

you end up with an array containing the string, and you can modify the array's contents to your heart's content:

```
string[0] = 'J';
```

However, it's possible to use string constants (the formal term is *string literals*) at other places in your code. Since they're arrays, the compiler generates pointers to their first elements when they're used in expressions, as usual.

That is, if you say,

```
char *p1 = "Hello";
int len = strlen("world");
it's almost as if you'd said
char internal_string_1[] = "Hello";
char internal_string_2[] = "world";
char *p1 = &internal_string_1[0];
int len = strlen(&internal_string_2[0]);
```

Here, the arrays named internal_string_1 and internal_string_2 are supposed to suggest the fact that the compiler is actually generating little temporary arrays every time you use a string constant in your code. *However*, the subtle fact is that the arrays which are "behind" the string constants are *not* necessarily modifiable. In particular, the compiler may store them in read-only-memory. Therefore, if you write

```
char *p3 = "Hello, world!";
p3[0] = 'J';
```

your programme may crash, because it may try to store a value (in this case, the character 'J') into nonwritable memory.

The moral is that whenever you're building or modifying strings, you have to make sure that the memory you're building or modifying them in is writable. That memory should either be an array you've allocated, or some memory which you've dynamically allocated by the techniques which we'll see in the next chapter.

Make sure that no part of your programme will ever try to modify a string which is actually one of the unnamed, unwritable arrays which the compiler generated for you in response to one of your string constants. (The only exception is array initialization, because if you write to such an array, you're writing to the array, not to the string literal which you used to initialize the array.)

EXAMPLE: BREAKING A LINE INTO "WORDS"

In an earlier assignment, an "extra credit" version of a

problem asked you to write a little checkbook balancing programme that accepted a series of lines of the form,

```
deposit 1000
check 10
check 12.34
deposit 50
check 20
```

It was a surprising nuisance to do this in an *ad hoc* way, using only the tools we had at the time. It was easy to read each line, but it was cumbersome to break it up into the word ("deposit" or "check") and the amount.

I find it very convenient to use a more general approach: first, break lines like these into a series of whitespace-separated words, then deal with each word separately. To do this, we will use an *array of pointers to* char, which we can also think of as an "array of strings," since a string is an array of char, and a pointer-to-char can easily point at a string. Here is the declaration of such an array:

```
char *words[10];
```

This is the first complicated C declaration we've seen: it says that words is an array of 10 pointers to char. We're going to write a function, getwords, which we can call like this:

```
int nwords;
nwords = getwords(line, words, 10);
```

where line is the line we're breaking into words, words is the array to be filled in with the (pointers to the) words, andnwords (the return value from getwords) is the number of words which the function finds. (As with getline, we tell the function the size of the array so that if the line should happen to contain more words than that, it won't overflow the array).

Here is the definition of the getwords function. It finds the beginning of each word, places a pointer to it in the array, finds the end of that word (which is signified by at least one whitespace character) and terminates the word by placing a '\0'character after it. (The '\0' character will overwrite the first whitespace character following the word.) Note that the original input string is therefore modified by getwords: if you were to try to print the input line after calling getwords, it would appear to contain only its first word (because of the first inserted '\0').

```
#include <stddef.h>
#include <ctype.h>
getwords(char *line, char *words[], int maxwords)
{
char *p = line;
int nwords = 0;
while(1)
{
while(isspace(*p))
p++;
if(*p == '\0')
return nwords;
words[nwords++] = p;
while(!isspace(*p) && *p != '\0')
p++;
if(*p == '\0')
return nwords;
*p++ = '\0';
if(nwords >= maxwords)
return nwords;
}
}
```

Each time through the outer while loop, the function tries to find another word. First it skips over whitespace (which might be leading spaces on the line, or the space(s) separating this word from the previous one). The isspace function is new: it's in the standard library, declared in the header file <ctype.h>, and it returns nonzero ("true") if the character you hand it is a space character (a space or a tab, or any other whitespace character there might happen to be).

When the function finds a non-whitespace character, it has found the beginning of another word, so it places the pointer to that character in the next cell of the words array. Then it steps though the word, looking at non-whitespace characters, until it finds another whitespace character, or the \0 at the end of the line. If it finds the \0, it's done with the entire line;

otherwise, it changes the whitespace character to a \0, to terminate the word it's just found, and continues. (If it's found as many words as will fit in the words array, it returns prematurely.)

Each time it finds a word, the function increments the number of words (nwords) it has found. Since arrays in C start at[0], the number of words the function has found so far is also the index of the cell in the words array where the next word should be stored. The function actually assigns the next word and increments nwords in one expression:

```
words[nwords++] = p;
```

You should convince yourself that this arrangement works, and that (in this case) the preincrement form

```
words[++nwords] = p;   /* WRONG */
```

would *not* behave as desired.

When the function is done (when it finds the \0 terminating the input line, or when it runs out of cells in the words array) it returns the number of words it has found.

Here is a complete example of calling getwords:

```
char line[] = "this is a test";
int i;
nwords = getwords(line, words, 10);
for(i = 0; i < nwords; i++)
printf("%s\n", words[i]);
```

Chapter 10

Memory Allocation

ALLOCATING MEMORY

A problem with many simple programs, including in particular little teaching programs such as we've been writing so far, is that they tend to use fixed-size arrays which may or may not be big enough.

We have an array of 100 ints for the numbers which the user enters and wishes to find the average of—what if the user enters 101 numbers? We have an array of 100 chars which we pass to getline to receive the user's input—what if the user types a line of 200 characters? If we're lucky, the relevant parts of the programme check how much of an array they've used, and print an error message or otherwise gracefully abort before overflowing the array. If we're not so lucky, a programme may sail off the end of an array, overwriting other data and behaving quite badly. In either case, the user doesn't get his job done. The answers all involve the standard library function malloc. Very simply, malloc returns a pointer to *n* bytes of memory which we can do anything we want to with. If we didn't want to read a line of input into a fixed-size array, we could usemalloc, instead.

Here's the first step:

```
#include <stdlib.h>
char *line;
int linelen = 100;
line = malloc(linelen);
/* incomplete — malloc's return value not checked
*/
```

```
getline(line, linelen);
```

malloc is declared in <stdlib.h>, so we #include that header in any programme that calls malloc. A "byte" in C is, by definition, an amount of storage suitable for storing one character, so the above invocation of malloc gives us exactly as many chars as we ask for.

We could illustrate the resulting pointer like this:

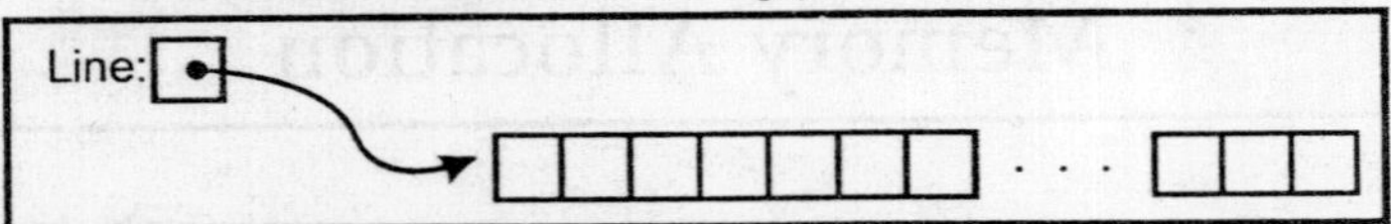

The 100 bytes of memory (not all of which are shown) pointed to by line are those allocated by malloc. (They are brand-new memory, conceptually a bit different from the memory which the compiler arranges to have allocated automatically for our conventional variables. The 100 boxes in the figure don't have a name next to them, because they're not storage for a variable we've declared.)

As a second example, we might have occasion to allocate a piece of memory, and to copy a string into it with strcpy:

```
char *p = malloc(15);
/* incomplete — malloc's return value not checked
*/
strcpy(p, "Hello, world!");
```

When copying strings, remember that all strings have a terminating \0 character. If you use strlen to count the characters in a string for you, that count will *not* include the trailing \0, so you must add one before calling malloc:

```
char *somestring, *copy;
...
copy = malloc(strlen(somestring) + 1);  /* +1
for \0 */
/* incomplete — malloc's return value not checked
*/
strcpy(copy, somestring);
```

What if we're not allocating characters, but integers? If we want to allocate 100 ints, how many bytes is that? If we know how big ints are on our machine (i.e. depending on whether we're using a 16- or 32-bit machine) we could try to compute it ourselves, but it's much safer and more portable to let C compute it for us. C has a sizeof operator, which computes the size, in bytes, of a variable or type. It's just what we need when calling malloc. To allocate space for 100ints, we could call

```
int *ip = malloc(100 * sizeof(int));
```

The use of the sizeof operator tends to look like a function call, but it's really an operator, and it does its work at compile time. Since we can use array indexing syntax on pointers, we can treat a pointer variable after a call to malloc almost exactly as if it were an array. In particular, after the above call to malloc initializes ip to point at storage for 100 ints, we can access ip[0], ip[1]... up to ip[99].

This way, we can get the effect of an array even if we don't know until run time how big the "array" should be. (In a later section we'll see how we might deal with the case where we're not even sure at the point we begin using it how big an "array" will eventually have to be.)

Our examples so far have all had a significant omission: they have not checked malloc's return value. Obviously, no real computer has an infinite amount of memory available, so there is no guarantee that malloc will be able to give us as much memory as we ask for. If we call malloc(100000000), or if we call malloc(10) 10,000,000 times, we're probably going to run out of memory.

When malloc is unable to allocate the requested memory, it returns a *null pointer*. A null pointer, remember, points definitively nowhere. It's a "not a pointer" marker; it's not a pointer you can use. (As we said in section 9.4, a null pointer can be used as a failure return from a function that returns pointers, and malloc is a perfect example.) Therefore, whenever you call malloc, it's vital to check the returned pointer before using it. If you call malloc, and it returns a null pointer, and you go off and use that null pointer as if it pointed somewhere, your programme probably won't last long. Instead, a programme should immediately check for a null pointer, and if it receives one, it should at the very least print an error message and exit, or perhaps figure out some way of proceeding without the memory it asked for. But it cannot go on to use the null pointer it got back from malloc in any way, because that null pointer by definition points nowhere. ("It cannot use a null pointer in any way" means that the programme cannot use the * or [] operators on such a pointer value, or pass it to any function that expects a valid pointer.)

A call to malloc, with an error check, typically looks something like this:

```
int *ip = malloc(100 * sizeof(int));
if(ip == NULL)
{
printf("out of memory\n");
exit or return
}
```

After printing the error message, this code should return to its caller, or exit from the programme entirely; it cannot proceed with the code that would have used ip.

Of course, in our examples so far, we've still limited ourselves to "fixed size" regions of memory, because we've been calling malloc with fixed arguments like 10 or 100. (Our call to getline is still limited to 100-character lines, or whatever number we set the linelen variable to; our ip variable still points at only 100 ints.) However, since the sizes are now values which can in principle be determined at run-time, we've at least moved beyond having to recompile the programme (with a bigger array) to accommodate longer lines, and with a little more work, we could arrange that the "arrays" automatically grew to be as large as required.

FREEING MEMORY

Memory allocated with malloc lasts as long as you want it to. It does not automatically disappear when a function returns, as automatic-duration variables do, but it does not have to remain for the entire duration of your programme, either. Just as you can use malloc to control exactly when and how much memory you allocate, you can also control exactly when you deallocate it.

In fact, many programs use memory on a transient basis. They allocate some memory, use it for a while, but then reach a point where they don't need that particular piece any more. Because memory is not inexhaustible, it's a good idea to deallocate (that is, release or *free*) memory you're no longer using.

Dynamically allocated memory is deallocated with the free function. If p contains a pointer previously returned bymalloc, you can call

```
free(p);
```

which will "give the memory back" to the stock of memory (sometimes called the "arena" or "pool") from which mallocrequests are satisfied. Calling free is sort of the ultimate in recycling: it costs you almost nothing, and the memory you give back is immediately usable by other parts of your programme. (Theoretically, it may even be usable by other programs.)

(Freeing unused memory is a good idea, but it's not mandatory. When your programme exits, any memory which it has allocated but not freed should be automatically released. If your computer were to somehow "lose" memory just because your programme forgot to free it, that would indicate a problem or deficiency in your operating system.)

Naturally, once you've freed some memory you must remember not to use it any more.

After calling,

```
free(p);
```

it is probably the case that p still points at the same memory. However, since we've given it back, it's now "available," and a later call to malloc might give that memory to some other part of your programme. If the variable p is a global variable or will otherwise stick around for a while, one good way to record the fact that it's not to be used any more would be to set it to a null pointer:

```
free(p);
p = NULL;
```

Now we don't even have the pointer to the freed memory any more, and (as long as we check to see that p is non-

NULLbefore using it), we won't misuse any memory via the pointer p.

When thinking about malloc, free, and dynamically-allocated memory in general, remember again the distinction between a pointer and what it points to. If you call malloc to allocate some memory, and store the pointer which mallocgives you in a local pointer variable, what happens when the function containing the local pointer variable returns?

If the local pointer variable has *automatic duration* (which is the default, unless the variable is declared static), it will disappear when the function returns. But for the pointer variable to disappear says nothing about the memory pointed to! That memory still exists and, as far as malloc and free are concerned, is still allocated. The only thing that has disappeared is the pointer variable you had which pointed at the allocated memory.

REALLOCATING MEMORY BLOCKS

Sometimes you're not sure at first how much memory you'll need. For example, if you need to store a series of items you read from the user, and if the only way to know how many there are is to read them until the user types some "end" signal, you'll have no way of knowing, as you begin reading and storing the first few, how many you'll have seen by the time you do see that "end" marker. You might want to allocate room for, say, 100 items, and if the user enters a 101st item before entering the "end" marker, you might wish for a way to say "uh, malloc, remember those 100 items I asked for? Could I change my mind and have 200 instead?"

In fact, you can do exactly this, with the realloc function. You hand realloc an old pointer (such as you received from an initial call to malloc) and a new size, and realloc does what it can to give you a chunk of memory big enough to hold the new size.

For example, if we wanted the ip variable from an earlier example to point at 200 ints instead of 100, we could try calling

```
ip = realloc(ip, 200 * sizeof(int));
```

Since you always want each block of dynamically-allocated memory to be contiguous (so that you can treat it as if it were an array), you and realloc have to worry about the case where realloc can't make the old block of memory bigger "in place," but rather has to relocate it elsewhere in order to find enough contiguous space for the new requested size.realloc does this by returning a new pointer. If realloc was able to make the old block of memory bigger, it returns the same pointer.

If realloc has to go elsewhere to get enough contiguous memory, it returns a pointer to the new memory, after copying your old data there. (In this case, after it makes the copy, it frees the old block.) Finally, if realloc can't find enough memory to satisfy the new request at all, it returns a null pointer.

Therefore, you usually don't want to overwrite your old pointer with realloc's return value until you've tested it to make sure it's not a null pointer.

You might use code like this:

```
int *newp;
newp = realloc(ip, 200 * sizeof(int));
if(newp != NULL)
ip = newp;
else {
printf("out of memory\n");
/* exit or return */
/* but ip still points at 100 ints */
}
```

If realloc returns something other than a null pointer, it succeeded, and we set ip to what it returned. (We've either setip to what it used to be or to a new pointer, but in either case, it points to where our data is now.) If realloc returns a null pointer, however, we hang on to our old pointer in ip which still points at our original 100 values.

Putting this all together, here is a piece of code which reads lines of text from the user, treats each line as an integer by calling atoi, and stores each integer in a dynamically-allocated "array":

```
#define MAXLINE 100
char line[MAXLINE];
int *ip;
int nalloc, nitems;
nalloc = 100;
ip = malloc(nalloc * sizeof(int));          /*
initial allocation */
if(ip == NULL)
{
printf("out of memory\n");
exit(1);
}
nitems = 0;
while(getline(line, MAXLINE) != EOF)
{
if(nitems >= nalloc)
{  /* increase allocation */
int *newp;
nalloc += 100;
newp = realloc(ip, nalloc * sizeof(int));
if(newp == NULL)
{
printf("out of memory\n");
exit(1);
}
ip = newp;
}
ip[nitems++] = atoi(line);
}
```

We use two different variables to keep track of the "array" pointed to by ip. nalloc is how many elements we've allocated, and nitems is how many of them are in use. Whenever we're about to store another item in the "array," ifnitems >= nalloc, the old "array" is full, and it's time to call realloc to make it bigger. Finally, we might ask what the return type of malloc and realloc is, if they are able to return pointers to char or pointers to int or (though we haven't seen it yet) pointers to any other type. The answer is that both of these functions are declared (in <stdlib.h>) as returning a type we haven't seen, void * (that is, pointer to void).

We haven't really seen type void, either, but what's going on here is that void * is specially defined as a "generic" pointer type, which may be used (strictly speaking, assigned to or from) any pointer type.

POINTER SAFETY

At the beginning of the previous chapter, we said that the hard thing about pointers is not so much manipulating them as ensuring that the memory they point to is valid. When a pointer doesn't point where you think it does, if you inadvertently access or modify the memory it points to, you can damage other parts of your programme, or (in some cases) other programs or the operating system itself!

When we use pointers to simple variables, as in section 10.1, there's not much that can go wrong. When we use pointers into arrays, as in section 10.2, and begin moving the pointers around, we have to be more careful, to ensure that the roving pointers always stay within the bounds of the array(s).

When we begin passing pointers to functions, and especially when we begin returning them from functions (as in the strstr function of section 10.4) we have to be more careful still, because the code using the pointer may be far removed from the code which owns or allocated the memory.

One particular problem concerns functions that return pointers. Where is the memory to which the returned pointer points? Is it still around by the time the function returns? The strstr function returns either a null pointer (which points definitively nowhere, and which the caller presumably checks for) or it returns a pointer which points into the input string, which the caller supplied, which is pretty safe.

One thing a function must *not* do, however, is return a pointer to one of its own, local, automatic-duration arrays. Remember that automatic-duration variables (which includes all non-static local variables), including automatic-duration arrays, are deallocated and disappear when the function returns. If a function returns a pointer to a local array, that pointer will be invalid by the time the caller tries to use it.

FILE POINTERS AND FOPEN

How will we specify that we want to access a particular data file? It would theoretically be possible to mention the name of a file each time it was desired to read from or write to it. But such an approach would have a number of drawbacks. Instead, the usual approach is that you mention the name of the file once, at the time you *open* it. Thereafter, you use some little token—in this case, the *file pointer*—which keeps track (both for your sake and the library's) of which file you're talking about. Whenever you want to read from or write to one of the files you're working with, you identify that file by using its file pointer (that is, the file pointer you obtained when you opened the file). As we'll see, you store file pointers in variables just as you store any other data you manipulate, so it is possible to have several files open, as long as you use distinct variables to store the file pointers.

You declare a variable to store a file pointer like this:

```
FILE *fp;
```

The type FILE is predefined for you by <stdio.h>. It is a data structure which holds the information the standard I/O library needs to keep track of the file for you. For historical reasons, you declare a variable which is a pointer to this FILEtype. The name of the variable can (as for any variable) be anything you choose; it is traditional to use the letters fp in the variable name (since we're talking about a file pointer). If you were reading from two files at once you'd probably use two file pointers:

```
FILE *fp1, *fp2;
```

If you were reading from one file and writing to another you might declare and input file pointer and an output file pointer:

```
FILE *ifp, *ofp;
```

Like any pointer variable, a file pointer isn't any good until it's initialized to point to something. (Actually, no variable of any type is much good until you've initialized it.) To actually open a file, and receive the "token" which you'll store in your file pointer variable, you call fopen. fopen accepts a file name (as a string) and a *mode* value indicating among other things whether you intend to read or write this file. (The mode variable is also a string.) To open the file input.dat for reading you might call

```
ifp = fopen("input.dat", "r");
```

The mode string "r" indicates reading. Mode "w" indicates writing, so we could open output.dat for output like this:

```
ofp = fopen("output.dat", "w");
```

The other values for the mode string are less frequently used. The third major mode is "a" for append. (If you use "w" to write to a file which already exists, its old contents will be discarded.) You may also add a + character to the mode string to indicate that you want to both read and write, or a b character to indicate that you want to do "binary" (as opposed to text) I/O.

One thing to beware of when opening files is that it's an operation which may fail. The requested file might not exist, or it might be protected against reading or writing. (These possibilities ought to be obvious, but it's easy to forget them.) fopenreturns a null pointer if it can't open the requested file, and it's important to check for this case before going off and usingfopen's return value as a file pointer. Every call to fopen will typically be followed with a test, like this:

```
ifp = fopen("input.dat", "r");
if(ifp == NULL)
{
printf("can't open file\n");
exit or return
}
```

If fopen returns a null pointer, and you store it in your file pointer variable and go off and try to do I/O with it, your programme will typically crash.

It's common to collapse the call to fopen and the assignment in with the test:

```
if((ifp = fopen("input.dat", "r")) == NULL)
```

```
{
printf("can't open file\n");
exit or return
}
```

I/O WITH FILE POINTERS

For each of the I/O library functions we've been using so far, there's a companion function which accepts an additional file pointer argument telling it where to read from or write to. The companion function to printf is fprintf, and the file pointer argument comes first. To print a string to the output.dat file we opened in the previous section, we might call

```
fprintf(ofp, "Hello, world!\n");
```

The companion function to getchar is getc, and the file pointer is its only argument. To read a character from theinput.dat file we opened in the previous section, we might call

```
int c;
c = getc(ifp);
```

The companion function to putchar is putc, and the file pointer argument comes last. To write a character tooutput.dat, we could call

```
putc(c, ofp);
```

Our own getline function calls getchar and so always reads the standard input. We could write a companionfgetline function which reads from an arbitrary file pointer:

```
#include <stdio.h>
/* Read one line from fp, */
/* copying it to line array (but no more than
max chars). */
/* Does not place terminating \n in line array.
*/
/* Returns line length, or 0 for empty line, or
EOF for end-of-file. */
int fgetline(FILE *fp, char line[], int max)
{
int nch = 0;
int c;
```

```
max = max - 1;  /* leave room for '\0' */
while((c = getc(fp)) != EOF)
{
if(c == '\n')
break;
if(nch < max)
{
line[nch] = c;
nch = nch + 1;
}
}
if(c == EOF && nch == 0)
return EOF;
line[nch] = '\0';
return nch;
}
```

Now we could read one line from ifp by calling

```
char line[MAXLINE];
...
fgetline(ifp, line, MAXLINE);
```

PREDEFINED STREAMS

Besides the file pointers which we explicitly open by calling fopen, there are also three predefined streams. stdin is a constant file pointer corresponding to standard input, and stdout is a constant file pointer corresponding to standard output. Both of these can be used anywhere a file pointer is called for; for example, getchar() is the same asgetc(stdin) and putchar(c) is the same as putc(c, stdout). The third predefined stream is stderr. Likestdout, stderr is typically connected to the screen by default. The difference is that stderr is not redirected when the standard output is redirected. For example, under Unix or MS-DOS, when you invoke,

```
programme > filename
```

anything printed to stdout is redirected to the file filename, but anything printed to stderr still goes to the screen. The intent behind stderr is that it is the "standard error output"; error messages printed to it will not disappear into an output file. For example, a more realistic way to print an error message when a file can't be opened would be,

```
if((ifp = fopen(filename, "r")) == NULL)
{
fprintf(stderr, "can't open file %s\n",
filename);
exit or return
}
```

where filename is a string variable indicating the file name to be opened. Not only is the error message printed tostderr, but it is also more informative in that it mentions the name of the file that couldn't be opened.

CLOSING FILES

Although you can open multiple files, there's a limit to how many you can have open at once. If your programme will open many files in succession, you'll want to close each one as you're done with it; otherwise the standard I/O library could run out of the resources it uses to keep track of open files. Closing a file simply involves calling fclose with the file pointer as its argument:

```
fclose(fp);
```

Calling fclose arranges that (if the file was open for output) any last, buffered output is finally written to the file, and that those resources used by the operating system (and the C library) for this file are released. If you forget to close a file, it will be closed automatically when the programme exits.

READING A DATA FILE

Suppose you had a data file consisting of rows and columns of numbers:

```
1  2   34
5  6   78
9  10  112
```

Suppose you wanted to read these numbers into an array. (Actually, the array will be an array of arrays, or a "multidimensional" array; see section 4.1.2.) We can write code to do this by putting together several pieces: thefgetline function we just showed, and the getwords function from chapter.

Assuming that the data file is namedinput.dat, the code would look like this:

```
#define MAXLINE 100
#define MAXROWS 10
#define MAXCOLS 10
int array[MAXROWS][MAXCOLS];
char *filename = "input.dat";
FILE *ifp;
char line[MAXLINE];
char *words[MAXCOLS];
int nrows = 0;
int n;
int i;
ifp = fopen(filename, "r");
if(ifp == NULL)
{
fprintf(stderr, "can't open %s\n", filename);
exit(EXIT_FAILURE);
}
while(fgetline(ifp, line, MAXLINE) != EOF)
{
if(nrows >= MAXROWS)
{
fprintf(stderr, "too many rows\n");
exit(EXIT_FAILURE);
}
n = getwords(line, words, MAXCOLS);
for(i = 0; i < n; i++)
array[nrows][i] = atoi(words[i]);
nrows++;
}
```

Each trip through the loop reads one line from the file, using fgetline. Each line is broken up into "words" usinggetwords; each "word" is actually one number.

The numbers are however still represented as strings, so

each one is converted to an int by calling atoi before being stored in the array. The code checks for two different error conditions (failure to open the input file, and too many lines in the input file) and if one of these conditions occurs, it prints an error message, and exits. The exit function is a Standard library function which terminates your programme.

Chapter 11

Variables and Arithmetic

FUNDAMENTALS

Here is where we start to look in detail at the bits that the last chapter chose to sweep under the carpet while it did its 'Instant C' introduction. The problem is, of course, the usual one of trying to introduce enough of the language to let you get a feel for what it's all about, without drowning beginners in a froth of detail that isn't essential at the time.

Because this is a lengthy chapter, and because it deliberately chooses to cover some subtle problems that are often missed out in introductory texts, you should make sure that you are in the right mood and proper frame of mind to read it.

The weary brain may find that the breaks for exercises are useful. We strongly recommend that you do actually attempt the exercises on the way through. They help to balance the weight of information, which otherwise turns into an indigestible lump.

THE ALPHABET OF C

This is an interesting area; alphabets are important. All the same, this is the one part of this chapter that you can read superficially first time round without missing too much. Read it to make sure that you've seen the contents once, and make a mental note to come back to it later on.

BASIC ALPHABET

Few computer languages bother to define their alphabet

rigorously. There's usually an assumption that the English alphabet augmented by a sprinkling of more or less arbitrary punctuation symbols will be available in every environment that is trying to support the language.

The assumption is not always borne out by experience. Older languages suffer less from this sort of problem, but try sendingC programs by Telex or restrictive e-mail links and you'll understand the difficulty.

The Standard talks about two different character sets: the one that programs are written in and the one that programs execute with. This is basically to allow for different systems for compiling and execution, which might use different ways of encoding their characters.

It doesn't actually matter a lot except when you are using character constants in the preprocessor, where they may not have the same value as they do at execution time. This behaviour is implementation-defined, so it must be documented.

The Standard requires that an alphabet of 96 symbols is available for C as follows:

Table. The Alphabet of C

---

a b c d e f g h i j k l m n o p q r s t u v w x y z

A B C D E F G H I J K L M N O P Q R S T U V W X Y Z

0 1 2 3 4 5 6 7 8 9

! " #%& ' () * +, -./

:; < = > ? [\] ^ _ {|} ~

space, horizontal and vertical tab

form feed, newline

It turns out that most of the commonly used computer alphabets contain all the symbols that are needed for C with a few notorious exceptions. The C alphabetic characters shown below are missing from the International Standards Organization ISO 646 standard 7-bit character set, which is as a subset of all the widely used computer alphabets.

[\] ^ { | } ~

To cater for systems that can't provide the full 96

characters needed by C, the Standard specifies a method of using the ISO 646 characters to represent the missing few; the technique is the use of *trigraphs*.

TRIGRAPHS

Trigraphs are a sequence of three ISO 646 characters that get treated as if they were one character in the C alphabet; all of the trigraphs start with two question marks ?? which helps to indicate that 'something funny' is going on. Table below shows the trigraphs defined in the Standard.

Table. Trigraphs

C character	Trigraph
#	??=
[	??(
]	??)
{	??<
}	??>
\	??/
|	??!
~	??-
^	??'

As an example, let's assume that your terminal doesn't have the # symbol.

To write the preprocessor line,

```
#define MAX 32767
```

isn't possible; you must use trigraph notation instead:

```
??=define MAX 32767
```

Of course trigraphs will work even if you do have a # symbol; they are there to help in difficult circumstances more than to be used for routine programming.

The ? 'binds to the right', so in any sequence of repeated ?s, only the two at the right could possibly be part of a trigraph, depending on what comes next—this disposes of any ambiguity.

It would be a mistake to assume that programs written to

be highly portable would use trigraphs 'in case they had to be moved to systems that only support ISO 646'. If your system can handle all 96 characters in the C alphabet, then that is what you should be using.

Trigraphs will only be seen in restricted environments, and it is extremely simple to write a character-by-character translator between the two representations. However, all compilers that conform to the Standard will recognize trigraphs when they are seen. Trigraph substitution is the very first operation that a compiler performs on its input text.

MULTIBYTE CHARACTERS

A very large proportion of day-to-day computing involves data that represents text of one form or another. Until recently, the rather chauvinist computing idustry has assumed that it is adequate to provide support for about a hundred or so printable characters (hence the 96 character alphabet of C), based on the requirements of the English language—not suprising, since the bulk of the development of commercial computing has been in the US market.

This alphabet (technically called the *repertoire*) fits conveniently into 7 or 8 bits of storage, which is why the US-ASCII character set standard and the architecture of mini and microcomputers both give very heavy emphasis to the use of 8-bit bytes as the basic unit of storage.

C also has a byte-oriented approach to data storage. The smallest individual item of storage that can be directly used in C is the byte, which is defined to be at least 8 bits in size. Older systems or architectures that are not designed explicitly to support this may incur a performance penalty when running C as a result, although there are not many that find this a big problem.

Perhaps there was a time when the English alphabet was acceptable for data processing applications worldwide—when computers were used in environments where the users could be expected to adapt—but those days are gone. Nowadays it is absolutely essential to provide for the storage and processing of textual material in the native alphabet of whoever wants to use the system. Most of the US and Western European language requirements can be squeezed together into a character set that still fits in 8 bits per character, but Asian and other languages simply cannot.

There are two general ways of extending character sets. One is to use a fixed number of bytes (often two) for every character. This is what the wide character support in C is designed to do. The other method is to use a shift-in shift-out coding scheme; this is popular over 8-bit communication links.

Imagine a stream of characters that looks like:

```
a b c <SI> a b g <SO> x y
```

where <SI> and <SO> mean 'switch to Greek' and 'switch back to English' respectively. A display device that agreed to use that method might well then display a, b, c, alpha, beta, gamma, x and y. This is roughly the scheme used by the shift-JIS Japanese standard, except that once the shift-in has been seen,*pairs* of characters together are used as the code for a single Japanese character. Alternative schemes exist which use more than one shift-in character, but they are less common.

The Standard now allows explicitly for the use of extended character sets. Only the 96 characters defined earlier are used for the C part of a programme, but in comments, strings, character constants and header names (these are really data, not part of the programme as such) extended characters are permitted if your environment supports them. The Standard lays down a number of pretty obvious rules about how you are allowed to use them which we will not repeat here. The most significant one is that a byte whose value is zero is interpreted as a *null character* irrespective of any shift state. That is important, because C uses a null character to indicate the end of strings and many library functions rely on it. An additional requirement is that multibyte sequences must start and end in the initial shift state.

The char type is specified by the Standard as suitable to hold the value of all of the characters in the 'execution character set', which will be defined in your system's documentation. This means that it could hold the value of 'a' or 'b' or even the "switch to Greek" character itself. Because of the shift-in shift-out mechanism, there would be no difference between the value stored in a char that was intended to represent 'a' or the Greek 'alpha' character. To do that would mean using a different representation - probably needing more than 8 bits, which on many systems would be too big for a char. That is why the Standard introduces the wchar_ttype.

STRUCTURE OF PROGRAMS

PROGRAMME LAYOUT

The examples so far have used the sort of indentation and line layout that is common in languages belonging to the same family as C. They are 'free format' languages and you are expected to use that freedom to lay the programme out in a way that enhances its readability and highlights its logical structure. Space (including horizontal tab) characters can be used for indentation anywhere except in identifiers or keywords without any effect on the meaning of the programme. New lines work in the same way as space and tab *except* on preprocessor command lines, which have a line-by-line structure. If a line is getting too long for comfort there are two things you can do. Generally it will be possible to replace one of the spaces by a newline and use simply two lines instead, as this example shows.

```
/* a long line */
a = fred + bill * ((this/ that) * sqrt(3.14159));
/* the same line */
a = fred + bill *
((this/ that) *
sqrt(3.14159));
```

If you're unlucky it may not be possible to break the lines like that. The preprocessor suffers most from the problem, because of its reliance on single-line 'statements'. To help, it's useful to know that the sequence 'backslash newline' becomes invisible to the C translation system. As a result, the sequence is valid even in unusual places such as the middle of identifiers, keywords, strings and so on. Only trigraphs are processed before this step.

```
/*
 * Example of the use of line joining
 */
#define important_but_long_preprocessor_text \
printf("this is effectively all ");\
printf("on a single line ");\
printf("because of line-joining\n");
```

The only time that you might want to use this way of breaking lines (outside of preprocessor control lines) is to prevent long strings from disappearing off the right-hand side of a programme listing. New lines are ***not*** permitted inside strings and character constants, so you might think that the following is a good idea.

```
/* not a good way of folding a string */
printf("This is a very very very\
long string\n");
```

That will certainly work, but for strings it is preferable to make use of the string-joining feature introduced by the Standard:

```
/* This string joining will not work in Old C
*/
printf("This is a very very very"
"long string\n");
```

The second example allows you to indent the continuation portion of the string without changing its meaning; adding indentation in the first example would have put the indentation into the string.

Incidentally, both examples contain what is probably a mistake. There is no space in front of the 'long' in the continuation string, which will contain the sequence 'verylong' as a result.

COMMENT

Comment, as has been said already, is introduced by the character pair /* and terminated by */. It is translated into a single space wherever it occurs and so it follows exactly the same rules that spaces do. It's important to realise that it doesn't simply disappear, which it used to do in Old C, and that it is not possible to put comment into strings or character constants. Comment in such a place becomes part of the string or constant:

```
/*"This is comment"*/
"/*The quotes mean that this is a string*/"
```

Old C was a bit hazy about what the deletion of comment implied.

You could argue that,

```
int/**/egral();
```

should have the comment deleted and so be taken by the compiler to be a call of a function named integral. The Standard C rule is that comment is to be read as if were a space, so the example must be equivalent to

```
int egral();
```

which declares a function egral that returns type int.

TRANSLATION PHASES

The various character translation, line joining, comment recognition and other early phases of translation must be specified to occur in a certain order. The Standard says that the translation is to proceed as if the phases occurred in this order (there are more phases, but these are the important ones):

- Trigraph translation.
- Line joining.
- Translate comment to space (but not in strings or character constants). At this stage, multiple white spaces may optionally be condensed into one.
- Translate the programme.

KEYWORDS AND IDENTIFIERS

After covering the underlying alphabet, we can look at more interesting elements of C. The most obvious of the language elements are *keywords* and *identifiers*; their forms are identical (although their meanings are different).

KEYWORDS

C keeps a small set of *keywords* for its own use. These keywords cannot be used as identifiers in the programme —

a common restriction with modern languages. Where users of Old C may be surprised is in the introduction of some new keywords; if those names were used as identifiers in previous programs, then the programs will have to be changed. It will be easy to spot, because it will provoke your compiler into telling you about invalid names for things. Here is the list of keywords used in Standard C; you will notice that none of them use upper-case letters.

Table. Keywords

aut–	double	int	struct
break	else	long	switch
case	enum	register	typedef
char	extern	return	union
const	float	short	unsigned
continue	for	signed	void
default	got–	sizeof	volatile
d–	if	static	while

The new keywords that are likely to surprise old programmers are: const, signed, void and volatile (although void has been around for a while). Eagle eyed readers may have noticed that some implementations of C used to use the keywords entry, asm, and fortran. These are not part of the Standard, and few will mourn them.

IDENTIFIERS

Identifier is the fancy term used to mean 'name'. In C, identifiers are used to refer to a number of things: we've already seen them used to name variables and functions. They are also used to give names to some things we haven't seen yet, amongst which are *labels* and the 'tags' of *structures, unions,* and *enums*.

The rules for the construction of identifiers are simple: you may use the 52 upper and lower case alphabetic characters, the 10 digits and finally the underscore '_', which is considered to be an alphabetic character for this purpose. The only restriction is the usual one; identifiers *must* start with an alphabetic character. Although there is no restriction on the length of identifiers in the Standard, this is a point that needs a bit of explanation. In Old C, as in Standard C, there has *never*been any restriction on the length of identifiers. The problem is that there was never any guarantee that more than a certain number of characters would be checked when names were compared for equality—in Old C this was eight characters, in Standard C this has changed to 31.

So, practically speaking, the new limit is 31 characters—although identifiers *may*be longer, they must differ in the first 31 characters if you want to be sure that your programs are portable. The Standard allows for implementations to supportlonger names if they wish to, so if you do use longer names, make sure that you don't rely on the checking stopping at 31. One of the most controversial parts of the Standard is the length of *external identifiers*. External identifiers are the ones that have to be visible outside the current source code file. Typical examples of these would be library routines or functions which have to be called from several different source files. The Standard chose to stay with the old restrictions on these external names: they are not guaranteed to be different unless they differ from each other in the first six characters. Worse than that, upper and lower case letters may be treated the same!

The reason for this is a pragmatic one: the way that most C compilation systems work is to use operating system specific tools to bind library functions into a C programme. These tools are outside the control of the C compiler writer, so the Standard has to impose realistic limits that are likely to be possible to meet. There is nothing to prevent any specific implementation from giving better limits than these, but for maximum portability the six monocase characters must be all that you expect. The Standard warns that it views both the use of only one case and any restriction on the length of external names to less than 31 characters as obsolescent features. A later standard may insist that the restrictions are lifted; let's hope that it is soon.

DECLARATION OF VARIABLES

It is noted that you have to declare the names of things before you can use them (the only exceptions to this rule are the names of functions returning int, because they are declared by default, and the names of*labels*).

You can do it either by using a *declaration,* which introduces just the name and type of something but allocates no storage, or go further by using a *definition,* which also allocates the space used by the thing being declared.

The distinction between declaration and definition is an important one, and it is a shame that the two words sound alike enough to cause confusion. From now on they will have to be used for their formal meaning, so if you are in doubt about the differences between them, refer back to this point.

The rules about what makes a declaration into a definition are rather complicated, so they will be deferred for a while. In the meantime, here are some examples and rule-of-thumb guidelines which will work for the examples that we have seen so far, and will do for a while to come.

```
/*
* A function is only defined if its body is
given
* so this is a declaration but not a definition
*/
int func_dec(void);
/*
* Because this function has a body, it is also
* a definition.
* Any variables declared inside will be
definitions,
* unless the keyword 'extern' is used.
* Don't use 'extern' until you understand it!
*/
int def_func(void){
float f_var;/* a definition */
int counter;/* another definition */
int rand_num(void);/* declare (but not define)
another function */
```

```
return(0);
}
```

INTEGRAL TYPES

The real types were the easy ones. The rules for the integral types are more complicated, but still tolerable, and these rules really should be learnt. Fortunately, the only types used in C for routine data storage are the real and integer types, or*structures* and *arrays* built up from them. C doesn't have special types for character manipulation or the handling of logical (boolean) quantities, but uses the integral types instead. Once you know the rules for the reals and the integers you know them all. We will start by looking at the various types and then the conversion rules.

PLAIN INTEGERS

There are two types of integer variables. Other types can be built from these, as we'll see, but the plain undecorated ints are the base. The most obvious of the pair is the 'signed' int, the less obvious is its close relative, the unsigned int. These variables are supposed to be stored in whatever is the most convenient unit for the machine running your programme.

The int is the natural choice for undemanding requirements when you just need a simple integral variable, say as a counter in a short loop. There isn't any guarantee about the number of bits that an int can hold, except that it will *always* be 16 or more. The standard header file <limits.h> details the actual number of bits available in a given implementation. Old C had no guarantee whatsoever about the length of an int, but consensus and common practice has always assumed at least 16 bits.

Actually, <limits.h> doesn't quite specify a number of bits, but gives maximum and minimum values for an int instead. The values it gives are 32767 and -32767 which implies 16 bits or more, whether ones or twos complement arithmetic is used. Of course there is nothing to stop a given implementation from providing a greater range in either direction. The range specified in the Standard for an unsigned int is 0 to at least 65535, meaning that it cannot be negative.

If you aren't used to thinking about the number of bits in a given variable, and are beginning to get worried about the portability implications of this apparently machine-dependent concern for the number of bits, then you're doing the right thing. C takes portability seriously and actually bothers to tell you what values and ranges are guaranteed to be safe.

The bitwise operators encourage you to think about the number of bits in a variable too, because they give direct access to the bits, which you manipulate one by one or in groups. Almost paradoxically, the overall result is that C programmers have a healthy awareness of portability issues which leads to more portable programs. This is *not* to say that you can't write C programs that are horribly non-portable!

CHARACTER VARIABLES

A bit less obvious than int is the other of the plain integral types, the char. It's basically just another sort of int, but has a different application. Because so many C programs do a lot of character handling, it's a good idea to provide a special type to help, especially if the range provided by an int uses up much more storage than is needed by characters.

The limits file tells us that three things are guaranteed about char variables: they have at least 8 bits, they can store a value of at least +127, and the minimum value of a char is zero or lower. This means that the only guaranteed range is 0–127. Whether or not char variables behave assigned or unsigned types is implementation defined.

In short, a character variable will probably take less storage than an int and will most likely be used for character manipulation. It's still an integer type though, and can be used for arithmetic, as this example shows.

```
include <limits.h>
include <stdio.h>
include <stdlib.h>
main(){
char c;
```

```
c = CHAR_MIN;
while(c != CHAR_MAX){
printf("%d\n", c);
c = c+1;
}
exit(EXIT_SUCCESS);
}
```

Running that programme is left as an exercise for the easily amused. If you are bothered about where CHAR_MIN and CHAR_MAX come from, find limits.h and read it.

Here's a more enlightening example. It uses character constants, which are formed by placing a character in single quotes:

```
'x'
```

Because of the rules of arithmetic, the type of this sort of constant turns out to beint, but that doesn't matter since their value is always small enough to assign them to char variables without any loss of precision. (Unfortunately, there is a related version where that guarantee does not hold. Ignore it for the moment.) When a character variable is printed using the %c format with printf, the appropriate character is output. You can use %d, if you like, to see what integer value is used to represent the character. Why %d? Because a char is just another integral type.

It's also useful to be able to read characters into a programme. The library functiongetchar is used for the job. It reads characters from the program's *standard input*and returns an int value suitable for storing into a char. The int value is for one reason only: not only does getchar return all possible character values, but it also returns an ***extra*** value to indicate that end-of-input has been seen. The range of achar might not be enough to hold this extra value, so the int has to be used.

The following programme reads its input and counts the number of commas and full stops that it sees. On end-of-input, it prints the totals.

```
#include <stdio.h>
#include <stdlib.h>
main(){
```

```
int this_char, comma_count, stop_count;
comma_count = stop_count = 0;
this_char = getchar();
while(this_char != EOF){
if(this_char == '.')
stop_count = stop_count+1;
if(this_char == ',')
comma_count = comma_count+1;
this_char = getchar();
}
printf("%d commas, %d stops\n", comma_count,
stop_count);
exit(EXIT_SUCCESS);
}
```

The two features of note in that example were the multiple assignment to the two counters and the use of the defined constant EOF. EOF is the value returned bygetchar on end of input (it stands for End Of File), and is defined in <stdio.h>. The multiple assignment is a fairly common feature of C programs.

Another example, perhaps. This will either print out the whole lower case alphabet, if your implementation has its characters stored consecutively, or something even more interesting if they aren't. C doesn't make many guarantees about the ordering of characters in internal form, so this programme produces *non-portable*results!

```
#include <stdio.h>
#include <stdlib.h>
main(){
char c;
c = 'a';
while(c <= 'z'){
printf("value %d char %c\n", c, c);
c = c+1;
}
exit(EXIT_SUCCESS);
}
```

Yet again this example emphasizes that a char is only

another form of integer variable and can be used just like any other form of variable. It is ***not*** a 'special' type with its own rules.

The space saving that a char offers when compared to an int only becomes worthwhile if a lot of them are being used. Most character-processing operations involve the use of not just one or two character variables, but large arrays of them. That's when the saving can become noticeable: imagine an array of 1024 ints.

On a lot of common machines that would eat up 4096 8-bit bytes of storage, assuming the common length of 4 bytes per int. If the computer architecture allows it to be done in a reasonably efficient way, the C implementor will probably have arranged for char variables to be packed one per byte, so the array would only use 1024 bytes and the space saving would be 3072 bytes.

Sometimes it doesn't matter whether or not a programme tries to save space; sometimes it does. At least C gives you the option of choosing an appropriate type.

COMPLICATED TYPES

The last two types were simple, in both their declaration and subsequent use. For serious systems programming they just aren't adequate in the precision of control over storage that they provide and the behaviour that they follow. To correct this problem, C provides extra forms of integral types, split into the categories ofsigned and unsigned. (Although both these terms are reserved words, they will also be used as adjectives.) The difference between the two types is obvious. Signed types are those that are capable of being negative, the unsigned types cannot be negative at any time. Unsigned types are usually used for one of two reasons: to get an extra bit of precision, or when the concept of being negative is simply not present in the data that is being represented. The latter is by far the better reason for choosing them.

Unsigned types also have the special property of never overflowing in arithmetic. Adding 1 to a signed variable that already contains the maximum possible positive number for its type will result in overflow, and the program's behaviour becomes undefined.

That can never happen with unsigned types, because they are defined to work 'modulo one greater than the maximum number that they can hold'.

What this means is best illustrated by example:

```
#include <stdio.h>
#include <stdlib.h>
main(){
unsigned int x;
x = 0;
while(x >= 0){
printf("%u\n", x);
x = x+1;
}
exit(EXIT_SUCCESS);
}
```

Assuming that the variable x is stored in 16 bits, then its range of values will be 0–65535 and that sequence will be printed endlessly.

The programme can't terminate: the test,

```
x >= 0
```

must always be true for an unsigned variable.

For both the signed and unsigned integral types there are three subtypes: short, ordinary and long. Taking those into account, here is a list of all of the possible integral types in C, except for the character types:

```
unsigned short int
unsigned int
unsigned long int
signed short int
signed int
signed long int
```

In the last three, the signed keyword is unnecessary because the int types are signed types anyway: you ***have*** to say unsigned to get anything different. It's also permissible, but not recommended, to drop the int keyword from any of those declarations provided that there is at least one other keyword present—the intwill be 'understood' to be present. For example long is equivalent to signed long int. The long and short kinds give you more control over the amount of space used to store variables.

Each has its own minimum range specified in <limits.h>which in practice means at least 16 bits in a short and an int, and at least 32 bits in a long, whether signed or unsigned. As always, an implementation can choose to give you more bits than the minimum if it wants to. The only restriction is that the limits must be equalled or bettered, and that you don't get more bits in a shorter type than a longer one (not an unreasonable rule).

The only character types are the signed char and the unsigned char. The difference between char and int variables is that, unless otherwise stated, allints are signed.

The same is not true for chars, which are signed or unsigned depending on the implementor's choice; the choice is presumably taken on efficiency grounds. You can of course explicitly force signed or unsignedness with the right keyword. The only time that it is likely to matter is if you are using character variables as extra short shorts to save more space.

SUMMARY

- The integral types are the short, long, signed, unsigned and plain ints.
- The commonest is the ordinary int, which is signed unless declared not to be.
- The char variables ***can*** be made signed or unsigned, as you prefer, but in the absence of indications to the contrary, they will be allocated the most efficient type.

PRINTING THE INTEGRAL TYPES

Once again you can use printf to print these various types. Character variables work exactly the same way that the other integral variables do, so you can use the standard format letters to print their contents—although the actual numbers stored in them are not likely to be very interesting. All of the integral types can be printed as if they were signed decimal numbers by using the %d format, or %ld for long types.

Other useful formats are shown in Table 2.5; notice that in every case a letter 'l' is put in front of the normal format letter if a long is to be printed. That's not just there to get the right result printed: the behaviour of printf is undefined if the wrong format is given.

Table. More Format Codes

Format	Use with
%c	char (in character form)
%d	decimal signed int, short, char
%u	decimal unsigned int, unsigned short, unsigned char
%x	hexadecimal int, short, char
%–	octal int, short, char
%ld	decimal signed long
%lu %lx %l–	as above, but for longs

EXPRESSIONS AND ARITHMETIC

Expressions in C can get rather complicated because of the number of different types and operators that can be mixed together. First, a bit of terminology. Expressions in C are built from combinations of*operators* and *operands,* so for example in this expression

```
x = a+b*(-c)
```

we have the operators =, + * and -. The operands are the variables x, a, b and c. You will also have noticed that parentheses can be used for grouping sub-expressions such as the -c. Most of C's unusually rich set of operators are either*binary operators,* which take two operands, or *unary operators,* which take only one. In the example, the - was being used as a unary operator, and is performing a different task from the binary subtraction operator which uses the same - symbol. It may seem like hair-splitting to argue that they are different operators when the job that they do seems conceptually the same, or at least similar. It's worth doing though, because, as you will find later, some of the operators have both a binary and a unary form where the two meanings bear no relation to each other; a good example would be the binary multiplication operator *, which in its unary form means indirection via a pointer variable!

A peculiarity of C is that operators may appear consecutively in expressions without the need for parentheses to separate them.

The previous example could have been written as,

```
x = a+b*-c;
```

and still have been a valid expression. Because of the number of operators that C has, and because of the strange way that assignment works, the *precedence* of the operators (and their *associativity*) is of much greater importance to the C programmer than in most other languages. It will be discussed fully after the introduction of the important arithmetic operators. Before that, we must investigate the type conversions that may occur.

CONVERSIONS

C allows types to be mixed in expressions, and permits operations that result in type conversions happening implicitly. This section describes the way that the conversions must occur. Old C programmers should read this carefully, because the rules have changed — in particular, the promotion of float to double, the promotions of short integral types and the introduction of *value preserving* rules are genuinely different in Standard C.

Although it isn't directly relevant at the moment, we must note that the integral and the floating types are jointly known as *arithmetic types* and that C also supports other types (notably pointer types). The rules that we discuss here are appropriate only in expressions that have arithmetic types throughout - additional rules come into play when expressions mix pointer types with arithmetic types and these are discussed much later.

There are various types of conversion in arithmetic expressions:

- The *integral promotions*
- Conversions between integral types

- Conversions between floating types
- Conversions between floating and integral types

Conversions between floating (real) types were discussed in Section 2.8; what we do next is to specify how the other conversions are to be performed, then look at*when* they are required. You will need to learn them by heart if you ever intend to programme seriously in C.

The Standard has, among some controversy, introduced what are known as *value preserving* rules, where a knowledge of the target computer is required to work out what the type of an expression will be. Previously, whenever an unsigned type occurred in an expression, you knew that the result had to be unsigned too. Now, the result will only be unsigned if the conversions demand it; in many cases the result will be an ordinary signed type.

The reason for the change was to reduce some of the surprises possible when you mix signed and unsigned quantities together; it isn't always obvious when this has happened and the intention is to produce the 'more commonly required' result.

INTEGRAL PROMOTIONS

No arithmetic is done by C at a precision shorter than int, so these conversions are implied almost whenever you use one of the objects listed below in an expression.

The conversion is defined as follows:

- Whenever a short or a char (or a *bitfield* or *enumeration type* which we haven't met yet) has the integral promotions applied
  - If an int can hold all of the values of the original type then the value is converted to int
  - Otherwise, the conversion will be to unsigned int

This preserves both the value and the sign of the original type. Note that whether a plain char is treated as signed or unsigned is implementation dependent.

These promotions are applied very often—they are applied as part of the *usual arithmetic conversions,* and to the operands of the shift, unary +, -, and ~operators. They are also applied when the expression in question is an argument to a function but no type information has been provided as part of a function prototype.

SIGNED AND UNSIGNED INTEGERS

A lot of conversions between different types of integers are caused by mixing the various flavours of integers in expressions. Whenever these happen, the integral promotions will already have been done. For all of them, if the new type can hold all of the values of the old type, then the value remains unchanged.

When converting from a signed integer to an unsigned integer whose length is equal to or longer than the original type, then if the signed value was nonnegative, its value is unchanged. If the value was negative, then it is converted to the signed form of the longer type and then made unsigned by conceptually adding it to one greater than the maximum that can be held in the unsigned type. In a twos complement system, this preserves the original bit-pattern for positive numbers and guarantees 'sign-extension' of negative numbers.

Whenever an integer is converted into a shorter unsigned type, there can be no 'overflow', so the result is defined to be 'the non-negative remainder on division by the number one greater than the largest unsigned number that can be represented in the shorter type'. That simply means that in a two's complement environment the low-order bits are copied into the destination and the high-order ones discarded.

Converting an integer to a shorter signed type runs into trouble if there is not enough room to hold the value. In that case, the result is implementation defined (although most old-timers would expect that simply the low-order bit pattern is copied).

That last item could be a bit worrying if you remember the integral promotions, because you might interpret it as follows—if I assign a char to another char, then the one on the right is first promoted to one of the kinds of int; could doing the assignment result in converting (say) an int to a char and provoking the 'implementation defined' clause? The answer is no, because assignment is specified not to involve the integral promotions, so you are safe.

FLOATING AND INTEGRAL

Converting a floating to an integral type simply throws away any fractional part. If the integral type can't hold the value that is left, then the behaviour is undefined—this is a sort of overflow.

As has already been said, going up the scale from float to double to long double, there is no problem with conversions—each higher one in the list can hold all the values of the lower ones, so the conversion occurs with no loss of information.

Converting in the opposite direction, if the value is outside the range that can be held, the behaviour is undefined. If the value *is* in range, but can't be held exactly, then the result is one of the two nearest values that *can* be held, chosen in a way that the implementation defines. This means that there will be a loss of precision.

ARITHMETIC CONVERSIONS

A lot of expressions involve the use of subexpressions of mixed types together with operators such as +, * and so on. If the operands in an expression have different types, then there will have to be a conversion applied so that a common resulting type can be established; these are the conversions:

- If either operand is a long double, then the other one is converted to long double and that is the type of the result.
- Otherwise, if either operand is a double, then the other one is converted todouble, and that is the type of the result.
- Otherwise, if either operand is a float, then the other one is converted tofloat, and that is the type of the result.
- Otherwise the integral promotions are applied to both operands and the following conversions are applied:

- If either operand is an unsigned long int, then the other one is converted to unsigned long int, and that is the type of the result.
- Otherwise, if either operand is a long int, then the other one is converted to long int, and that is the type of the result.
- Otherwise, if either operand is an unsigned int, then the other one is converted to unsigned int, and that is the type of the result.
- Otherwise, both operands must be of type int, so that is the type of the result.

The Standard contains a strange sentence: 'The values of floating operands and of the results of floating expressions may be represented in greater precision and range than that required by the type; the types are not changed thereby'. This is in fact to allow the Old C treatment of floats. In Old C, float variables were automatically promoted to double, the way that the integral promotions promotechar to int. So, an expression involving purely float variables may be done as if they were double, but the type of the result must appear to be float. The only effect is likely to be on performance and is not particularly important to most users.

Whether or not conversions need to be applied, and if so which ones, is discussed at the point where each operator is introduced.

In general, the type conversions and type mixing rules don't cause a lot of trouble, but there is one pitfall to watch out for. Mixing signed and unsigned quantities is fine until the signed number is negative; then its value can't be represented in an unsigned variable and something has to happen. The standard says that to convert a negative number to unsigned, the largest possible number that can be held in the unsigned plus one is added to the negative number; that is the result. Because there can be no overflow in an unsigned type, the result always has a defined value. Taking a 16-bit int for an example, the unsigned version has a range of 0–65535. Converting a signed value of -7 to this type involves adding 65536, resulting in 65529. What is happening is that the

Standard is enshrining previous practice, where the bit pattern in the signed number is simply assigned to the unsigned number; the description in the standard is exactly what would happen if you did perform the bit pattern assignment on a two's complement computer. The one's complement implementations are going to have to do some real work to get the same result.

Putting it plainly, a small magnitude negative number will result in a large positive number when converted to unsigned. If you don't like it, suggest a better solution—it is plainly a mistake to try to assign a negative number to an unsigned variable, so it's your own fault. Well, it's easy to say 'don't do it', but it can happen by accident and the results can be *very* surprising. Look at this example.

```
#include <stdio.h>
#include <stdlib.h>
main(){
int i;
unsigned int stop_val;
stop_val = 0;
i = -10;
while(i <= stop_val){
printf("%d\n", i);
i = i + 1;
}
exit(EXIT_SUCCESS);
}
```

Example: You might expect that to print out the list of values from -10 to 0, but it won't. The problem is in the comparison. The variable i, with a value of -10, is being compared against an unsigned 0. By the rules of arithmetic (check them) we must convert both types to unsigned int first, then make the comparison. The -10becomes at least 65526 (see <limits.h>) when it's converted, and is plainly somewhat larger than 0, so the loop is never executed. The moral is to steer clear of unsigned numbers unless you really have to use them, and to be perpetually on guard when they are mixed with signed numbers.

WIDE CHARACTERS

The Standard, as we've already said, now makes allowances for extended character sets. You can either use the shift-in shift-out encoding method which allows the multibyte charactes to be stored in ordinary C strings (which are really arrays of chars, as we explore later), or you can use a representation that uses more than one byte of storage per character for every character.

The use of shift sequences only works if you process the characters in strict order; it is next to useless if you want to create an array of characters and access them in non-sequential order, since the actual index of each char in the array and the logical index of each of the encoded characters are not easily determined. Here's the illustration we used before, annotated with the actual and the logical array indexes:

```
0 1 2 3 4 5 6 7 8 9 (actual array index)
a b c <SI> a b g <SO> x y
0 1 2 3 4 5 6 7 (logical index)
```

We're still in trouble even if we do manage to use the index of 5 to access the 'correct' array entry, since the value retrieved is indistinguishable from the value that encodes the letter 'g' anyhow.

Clearly, a better approach for this sort of thing is to come up with a distinct value for all of the characters in the character set we are using, which may involve more bits than will fit into a char, and to be able to store each one as a separate item without the use of shifts or other position-dependent techniques. That is what the wchar_t type is for.

Although it is always a synonym for one of the other integral types, wchar_t (whose definition is found in <stddef.h>) is defined to be the implementation-dependent type that should be used to hold extended characters when you need an array of them. The Standard makes the following guarantees about the values in a wide character:

- A wchar_t can hold distinct values for each member of the largest character set supported by the implementation.
- The null character has the value of zero.

- Each member of the basic character set is encoded in awchar_t with the same value as it has in a char.

There is further support for this method of encoding characters. Strings, which we have already seen, are implemented as arrays of char, even though they look like this:

```
"a string"
```

To get strings whose type is wchar_t, simply prefix a string with the letter L.

For example:

```
L"a string"
```

In the two examples, it is very important to understand the differences. Strings are implemented as arrays and although it might look odd, it is entirely permissible to use array indexing on them:

```
"a string"[4]
L"a string"[4]
```

are both valid expressions. The first results in an expression whose type is charand whose value is the internal representation of the letter 'r' (remember arrays index from zero, not one). The second has the type wchar_t and also has the value of the internal representation of the letter 'r'.

It gets more interesting if we are using extended characters. If we use the notation <a>, <b>, and so on to indicate 'additional' characters beyond the normal character set which are encoded using some form of shift technique, then these examples show the problems.

```
"abc<a><b>"[3]
L"abc<a><b>"[3]
```

The second one is easiest: it has a type of wchar_t and the appropriate internal encoding for whatever <a> is supposed to be—say the Greek letter alpha. The first one is unpredictable. Its type is unquestionably char, but its value is probably the value of the 'shift-in' marker.

As with strings, there are also wide character constants.

```
'a'
```

has type char and the value of the encoding for the letter 'a'.

```
L'a'
```

is a constant of type wchar_t. If you use a multibyte character in the first one, then you have the same sort of thing as if you had written,

```
'xy'
```

—multiple characters in a character constant (actually, this is valid but means something funny). A single multibyte character in the second example will simply be converted into the appropriate wchar_t value.

If you don't understand all the wide character stuff, then all we can say is that we've done our best to explain it. Come back and read it again later, when it might suddenly click. In practice it does manage to address the support of extended character sets in C and once you're used to it, it makes a lot of sense.

Exercise Assuming that chars, ints and longs are respectively 8, 16 and 32 bits long, and that char defaults to unsigned char on a given system, what is the resulting type of expressions involving the following combinations of variables, after the usual arithmetic conversions have been applied?

- Simply signed char.
- Simply unsigned char.
- Int, unsigned int.
- Unsigned int, long.
- Int, unsigned long.
- Char, long.
- Char, float.
- Float, float.
- Float, long double.

CASTS

From time to time you will find that an expression turns out not to have the type that you wanted it to have and you would like to force it to have a different type. That is what *casts* are for. By putting a type name in parentheses, for example,

```
(int)
```

you create a unary operator known as a *cast*. A cast turns the value of the expression on its right into the indicated type. If, for example, you were dividing two integers a/b then the expression would use integer division and discard any remainder. To force the fractional part to be retained, you could either use some intermediate float variables, or a cast.

This example does it both ways:

```
#include <stdio.h>
#include <stdlib.h>
/*
* Illustrates casts.
* For each of the numbers between 2 and 20,
* print the percentage difference between it
and the one
* before
*/
main(){
int curr_val;
float temp, pcnt_diff;
curr_val = 2;
while(curr_val <= 20){
/*
*% difference is
* 1/(curr_val)*100
*/
temp = curr_val;
pcnt_diff = 100/temp;
printf("Per cent difference at %d is %f\n",
curr_val, pcnt_diff);
/*
* Or, using a cast:
*/
pcnt_diff = 100/(float)curr_val;
printf("Per cent difference at %d is %f\n",
curr_val, pcnt_diff);
curr_val = curr_val + 1;
}
exit(EXIT_SUCCESS);
}
```

Example: The easiest way to remember how to write a cast

is to write down exactly what you would use to declare a variable of the type that you want. Put parentheses around the entire declaration, then delete the variable name; that gives you the cast. Table shows a few simple examples—some of the types shown will be new to you, but it's the complicated ones that illustrate best how casts are written.

Table. Casts

Declaration	Cast	Type
int x;	(int)	int
float f;	(float)	float
char x[30];	(char [30])	array of char
int *ip;	(int *)	pointer to int
int (*f)();	(int (*)())	pointer to function
	returning int	

OPERATORS

MULTIPLICATIVE OPERATORS

Or, put another way, multiplication *, division / and the remainder operator %. Multiplication and division do what is expected of them for both real and integral types, with integral division producing a truncated result. The truncation is towards zero. The remainder operator is only defined to work with integral types, because the division of real numbers supposedly doesn't produce a remainder.

If the division is not exact and neither operand is negative, the result of / is positive and rounded toward zero—to get the remainder, use %.

For example,

```
9/2 == 4
9%2 == 1
```

If either operand is negative, the result of / may be the nearest integer to the true result on either side, and the sign of the result of % may be positive or negative. Both of these features are implementation defined.

It is always true that the following expression is equal to zero:

```
(a/b)*b + a%b - a
```

unless b is zero. The usual arithmetic conversions are applied to both of the operands.

ADDITIVE OPERATORS

Addition + and subtraction - also follow the rules that you expect. The binary operators and the unary operators both have the same symbols, but rather different meanings. For example, the expressions a+b and a-b both use a binary operator (the + or - operators), and result in addition or subtraction. The unary operators with the same symbols would be written +b or -b.

The unary minus has an obvious function—it takes the negative value of its operand; what does the unary plus do? In fact the answer is almost nothing. The unary plus is a new addition to the language, which balances the presence of the unary minus, but doesn't have any effect on the value of the expression. Very few Old C users even noticed that it was missing.

The usual arithmetic conversions are applied to both of the operands of the binary forms of the operators. Only the integral promotions are performed on the operands of the unary forms of the operators.

THE BITWISE OPERATORS

One of the great strengths of C is the way that it allows systems programmers to do what had, before the advent of C, always been regarded as the province of the assembly code programmer. That sort of code was by definition highly non-portable.

As C demonstrates, there isn't any magic about that sort of thing, and into the bargain it turns out to be surprisingly portable. What is it? It's what is often referred to as 'bit-twiddling'—the manipulation of individual bits in integer variables. None of the bitwise operators may be used on real operands because they aren't considered to have individual or accessible bits.

There are six bitwise operators, listed in Table 2.7, which also shows the arithmetic conversions that are applied.

Table. Bitwise Operators

Operator	Effect	Conversions
&	bitwise AND	usual arithmetic conversions
|	bitwise OR	usual arithmetic conversions
^	Bitwise XOR	usual arithmetic conversions
<<	left shift	integral promotions
>>	right shift	integral promotions
~	one's complement	integral promotions

Only the last, the one's complement, is a unary operator. It inverts the state of every bit in its operand and has the same effect as the unary minus on a one's complement computer. Most modern computers work with two's complement, so it isn't a waste of time having it there.

Illustrating the use of these operators is easier if we can use hexadecimal notation rather than decimal, so now is the time to see hexadecimal constants. Any number written with 0x at its beginning is interpreted as hexadecimal; both 15 and 0xf(or 0XF) mean the same thing. Try running this or, better still, try to predict what it does first and then try running it.

```
#include <stdio.h>
#include <stdlib.h>
main(){
int x,y;
x = 0; y = ~0;
while(x != y){
printf("%x & %x = %x\n", x, 0xff, x&0xff);
printf("%x | %x = %x\n", x, 0x10f, x|0x10f);
printf("%x ^ %x = %x\n", x, 0xf00f, x^0xf00f);
printf("%x >> 2 = %x\n", x, x >> 2);
printf("%x << 2 = %x\n", x, x << 2);
x = (x << 1) | 1;
}
exit(EXIT_SUCCESS);
}
```

The way that the loop works in that example is the first

thing to study. The controlling variable is x, which is initialized to zero. Every time round the loop it is compared against y, which has been set to a word-length independent pattern of all 1s by taking the one's complement of zero. At the bottom of the loop, x is shifted left once and has 1 ORed into it, giving rise to a sequence that starts 0, 1,11, 111, ... in binary.

For each of the AND, OR, and XOR (exclusive OR) operators, x is operated on by the operator and some other interesting operand, then the result printed.

The left and right shift operators are in there too, giving a result which has the type and value of their left-hand operand shifted in the required direction a number of places specified by their right-hand operand; the type of both of the operands must be integral.

Bits shifted off either end of the left operand simply disappear. Shifting by more bits than there are in a word gives an implementation dependent result. Shifting left guarantees to shift zeros into the low-order bits.

Right shift is fussier. Your implementation is allowed to choose whether, when shifting signed operands, it performs a logical or arithmetic right shift. This means that a logical shift shifts zeros into the most significant bit positions; an arithmetic shift copies the current contents of the most significant bit back into itself.

The position is clearer if an unsigned operand is right shifted, because there is no choice: it must be a logical shift. For that reason, whenever right shift is being used, you would expect to find that the thing being shifted had been declared to be unsigned, or cast to unsigned for the shift, as in the example:

```
int i,j;
i = (unsigned)j >> 4;
```

The second (right-hand) operand of a shift operator does not have to be a constant; any integral expression is legal. Importantly, the rules involving mixed types of operands do not apply to the shift operators. The result of the shift has the same type as the thing that got shifted (after the integral promotions), and depends on nothing else.

Now something different; one of those little tricks that C programmers find helps to write better programs. If for any reason you want to form a value that has 1s in all but its least significant so-many bits, which are to have some other pattern in them, you don't have to know the word length of the machine.

For example, to set the low order bits of an int to 0x0f0 and all the other bits to 1, this is the way to do it:

```
int some_variable;
some_variable = ~0xf0f;
```

The one's complement of the desired low-order bit pattern has been one's complemented. That gives exactly the required result and is completely independent of word length; it is a very common sight in C code.

There isn't a lot more to say about the bit-twiddling operators, and our experience of teaching C has been that most people find them easy to learn. Let's move on.

THE ASSIGNMENT OPERATORS

No, that isn't a mistake, 'operators' was meant to be plural. C has several assignment operators, even though we have only seen the plain = so far.

An interesting thing about them is that they are all like the other binary operators; they take two operands and produce a result, the result being usable as part of an expression. In this statement,

```
x = 4;
```

the value 4 is assigned to x. The result has the type of x and the value that was assigned.

It can be used like this,

```
a = (x = 4);
```

where a will now have the value 4 assigned to it, after x has been assigned to. All of the simpler assignments that we have seen until now (except for one example) have simply discarded the resulting value of the assignment, even though it is produced.

It's because assignment has a result that an expression like,

```
a = b = c = d;
```

works. The value of d is assigned to c, the result of that is assigned to b and so on. It makes use of the fact that expressions involving only assignment operators are evaluated from right to left, but is otherwise like any other expression.

If you look back to the section describing 'conversions', there is a description of what happens if you convert longer types to shorter types: that is what happens when the left-hand operand of an assignment is shorter than the right-hand one. No conversions are applied to the right-hand operand of the simple assignment operator.

The remaining assignment operators are the compound assignment operators. They allow a useful shorthand, where an assignment containing the same left- and right-hand sides can be compressed; for example

```
x = x + 1;
```

can be written as

```
x += 1;
```

using one of the compound assignment operators. The result is the same in each case. It is a useful thing to do when the left-hand side of the operator is a complicated expression, not just a variable; such things occur when you start to use arrays and pointers.

Most experienced C programmers tend to use the form given in the second example because somehow it 'feels better', a sentiment that no beginner has ever been known to agree with. Table lists the compound assignment operators; you will see them used a lot from now on.

Table. Compound Assignment Operators

*=	/=	%=
+=	-=	
&=	|=	^=
>>=	<<=	

In each case, arithmetic conversions are applied as if the expression had been written out in full, for example as if a+=b had been written a=a+b. Reiterating: the result of an assignment operator has both the value and the type of the object that was assigned to.

INCREMENT AND DECREMENT OPERATORS

It is so common to simply add or subtract 1 in an expression that C has two special unary operators to do the job. The increment operator ++ adds 1, the decrement — subtracts 1.

They are used like this:

```
x++;
++x;
x—;
—x;
```

where the operator can come either before or after its operand. In the cases shown it doesn't matter where the operator comes, but in more complicated cases the difference has a definite meaning and must be used properly.

Here is the difference being used.

```
#include <stdio.h>
#include <stdlib.h>
main(){
int a,b;
a = b = 5;
printf("%d\n", ++a+5);
printf("%d\n", a);
printf("%d\n", b++ +5);
printf("%d\n", b);
exit(EXIT_SUCCESS);
}
```

The results printed were,

```
11
6
10
6
```

The difference is caused by the different positions of the operators. If the inc/decrement operator appears in front of the variable, then its value is changed by one and the *new* value is used in the expression. If the operator comes after the variable, then the *old* value is used in the expression and the vari~ble's value is changed afterwards. C programmers never add or subtract one with statements like this, x += 1;

they invariably use one of,

x++;/* or */ ++x;

as a matter of course. A warning is in order though: it is not safe to use a variable more than once in an expression if it has one of these operators attached to it. There is no guarantee of when, within an expression, the affected variable will actually change value. The compiler might choose to 'save up' all of the changes and apply them at once, so an expression like this,

```
y = x++ + —x;
```

does not guarantee to assign twice the original value of x to y

It might be evaluated as if it expanded to this instead:

```
y = x + (x-1);
```

because the compiler notices that the overall effect on the value of x is zero. The arithmetic is done exactly as if the full addition expression had been used, for example x=x+1, and the usual arithmetic conversions apply.

Exercise Given the following variable definitions:

```
int i1, i2;
float f1, f2;
```

- How would you find the remainder when i1 is divided by i2?
- How would you find the remainder when i1 is divided by the value of f1, treating f1 as an integer?
- What can you predict about the sign of the remainders calculated in the previous two questions?
- What meanings can the - operator have?
- How would you turn off all but the low-order four bits in i1?
- How would you turn on all the low-order four bits in i1?
- How would you turn off only the low-order four bits in i1?
- How would you put into i1 the low-order 8 bits in i2, but swapping the significance of the lowest four with the next
- What is wrong with the following expression?

```
f2 = ++f1 + ++f1;
```

PRECEDENCE AND GROUPING

After looking at the operators we have to consider the way that they work together. For things like addition it may not seem important; it hardly matters whether,

```
a + b + c
is done as
(a + b) + c
or
a + (b + c)
```

does it? Well, yes in fact it does. If a+b would overflow and c held a value very close to -b, then the second grouping might give the correct answer where the first would cause undefined behaviour.

The problem is much more obvious with integer division:

```
a/b/c
```

gives very different results when grouped as

```
a/(b/c)
or
(a/b)/c
```

If ycu don't believe that, try it with a=10, b=2, c=3. The first gives 10/(2/3); 2/3 in integer division gives 0, so we get 10/0 which immediately overflows. The second grouping gives (10/2), obviously 5, which divided by 3 gives 1.

The grouping of operators like that is known as *associativity*. The other question is one of *precedence*, where some operators have a higher priority than others and force evaluation of sub-expressions involving them to be performed before those with lower precedence operators. This is almost universal practice in high-level languages, so we 'know' that,

```
a + b * c + d
groups as
a + (b * c) + d
```

indicating that multiplication has higher precedence than addition. The large set of operators in C gives rise to 15 levels of precedence! Only very boring people bother to remember them all. The complete list is given in Table 2.9, which indicates both precedence and associativity. Not all of the operators have been mentioned yet. Beware of the use of the same symbol for both unary and binary operators: the table indicates which are which.

Table. Operator Precedence and Associativity

Operator	Direction	Notes
() [] ->.	left to right	1
! ~ ++ — - + (cast) * & sizeof	right to left	all unary
*/%	left to right	binary
+ -	left to right	binary
<< >>	left to right	binary
< <= > >=	left to right	binary
== !=	left to right	binary
&	left to right	binary
^	left to right	binary
|	left to right	binary
&&	left to right	binary
| |	left to right	binary
?:	right to left	2
= += and all combined assignment	right to left	binary
,	left to right	binary

- Parentheses are for expression grouping, *not* function call.
- This is unusual..

The question is, what can you do with that information, now that it's there? Obviously it's important to be able to work out both how to write expressions that evaluate in the proper order, and also how to read other people's. The technique is this: first, identify the unary operators and the operands that they refer to. This isn't such a difficult task but it takes some practice, especially when you discover that operators such as unary * can be applied an arbitrary number of times to their operands; this expression

```
a*****b
```

means a multiplied by *something*, where the something is an expression involving b and several unary * operators.

It's not too difficult to work out which are the unary operators; here are the rules.

- ++ and - are always unary operators.

- The operator immediately to the right of an operand is a binary operator unless (1) applies, when the operator to its right is binary.
- All operators to the left of an operand are unary unless (2) applies.

Because the unary operators have very high precedence, you can work out what they do before worrying about the other operators. One thing to watch out for is the way that ++ and — can be before or after their operands; the expression,

```
a + -b++ + c
```

has two unary operators applied to b. The unary operators all associate right to left, so although the - comes first when you read the expression, it really parenthesizes (for clarity) like this:

```
a + -(b++) + c
```

The case is a little clearer if the prefix, rather than the postfix, form of the increment/decrement operators is being used. Again the order is right to left, but at least the operators come all in a row.

After sorting out what to do with the unary operators, it's easy to read the expression from left to right. Every time you see a binary operator, remember it. Look to the right: if the next binary operator is of a lower precedence, then the operator you just remembered is part of a subexpression to evaluate before anything else is seen.

If the next operator is of the same precedence, keep repeating the procedure as long as equal precedence operators are seen. When you eventually find a lower precedence operator, evaluate the subexpression on the left according to the associativity rules.

If a higher precedence operator is found on the right, forget the previous stuff: the operand to the left of the higher precedence operator is part of a subexpression separate from anything on the left so far. It belongs to the new operator instead. If that lot isn't clear don't worry. A lot of C programmers have trouble with this area and eventually learn to parenthesize these expressions 'by eye', without ever using formal rules.

What *does* matter is what happens when you have fully parenthesized these expressions. Remember the 'usual arithmetic conversions'? They explained how you could predict the type of an expression from the operands involved. Now, even if you mix all sorts of types in a complicated expression, the types of the subexpressions are determined only from the the types of the operands in the subexpression. Look at this.

```
#include <stdio.h>
#include <stdlib.h>
main(){
int i,j;
float f;
i = 5; j = 2;
f = 3.0;
f = f + j/ i;
printf("value of f is %f\n", f);
exit(EXIT_SUCCESS);
}
```

The value printed is 3.0000, not 5.0000—which might surprise some, who thought that because a float was involved the whole statement involving the division would be done in that real type.

Of course, the division operator had only int types on either side, so the arithmetic was done as integer division and resulted in zero. The addition had a float and an int on either side, so the conversions meant that the int was converted tofloat for the arithmetic, and that was the correct type for the assignment, so there were no further conversions.

The previous section on casts showed one way of changing the type of an expression from its natural one to the one that you want.

Be careful though:

```
(float)(j/i)
```

would still use integer division, then convert the result to float. To keep the remainder, you should use,

```
(float)j/i
```

which would force real division to be used.

PARENTHESES

C allows you to override the normal effects of precedence and associativity by the use of parentheses as the examples have illustrated. In C, the parentheses had no further meaning, and in particular did *not* guarantee anything about the order of evaluation in expressions like these:

```
int a, b, c;
a+b+c
(a+b)+c;
a+(b+c);
```

You used to need to use explicit temporary variables to get a particular order of evaluation—something that matters if you know that there are risks of overflow in a particular expression, but by forcing the evaluation to be in a certain order you can avoid it.

Standard C says that evaluation must be done in the order indicated by the precedence and grouping of the expression, unless the compiler can tell that the result will not be affected by any regrouping it might do for optimization reasons.

So, the expression a = 10+a+b+5; cannot be rewritten by the compiler as a = 15+a+b; unless it can be guaranteed that the resulting value of a will be the same for all combinations of initial values of a and b.

That would be true if the variables were both unsigned integral types, or if they were signed integral types but in that particular implementation overflow did not cause a run-time exception and overflow was reversible.

SIDE EFFECTS

To repeat and expand the warning given for the increment operators: it is unsafe to use the same variable more than once in an expression if evaluating the expression changes the variable and the new value could affect the result of the expression.

This is because the change(s) may be 'saved up' and only applied at the end of the statement. So f = f+1; is safe even though f appears twice in a value-changing expression, f++; is also safe, but f = f++; is unsafe.

CONSTANTS

INTEGER CONSTANTS

The normal integral constants are obvious: things like 1, 1034 and so on. You can put l or L at the end of an integer constant to force it to be long. To make the constant unsigned, one of u or U can be used to do the job.

Integer constants can be written in hexadecimal by preceding the constant with 0xor 0X and using the upper or lower case letters a, b, c, d, e, f in the usual way.

Be careful about octal constants. They are indicated by starting the number with 0and only using the digits 0, 1, 2, 3, 4, 5, 6, 7. It is easy to write 015 by accident, or out of habit, and not to realise that it is not in decimal. The mistake is most common with beginners, because experienced C programmers already carry the scars.

The Standard has now invented a new way of working out what type an integer constant is. In the old days, if the constant was too big for an int, it got promoted to a long (without warning). Now, the rule is that a plain decimal constant will be fitted into the first in this list,

```
int long unsigned long
that can hold the value.
Plain octal or hexadecimal constants will use
this list
int unsigned int long unsigned long
If the constant is suffixed by u or U:
unsigned int unsigned long
If it is suffixed by l or L:
long unsigned long
```

and finally, if it suffixed by both u or U and l or L, it can only be an unsigned long.

All that was done to try to give you 'what you meant'; what it does mean is that it is hard to work out exactly what the type of a constant expression is if you don't know something about the hardware. Hopefully, good compilers will warn when a constant is promoted up to another length and the U or L etc. is not specified.

A nasty bug hides here:

```
printf("value of 32768 is %d\n", 32768);
```

On a 16-bit two's complement machine, 32768 will be a long by the rules given above. But printf is only expecting an int as an argument (the %d indicates that). The type of the argument is just wrong. For the ultimate in safety-conscious programming, you should cast such cases to the right type:

```
printf("value of 32768 is %d\n", (int)32768);
```

It might interest you to note that there are no negative constants; writing -23 is an expression involving a positive constant and an operator.

Character constants actually have type int (for historical reasons) and are written by placing a sequence of characters between single quote marks:

```
'a'
'b'
'like this'
```

Wide character constants are written just as above, but prefixed with L:

```
L'a'
L'b'
L'like this'
```

Regrettably it *is* valid to have more than one character in the sequence, giving a machine-dependent result. Single characters are the best from the portability point of view, resulting in an ordinary integer constant whose value is the machine representation of the single character. The introduction of extended characters may cause you to stumble over this by accident; if '<a>' is a multibyte character (encoded with a shift-in shift-out around it) then '<a>' will be a plain character constant, but containing several characters, just like the more obvious 'abcde'. This is bound to lead to trouble in the future; let's hope that compilers will warn about it.

To ease the way of representing some special characters that would otherwise be hard to get into a character constant (or hard to read; does ' ' contain a space or a tab?), there is what is called an escape sequence which can be used instead. Table shows the *escape sequences* defined in the Standard.

Table. C escape sequences

Sequence	Represents
\a	audible alarm
\b	backspace
\f	form feed
\n	newline
\r	carriage return
\t	tab
\v	vertical tab
\\	backslash
\'	quote
\"	double quote
\?	question mark

It is also possible to use numeric escape sequences to specify a character in terms of the internal value used to represent it. A sequence of either \oooor \xhhhh, where the ooo is up to three octal digits and hhhh is any number of hexadecimal digits respectively.

A common version of it is '\033', which is used by those who know that on an ASCII based machine, octal 33 is the ESC (escape) code.

Beware that the hexadecimal version will absorb any number of valid following hexadecimal digits; if you want a string containing the character whose value is hexadecimal ff followed by a letter f, then the safe way to do it is to use the string joining feature:

"\xff" "f"

The string

"\xfff"

only contains one character, with all three of the fs eaten up in the hexadecimal sequence.

Some of the escape sequences aren't too obvious, so a brief explanation is needed. To get a single quote as a character constant you type '\'', to get a question mark you may have to use '\?'; not that it matters in that example, but to get two of them in there you can't use '??', because the sequence ??' is a trigraph! You would have to use '\?\?'. The escape \" is only necessary in strings, which will come later.

There are two distinct purposes behind the escape sequences. It's obviously necessary to be able to represent characters such as single quote and backslash unambiguously: that is one purpose. The second purpose applies to the following sequences which control the motions of a printing device when they are sent to it, as follows:

```
\a
Ring the bell if there is one. Do not move.
\b
Backspace.
\f
Go to the first position on the 'next page',
whatever that may mean for the output device.
\n
Go to the start of the next line.
\r
Go back to the start of the current line.
\t
Go to the next horizontal tab position.
\v
Go to the start of the line at the next vertical
tab position.
```

For \b, \t, \v, if there is no such position, the behaviour is unspecified. The Standard carefully avoids mentioning the physical directions of movement of the output device which are not necessarily the top to bottom, left to right movements common in Western cultural environments.

It is guaranteed that each escape sequence has a unique integral value which can be stored in a char.

REAL CONSTANTS

These follow the usual format:

```
1.0
2.
.1
2.634
```

```
.125
2.e5
2.e+5
.125e-3
2.5e5
3.1E-6
```

and so on. For readability, even if part of the number is zero, it is a good idea to show it:

```
1.0
0.1
```

The exponent part shows the number of powers of ten that the rest of the number should be raised to, so

```
3.0e3
```

is equivalent in value to the integer constant

```
3000
```

As you can see, the e can also be E. These constants all have type double unless they are suffixed with f or F to mean float or l or L to mean long double. For completeness, here is the formal description of a real constant:

A real constant is one of:

- A *fractional constant* followed by an optional *exponent.*
- A *digit sequence* followed by an *exponent*.

In either case followed by an optional one of f, l, F, L, where:

- A *fractional constant* is one of:
  - An optional *digit sequence* followed by a decimal point followed by a*digit sequence.*
  - A *digit sequence* followed by a decimal point.

Chapter 12

Functions

CHANGES

The worst feature of Old C was that there was no way to declare the number and types of a function's arguments and to have the compiler check that the use of the function was consistent with its declaration. Although it didn't do a lot of damage to the success of C, it did result in portability and maintainability problems that we all could have done without.

The Standard has changed that state of affairs. You can now declare functions in a way that allows their use to be checked, and which is also largely compatible with the old style (so old programs still work, provided they had no errors before). Another useful feature is a portable way of using functions with a variable number of arguments, like printf, which used to be non-portable; the only way to implement it relied upon intimate knowledge of the hardware involved.

The Standard's way of fixing this problem was in large measure to plagiarize fromC++, which had already tried out the new ideas in practice. This model has been so successful that lots of 'Old' C compilers adopted it on their way to conforming to the Standard. The Standard still retains compatibility with Old C function declarations, but that is purely for the benefit of existing programs. Any new programs should make full use of the much tighter checking that the Standard permits and strenuously avoid the old syntax.

TYPE OF FUNCTIONS

All functions have a type: they return a value of that type

whenever they are used. The reason that C doesn't have 'procedures', which in most other languages are simply functions without a value, is that in C it is permissible (in fact well-nigh mandatory) to discard the eventual value of most expressions. If that surprises you, think of an assignment

```
a = 1;
```

That's a perfectly valid assignment, but don't forget that it has a value too. The value is discarded. If you want a bigger surprise, try this one:

```
1;
```

That is an expression followed by a semicolon. It is a well formed statement according to the rules of the language; nothing wrong with it, it is just useless. A function used as a procedure is used in the same way—a value is *always*returned, but you don't use it:

```
f(argument);
```

is also an expression with a discarded value.

It's all very well saying that the value returned by a function can be ignored, but the fact remains that if the function really ***does*** return a value then it's probably a programming error not to do something with it. Conversely, if no useful value is returned then it's a good idea to be able to spot anywhere that it is used by mistake. For both of those reasons, functions that don't return a useful value should be declared to be void.

Functions can return any type supported by C (except for arrays and functions), including the pointers, structures and unions which are described in later chapters. For the types that can't be returned from functions, the restrictions can often be sidestepped by using pointers instead.

All functions can be called recursively.

DECLARING FUNCTIONS

Unfortunately, we are going to have to use some jargon now. This is one of the times that the use of an appropriate technical term really does reduce the amount of repetitive descriptive text that would be needed. With a bit of luck, the result is a shorter, more accurate and less confusing explanation. Here are the terms.

`declaration`

The point at which a name has a type associated with it.

`definition`

Also a declaration, but at this point some storage is reserved for the named object. The rules for what makes a declaration into a definition can be complicated, but are easy for functions: You turn a function declaration into a definition by providing a body for the function in the form of a compound statement.

`formal parameters`
`parameters`

These are the names used inside a function to refer to its arguments.

`actual arguments`
`arguments`

These are the values used as arguments when the function is actually called. In other words, the values that the *formal parameters* will have on entry to the function.

The terms 'parameter' and 'argument' do tend to get used as if they were interchangeable, so don't read too much into it if you see one or the other in the text below.

If you use a function before you declare it, it is implicitly declared to be 'function returning int'. Although this will work, and was widely used in Old C, in Standard C it is bad practice—the use of undeclared functions leads to nasty problems to do with the number and type of arguments that are expected for them. All functions should be fully declared before they are used. For example, you might be intending to use a function in a private library called, say, aax1. You know that it takes no arguments and returns a double.

Here is how it should be declared:

```
double aax1(void);
and here is how it might be used:
main(){
double return_v, aax1(void);
return_v = aax1();
exit(EXIT_SUCCESS);
}
```

The declaration was an interesting one. It defined return_v, actually causing a variable to come into existence. It also declared aax1 without defining it; as we know, functions only become *defined* when a body is provided for them. Without a declaration in force, the default rules mean that aax1 would have been assumed to be int, even though it really does return a double—which means that your programme will have undefined behaviour. Undefined behaviour is disastrous!

The presence of void in the argument list in the declaration shows that the function really takes no arguments. If it had been missing, the declaration would have been taken to give no information about the function's arguments. That way, compatibility with Old C is maintained at the price of the ability of the compiler to check.

To *define* a function you also have to provide a body for it, in the form of a compound statement. Since no function can itself contain the definition of a function, functions are all separate from each other and are only found at the outermost level of the program's structure. Here is a possible definition for the function aax1.

```
double
aax1(void) {
/* code for function body */
return (1.0);
}
```

It is unusual for a block-structured language to prohibit you from defining functions inside other functions, but this is one of the characteristics of C. Although it isn't obvious, this helps to improve the run-time performance of C by reducing the housekeeping associated with function calls.

THE RETURN STATEMENT

The return statement is very important. Every function except those returning voidshould have at least one, each return showing what value is supposed to be returned at that point. Although it is possible to return from a function by falling through the last }, unless the function returns void an unknown value will be returned, resulting in undefined behaviour.

Here is another example function. It uses getchar to read characters from the programme input and returns whatever it sees except for space, tab or newline, which it throws away.

```
#include <stdio.h>
int
non_space(void){
int c;
while ((c=getchar ())=='\t' || c== '\n' || c=='
')
;/* empty statement */
return (c);
}
```

Look at the way that all of the work is done by the test in the while statement, whose body was an empty statement. It is not an uncommon sight to see the semicolon of the empty statement sitting there alone and forlorn, with only a piece of comment for company and readability. Please, please, never write it like this:

```
while (something);
```

with the semicolon hidden away at the end like that. It's too easy to miss it when you read the code, and to assume that the following statement is under the control of the while.

The type of expression returned must match the type of the function, or be capable of being converted to it as if an assignment statement were in use. For example, a function declared to return double could contain

```
return (1);
```

and the integral value will be converted to double. It is also possible to have justreturn without any expression—but this is probably a programming error unless the function returns void. Following the return with an expression is *not* permitted if the function returns void.

ARGUMENTS TO FUNCTIONS

Before the Standard, it was not possible to give any information about a function's arguments except in the definition of the function itself. The information was only used in the body of the function and was forgotten at the end. In those bad old days, it was quite possible to define a function that had three double arguments and only to pass it one int, when it was called.

The programme would compile normally, but simply not work properly. It was considered to be the programmer's job to check that the number and the type of arguments to a function matched correctly. As you would expect, this turned out to be a first-rate source of bugs and portability problems.

Here is an example of the definition and use of a function with arguments, but omitting for the moment to declare the function fully.

```
#include <stdio.h>
#include <stdlib.h>
main(){
void pmax();/* declaration */
int i,j;
for(i = -10; i <= 10; i++){
for(j = -10; j <= 10; j++){
pmax(i,j);
}
}
exit(EXIT_SUCCESS);
}
/*
* Function pmax.
* Returns: void
* Prints larger of its two arguments.
*/
void
pmax(int a1, int a2){/* definition */
int biggest;
if(a1 > a2){
biggest = a1;
}else{
biggest = a2;
}
```

```
printf("larger of %d and %d is %d\n",
a1, a2, biggest);
}
```

To start with, notice the careful declaration that pmaxreturns void. In the function definition, the matching void occurs on the line before the function name. The reason for writing it like that is purely one of style; it makes it easier to find function definitions if their names are always at the beginning of a line.

The function declaration (in main) gave no indication of any arguments to the function, yet the use of the function a couple of lines later involved two arguments. That is permitted by both the old and Standard versions of C, but *must nowadays be considered to be bad practice*. It is much better to include information about the arguments in the declaration too, as we will see. The old style is now an 'obsolescent feature' and may disappear in a later version of the Standard.

Now on to the function definition, where the body is supplied. The definition shows that the function takes two arguments, which will be known as a1 and a2 throughout the body of the function. The types of the arguments are specified too, as can be seen. In the function definition you don't *have* to specify the type of each argument because they will default to int, but this is bad style. If you adopt the practice of always declaring arguments, even if they do happen to be int, it adds to a reader's confidence. It indicates that you meant to use that type, instead of getting it by accident: it wasn't simply forgotten.

The definition of pmax could have been this:

```
/* BAD STYLE OF FUNCTION DEFINITION */
void
pmax(a1, a2){
/* and so on */
```

The proper way to declare and define functions is through the use of *prototypes*.

FUNCTION PROTOTYPES

The introduction of *function prototypes* is the biggest

change of all in the Standard. A function prototype is a function declaration or definition which includes information about the number and types of the arguments that the function takes.

Although you are allowed not to specify any information about a function's arguments in a declaration, it is purely because of backwards compatibility with Old C and should be avoided.

A declaration without any information about the arguments is *not* a prototype.

Here's the previous example 'done right'.

```
#include <stdio.h>
#include <stdlib.h>
main(){
void pmax(int first, int second);/*declaration*/
int i,j;
for(i = -10; i <= 10; i++){
for(j = -10; j <= 10; j++){
pmax(i,j);
}
}
exit(EXIT_SUCCESS);
}
void
pmax(int a1, int a2){/*definition*/
int biggest;
if(a1 > a2){
biggest = a1;
}
else{
biggest = a2;
}
printf("largest of %d and %d is %d\n",
a1, a2, biggest);
}
```

This time, the declaration provides information about the function arguments, so it's a prototype. The names first and second are not an essential part of the declaration, but they are allowed to be there because it makes it easier to refer to named arguments when you're documenting the use of the function. Using them, we can describe the function simply by giving its declaration,

```
void pmax (int xx, int yy);
```

and then say that pmax prints whichever of the arguments xx or yy is the larger. Referring to arguments by their position, which is the alternative (e.g. the fifth argument), is tedious and prone to miscounting.

All the same, you can miss out the names if you want to. This declaration is entirely equivalent to the one above.

```
void pmax (int,int);
```

All that is needed is the type names.

For a function that has no arguments the declaration is

```
void f_name (void);
```

and a function that has one int, one double and an unspecified number of other arguments is declared this way:

```
void f_name (int,double...);
```

The ellipsis (...) shows that other arguments follow. That's useful because it allows functions like printf to be written. Its declaration is this:

```
int printf (const char *format_string...)
```

where the type of the first argument is 'pointer to const char'; we'll discuss what that means later. Once the compiler knows the types of a function's arguments, having seen them in a prototype, it's able to check that the use of the function conforms to the declaration.

If a function is called with arguments of the wrong type, the presence of a prototype means that the actual argument is converted to the type of the formal argument 'as if by assignment'. Here's an example: a function is used to evaluate a square root using Newton's method of successive approximations.

```
#include <stdio.h>
#include <stdlib.h>
#define DELTA 0.0001
main(){
double sq_root(double);/* prototype */
int i;
```

```
for(i = 1; i < 100; i++){
printf("root of %d is %f\n", i, sq_root(i));
}
exit(EXIT_SUCCESS);
}
double
sq_root(double x){/* definition */
double curr_appx, last_appx, diff;
last_appx = x;
diff = DELTA+1;
while(diff > DELTA){
curr_appx = 0.5*(last_appx
+ x/last_appx);
diff = curr_appx - last_appx;
if(diff < 0)
diff = -diff;
last_appx = curr_appx;
}
return(curr_appx);
}
```

The prototype tells everyone that sq_root takes a single argument of type double. The argument actually passed in the main function is an int, so it has to be converted to double first. The critical point is that if no prototype had been seen, C would assume that the programmer had meant to pass an int and an int is what would be passed. The Standard simply notes that this results in undefined behaviour, which is as understated as saying that catching rabies is unfortunate. This is a *very serious error* and has led to many, many problems in Old C programs.

The conversion of int to double could be done because the compiler had seen a protoytpe for the function and knew what to do about it. As you would expect, there are various rules used to decide which conversions are appropriate, so we need to look at them next.

ARGUMENT CONVERSIONS

When a function is called, there are a number of possible

conversions that will be applied to the values supplied as argumeents depending on the presence or absence of a prototype. Let's get one thing clear: although you *can* use these rules to work out what to do if you haven't used prototypes, it is a recipe for pain and misery in the long run. The rules mention the *default argument promotions and compatible type*. Where they are used, the default argument promotions are:

- Apply the integral promotions to the value of each argument
- If the type of the argument is float it is converted to double

The introduction of prototypes (amongst other things) has increased the need for precision about 'compatible types', which was not much of an issue in Old C. For the moment, we will simply work on the basis that if two types are the same, they are indisputably compatible.

The conversions are applied according to these rules (which are intended to be guidance on how to apply the Standard, not a direct quote):

- At the point of calling a function, if no prototype is in scope, the arguments all undergo the default argument promotions. Furthermore:
  - If the number of arguments does not agree with the number of formal parameters to the function, the behaviour is undefined.
  - If the function definition was not a definition containing a prototype, then the type of the actual arguments after promotion must be*compatible* with the types of the formal parameters in the definition after they too have had the promotions applied. Otherwise the behaviour is undefined.
  - If the function definition was a definition containing a prototype, and the types of the actual arguments after promotion are not compatible with the formal parameters in the prototype, then the behaviour is undefined. The behaviour is also undefined it the prototype

included ellipsis (, ...).

- At the point of calling a function, if a prototype *is* in scope, the arguments are converted, as if by assignment, to the types specified in the prototype. Any arguments which fall under the variable argument list category (specified by the ... in the prototype) still undergo the default argument conversions.

It *is* possible to write a programme so badly that you have a prototype in scope when you call the function, but for the function definition itself not to have a prototype. Why anyone should do this is a mystery, but in this case, the function that is called must have a type that is *compatible* with the apparent type at the point of the call.

FUNCTION DEFINITIONS

Function prototypes allow the same text to be used for both the declaration and definition of a function. To turn a declaration:

```
double
some_func(int a1, float a2, long double a3);
```

into a definition, we provide a body for the function:

```
double
some_func(int a1, float a2, long double a3){
/* body of function */
return(1.0);
}
```

by replacing the semicolon at the end of the declaration with a compound statement. In either a definition or a declaration of a function, it serves as a prototype if the parameter types are specified; both of the examples above are prototypes. The Old C syntax for the declaration of a function's formal arguments is still supported by the Standard, although it should not be used by new programs.

It looks like this, for the example above:

```
double
some_func(a1, a2, a3)
```

```
int a1;
float a2;
long double a3;
{
/* body of function */
return(1.0);
}
```

Because no type information is provided for the parameters at the point where they are named, this form of definition does *not* act as a prototype. It declares only the return type of the function; nothing is remembered by the compiler about the types of the arguments at the end of the definition.

- Functions can be called recursively.
- Functions can return any type that you can declare, except for arrays and functions (you can get around that restriction to some extent by using pointers). Functions returning no value should return void.
- Always use function prototypes.
- Undefined behaviour results if you call or define a function anywhere in a programme unless either
  - a prototype is *always* in scope for *every call* or definition, or
  - you are very, very careful.
- Assuming that you *are* using prototypes, the values of the arguments to a function call are converted to the types of the formal parameters exactly as if they had been assigned using the = operator.
- Functions taking no arguments should have a prototype with (void) as the argument specification.
- Functions taking a variable number of arguments must take at least one named argument; the variable arguments are indicated by ... as shown:
- int

```
vfunc(int x, float y...);
```

COMPOUND STATEMENTS AND DECLARATIONS

As we have seen, functions always have a compound

statement as their body. It is possible to declare new variables inside any compound statement; if any variables of the same name already exist, then the old ones are hidden by the new ones within the new compound statement. This is the same as in every other block-structured language. C restricts the declarations to the head of the compound statement (or 'block'); once any other kind of statement has been seen in the block, declarations are no longer permitted within that block.

How can it be possible for names to be hidden? The following example shows it happening:

```
int a;/* visible from here onwards */
void func(void){
float a;/* a different 'a' */
{
char a;/* yet another 'a' */
}
/* the float 'a' reappears */
}
/* the int 'a' reappears */
```

Example: A name declared inside a block hides any outer versions of the same name until the end of the block where it is declared. Inner blocks can also re-declare that name—you can do this for ever.

The *scope* of a name is the range in which it has meaning. Scope starts from the point at which the name is mentioned and continues from there onwards to the end of the block in which it is declared. If it is external (outside of any function) then it continues to the end of the file. If it is internal (inside a function), then it disappears at the end of the block containing it. The scope of any name can be suspended by redeclaring the name inside a block.

Using knowledge of the scope rules, you can play silly tricks like this one:

```
main () {}
int i;
f () {}
f2 () {}
```

Now f and f2 can use i, but main can't, because the

declaration of the variable comes later than that of main. This is not an aspect that is used very much, but it is implicit in the way that C processes declarations. It is a source of confusion for anyone reading the file (external declarations are generally expected to precede any function definitions in a file) and should be avoided.

The Standard has changed things slightly with respect to a function's formal parameters. They are now considered to have been declared inside the first compound statement, even though textually they aren't: this goes for both the new and old ways of function definition. So, if a function has a formal parameter with the same name as something declared in the outermost compound statement, this causes an error which will be detected by the compiler.

In Old C, accidental redefinition of a function's formal parameter was a horrible and particularly difficult mistake to track down.

Here is what it would look like:

```
/* erroneous redeclaration of arguments */
func(a, b, c){
int a;/* AAAAgh! */
}
```

The pernicious bit is the new declaration of a in the body of the function, which hides the parameter called a. Since the problem has now been eliminated we won't investigate it any further.

RECURSION AND ARGUMENT

So far, we've seen how to give functions a type (how to declare the return value and the type of any arguments the function takes), and how the definition is used to give the body of the function. Next we need to see what the arguments can be used for.

CALL BY VALUE

The way that C treats arguments to functions is both simple and consistent, with no exceptions to the single rule. When a function is called, any arguments that are provided by the caller are simply treated as expressions. The value of each expression has the appropriate conversions applied and is then used to initialize the corresponding formal parameter in the called function, which behaves in exactly the same way as any other local variables in the function. It's illustrated here:

```
void called_func(int, float);
main(){
called_func(1, 2*3.5);
exit(EXIT_SUCCESS);
}
void
called_func(int iarg, float farg){
float tmp;
tmp = iarg * farg;
}
```

The arguments to called_func in main are two expressions, which are evaluated. The value of each expression is used to initialize the parameters iarg and farg incalled_func, and the parameters are indistinguishable from the other local variable declared in called_func, which is tmp.

The initialization of the formal parameters is the last time that any communication occurs between the caller and the called function, except for the return value.

For those who are used to FORTRAN and var arguments in Pascal, where a function ***can*** change the values of its arguments: forget it. You cannot affect the values of a function's actual arguments by anything that you try. Here is an example to show what we mean.

```
#include <stdio.h>
#include <stdlib.h>
main(){
void changer(int);
int i;
i = 5;
printf("before i=%d\n", i);
changer(i);
printf("after i=%d\n", i);
exit(EXIT_SUCCESS);
```

```
}
void
changer(int x){
while(x){
printf("changer: x=%d\n", x);
x-;
}
}
The result of running that is:
before i=5
changer: x=5
changer: x=4
changer: x=3
changer: x=2
changer: x=1
after i=5
```

The function changer uses its formal parameter x as an ordinary variable—which is exactly what it is. Although the value of x is changed, the variable i (in main) is unaffected. That is the whole point—the arguments in C are passed into a function by their value only, no changes made by the function are passed back.

RECURSION

With argument passing safely out of the way we can look at recursion. Recursion is a topic that often provokes lengthy and unenlightening arguments from opposing camps. Some think it is wonderful, and use it at every opportunity; some others take exactly the opposite view. Let's just say that when you need it, you really *do* need it, and since it doesn't cost much to put into a language, as you would expect, C supports recursion.

Every function in C may be called from any other or itself. Each invocation of a function causes a new allocation of the variables declared inside it. In fact, the declarations that we have been using until now have had something missing: the keyword auto, meaning 'automatically allocated'.

```
/* Example of auto */
```

```
main(){
auto int var_name;
.
.
.
}
```

The storage for auto variables is automatically allocated and freed on function entry and return. If two functions both declare large automatic arrays, the programme will only have to find room for both arrays if both functions are active at the same time. Although auto is a keyword, it is never used in practice because it's the default for internal declarations and is invalid for external ones. If an explicit initial value (see ' initialization') isn't given for an automatic variable, then its value will be unknown when it is declared. In that state, any use of its value will cause undefined behaviour.

The real problem with illustrating recursion is in the selection of examples. Too often, simple examples are used which don't really get much out of recursion. The problems where it really helps are almost always well out of the grasp of a beginner who is having enough trouble trying to sort out the difference between, say, definition and declaration without wanting the extra burden of having to wrap his or her mind around a new concept as well. The chapter on data structures will show examples of recursion where it is a genuinely useful technique.

The following example uses recursive functions to evaluate expressions involving single digit numbers, the operators *, %, /, +, - and parentheses in the same way that C does. (Stroustrup[1], in his book about C++, uses almost an identical example to illustrate recursion. This happened purely by chance.) The whole expression is evaluated and its value printed when a character not in the 'language' is read. For simplicity no error checking is performed. Extensive use is made of the ungetc library function, which allows the last character read bygetchar to be 'unread' and become once again the next character to be read. Its second argument is one of the things declared in stdio.h.

Those of you who understand BNF notation might like to know that the expressions it will understand are described as follows:

```
<primary>::= digit | (<exp>)
<unary>::= <primary> | -<unary> | +<unary>
<mult>::= <unary> | <mult> * <unary> |
<mult>/ <unary> | <mult>%<unary>
<exp>::= <exp> + <mult> | <exp> - <mult> | <mult>
```

The main places where recursion occurs are in the function unary_exp, which calls itself, and at the bottom level where primary calls the top level all over again to evaluate parenthesized expressions.

If you don't understand what it does, try running it. Trace its actions by hand on inputs such as

```
1
1+2
1+2 * 3+4
1+--4
1+(2*3)+4
```

That should keep you busy for a while!

```
/*
* Recursive descent parser for simple C
expressions.
* Very little error checking.
*/
#include <stdio.h>
#include <stdlib.h>
int expr(void);
int mul_exp(void);
int unary_exp(void);
int primary(void);
main(){
int val;
for(;;){
printf("expression: ");
val = expr();
if(getchar() != '\n'){
printf("error\n");
```

```
while(getchar() != '\n')
;/* NULL */
} else{
printf("result is %d\n", val);
}
}
exit(EXIT_SUCCESS);
}
int
expr(void){
int val, ch_in;
val = mul_exp();
for(;;){
switch(ch_in = getchar()){
default:
ungetc(ch_in,stdin);
return(val);
case '+':
val = val + mul_exp();
break;
case '-':
val = val - mul_exp();
break;
}
}
}
int
mul_exp(void){
int val, ch_in;
val = unary_exp();
for(;;){
switch(ch_in = getchar()){
default:
ungetc(ch_in, stdin);
return(val);
case '*':
val = val * unary_exp();
break;
```

```
case '/':
val = val/ unary_exp();
break;
case '%':
val = val % unary_exp();
break;
}
}
}
int
unary_exp(void){
int val, ch_in;
switch(ch_in = getchar()){
default:
ungetc(ch_in, stdin);
val = primary();
break;
case '+':
val = unary_exp();
break;
case '-':
val = -unary_exp();
break;
}
return(val);
}
int
primary(void){
int val, ch_in;
ch_in = getchar();
if(ch_in >= '0' && ch_in <= '9'){
val = ch_in - '0';
goto out;
}
if(ch_in == '('){
val = expr();
getchar();/* skip closing ')' */
goto out;
```

```
}
printf("error: primary read %d\n", ch_in);
exit(EXIT_FAILURE);
out:
return(val);
}
```

LINKAGE

Although the simple examples have carefully avoided the topic, we now have to look into the effects of scope and linkage, terms used to describe the accessibility of various objects in a C programme. Why bother? It's because realistic programs are built up out of multiple files and of course libraries. It is clearly crucial that functions in one file should be able to refer to functions (or other objects) in other files and libraries; naturally there are a number of concepts and rules that apply to this mechanism.

If you are relatively new to C, there are more important subjects to cover first. Come back to this stuff later instead.

There are essentially two types of object in C: the internal and external objects. The distinction between external and internal is to do with functions: anything declared outside a function is external, anything inside one, including its formal parameters, is internal. Since no function can be defined inside another, functions themselves are always external. At the outermost level, a C programme is a collection of *external objects*.

The term used by the Standard to describe the accessibility of objects from one file to another, or even within the same file, is *linkage*. There are three types of linkage: *external linkage, internal linkage* and *no linkage*. Anything internal to a function—its arguments, variables and so on—*always* has no linkage and so can only be accessed from inside the function itself. (The way around this is to declare something inside a function but prefix it with the keyword extern which says 'it isn't really internal', but we needn't worry about that just yet.)

Objects that have external linkage are all considered to be located at the outermost level of the programme; this is the default linkage for functions and anything declared outside of a function. *All instances of a particular name with external linkage refer to the same object in the programme.* If two or more declarations of the same name have external linkage but incompatible types, then you've done something very silly and have undefined behaviour. The most obvious example of external linkage is the printf function, whose declaration in <stdio.h>is

```
int printf(const char *...);
```

From that we can tell that it's a function returning int and with a particular prototype—so we know everything about its type. We also know that it has external linkage, because that is the default for every external object. As a result, everywhere that the name print is used with external linkage, we are referring to this function.

Quite often, you want to be able to declare functions and other objects within a single file in a way that allows them to reference each other but ***not*** to be accessible from outside that file. This is often necessary in the modules that support library functions, where the additional framework that makes those functions work is not interesting to the user and would be a positive nuisance if the names of those things became visible outside the module. You do it through the use of *internal linkage.*

Names with internal linkage only refer to the same object within a single source file. You do this by prefixing their declarations with the keyword static, which changes the linkage of external objects from external linkage to internal linkage. It is also possible to declare internal objects to be static, but that has an entirely different meaning which we can defer for the moment.

It's confusing that the types of linkage and the types of object are both described by the terms 'internal' and 'external'; this is to some extent historical. C archaeologists may know that at one time the two were equivalent and one implied the other—for us it's unfortunate that the terms remain but the meanings have diverged.

To summarize:

Table. Linkage and accessibility

Type of linkage	Type of object	Accessibility
external	external	throughout the programme
internal	external	a single file
none	internal	local to a single function

Finally, before we see an example, it is important to know that all objects with external linkage must have one and only one definition, although there can be as many compatible declarations as you like.

Here's the example:

```
/* first file */
int i;/* definition */
main () {
void f_in_other_place (void);/* declaration */
i = 0
}
/* end of first file */
/* start of second file */
extern int i;/* declaration */
void f_in_other_place (void){/* definition */
i++;
}
/* end of second file */
```

Although the full set of rules is a bit more complex, the basic way of working out what constitutes a definition and a declaration is not hard:

- A function declaration without a body for the function is just a declaration.
- A function declaration with a body for the function is a definition.
- At the external level, a declaration of an object (like the variablei) is a definition unless it has the keyword extern in front of it, when it is a declaration only.

In the example it's easy to see that each file is able to access the objects defined in the other by using their names. Just from that example alone you should be able to work out how to construct programs with multiple files and functions and variables declared or defined as appropriate in each of them.

Here's another example, using static to restrict the accessibility of functions and other things.

```
/* example library module */
/* only 'callable' is visible outside */
static buf [100];
static length;
static void fillup(void);
int
callable (){
if (length ==0){
fillup ();
}
return (buf [length—]);
}
static void
fillup (void){
while (length <100){
buf [length++] = 0;
}
}
```

A user of this module can safely re-use the names declared here, length, buf, and fillup, without any danger of surprising effects. Only the name callable is accessible outside this module.

A very useful thing to know is that any external object that has no other initalizer (and except for functions we haven't seen any initializers yet) is always set to the value of zero before the programme starts. This is widely used and relied on—the previous example relies on it for the initial value of length.

EFFECT OF SCOPE

There's one additional complicating factor beyond simply linkage. Linkage allows you to couple names together on a per-programme or a per-file basis, but scope determines the visibility of the names. Fortunately, the rules of scope are completely independent of anything to do with linkage, so you don't have to remember funny combinations of both.

What introduces the complexity is the dreaded extern keyword. The nice regular block structure gets blown to pieces with this, which although at a first glance is simple and obvious, does some very nasty things to the fabric of the language. We've already seen it used to ensure that the declaration of something at the outer block level (the external level) of the programme is a declaration and not a definition (but beware: you can still override the extern by, for example, providing an*initializer* for the object).

Unless you prefix it with extern, the declaration of any data object (not a function) at the outer level is also a definition. Look back to Example 4.9 to see this in use.

All function declarations implicitly have the extern stuck in front of them, whether or not you put it there too. These two ways of declaring some_function are equivalent and are always declarations:

```
void some_function(void);
extern void some_function(void);
```

The thing that mysteriously turns those declarations into definitions is that when you also provide the body of the function, that is effectively the initializer for the function, so the comment about initializers comes into effect and the declaration becomes a definition. So far, no problem.

Now, what is going on here?

```
void some_function(void){
int i_var;
extern float e_f_var;
}
void another_func(void){
int i;
i = e_f_var;/* scope problem */
}
```

What happened was that although the declaration of e_f_var declares that something called e_f_var is of type float and is accessible throughout the entire programme, the *scope* of the name disappears at the end of the function that contains it. That's why it is meaningless inside another_func—the name ofe_f_var is out of scope, just as much as i_var is.

So what use is that? It's sometimes handy if you only want to make use of an external object from within a single function. If you followed the usual practice and declared it at the head of the particular source file, then there is no easy way for the reader of that file to see which functions actually use it. By restricting the access and the scope of the name to the place where is needed, you do communicate to a later reader of the programme that this is a very restricted use of the name and that there is no intention to make widespread use of it throughout the file. Of course, any half-way decent cross-reference listing would communicate that anyway, so the argument is a bit hard to maintain.

There's a set of guidelines for how to get the results that are most often wanted from multi-file construction, and a good deal more detail on what happens when you mix extern, static and internal and external declarations. It isn't the sort of reading that you're likely to do for pleasure, but it does answer the 'what if' questions.

INTERNAL STATIC

You are also allowed to declare internal objects as static. Internal variables with this attribute have some interesting properties: they are initialized to zero when the programme starts, they retain their value between entry to and exit from the statement containing their declaration and there is only one copy of each one, which is shared between all recursive calls of the function containing it.

Internal statics can be used for a number of things. One is to count the number of times that a function has been called; unlike ordinary internal variables whose value is lost after leaving their function, statics are convenient for this.

Here's a function that always returns a number between 0 and 15, but remembers how often it was called.

```
int
small_val (void) {
static unsigned count;
```

```
count ++;
return (count % 16);
}
```

They can help detect excessive recursion:

```
void
r_func (void){
static int depth;
depth++;
if (depth > 200) {
printf ("excessive recursion\n");
exit (1);
}
else {
/* do usual thing,
* not shown here.
* This last action
* occasionally results in another
* call on r_func()
*/
x_func();
}
depth—;
}
```

Chapter 13

Arrays and Pointers

IMPORTANCE

The arithmetic data types and operators of C are interesting but hardly rivetting. They show, collectively, a certain imagination and spirit that has stamped C with a special flavour, but they form the sauce, not the meat, of this particular dish. For most users, it's functions and the parts of the language covered in this chapter that provide the real feel of C.

For the new reader, this is the part of the language that causes the biggest problems. Most beginners with C are at least familiar with the use of arithmetic, functions and arrays; those are not the problem areas. The difficulties arise when we get on to the structured types (structures and unions), and the way that C just wouldn't be C without the use of pointers.

Pointers aren't a feature that you can choose to ignore. They're used everywhere; their influence affects the whole language and must be the single most noticeable feature of all but the simplest C programs. If you think that this is one of the bits you can skip because it's hard and doesn't look too important, you are wrong! Most of the examples used so far in this book have had pointers used in them (although not obviously), so you might as well accept the inevitable and learn how to use them properly.

EFFECT OF STANDARD

The new Standard has left very little mark on the contents of this chapter; a lot of it would be nearly word for word the same even if it only talked about Old C. The inference to be drawn is that nothing was wrong with the old version of the language, and that there was nothing to be gained by fixing what wasn't broken. This may be received with some relief by those readers who already knew this part of the old language and who, like the Committee, felt that it was good enough to leave alone.

Even so, the introduction of *qualified types* by the Standard does add some complexity to this chapter. The rules about exactly how the various arithmetic and relational operators work when they are applied to pointers have been clarified, which adds bulk to the text but has not changed things substantially. In the early examples we do not pay a lot of attention to them, but after that they are introduced gradually and where appropriate.

ARRAYS

Like other languages, C uses arrays as a way of describing a collection of variables with identical properties. The group has a single name for all of the members, with the individual members being selected by an *index*.

Here's an array being declared:

```
double ar[100];
```

The name of the array is ar and its members are accessed as ar[0] through toar[99] inclusive, as Figure shows.

Fig. 100 Element Srray

Each of the hundred members is a separate variable whose type is double. Without exception, all arrays in C are numbered from 0 up to one less than the bound given in the declaration. This is a prime cause of surprise to beginners—watch out for it. For simple examples of the use of arrays, look back at earlier chapters where several problems are solved with their help.

One important point about array declarations is that they don't permit the use of varying subscripts. The numbers given must be constant expressions which can be evaluated at compile time, not run time. For example, this function incorrectly tries to use its argument in the size of an array declaration:

```
f(int x){
char var_sized_array[x];/* FORBIDDEN */
}
```

It's forbidden because the value of x is unknown when the programme is compiled; it's a run-time, not a compile-time, value.

MULTIDIMENSIONAL ARRAYS

Multidimensional arrays can be declared like this:

```
int three_dee[5][4][2];
int t_d[2][3]
```

The use of the brackets gives a clue to what is going on. If you refer to the precedence table given, you'll see that [] associates left to right and that, as a result, the first declaration gives us a five-element array called three_dee. The members of that array are each a four element array whose members are an array of two ints. We have declared arrays of arrays, as Figure shows for two dimensions.

t.d[0]			t.d[1]		
t.d [0] [0]	t.d [0] [1]	t.d [0] [2]	t.d [1] [0]	t.d [1] [1]	t.d [1] [2]

Fig. Two-Dimensional Array, Showing Layout

In the diagram, you will notice that t_d[0] is one element, immediately followed byt_d[1] (there is no break). It so happens that both of those elements are themselves arrays of three integers. Because of C's storage layout rules,t_d[1][0] is immediately after t_d[0][2]. It would be possible (but very poor practice) to access t_d[1][0] by making use of the lack of array-bound checking in C, and to use the expression t_d[0][3]. That is not recommended—apart from anything else, if the declaration of t_d ever changes, then the results will be likely to surprise you.

That's all very well, but does it really matter in practice? Not much it's true; but it is interesting to note that in terms of actual machine storage layout the rightmost subscript 'varies fastest'. This has an impact when arrays are accessed via pointers. Otherwise, they can be used just as would be expected; expressions like these are quite in order:

```
three_dee[1][3][1] = 0;
three_dee[4][3][1] += 2;
```

The second of those is interesting for two reasons. First, it accesses the very last member of the entire array—although the subscripts were declared to be[5][4][2], the highest usable subscript is always one less than the one used in the declaration. Second, it shows where the combined assignment operators are a real blessing.

For the experienced C programmer it is much easier to tell that only one array member is being accessed, and that it is being incremented by two.

Other languages would have to express it like this:

```
three_dee[4][3][1] = three_dee[4][3][1] + 2;
```

It takes a conscious effort to check that the same array member is being referenced on both sides of the assignment. It makes thing easier for the compiler too: there is only one array indexing calculation to do, and this is likely to result in shorter, faster code.

Of course a clever compiler would notice that the left- and right-hand sides look alike and would be able to generate equally efficient code—but not all compilers are clever and there are lots of special cases where even clever compilers are unable to make use of the information.

POINTERS

Using pointers is a bit like riding a bicycle. Just when you think that you'll never understand them—suddenly you do! Once learned the trick is hard to forget. There's no real magic to pointers, and a lot of readers will already be familiar with their use.

The only peculiarity of C is how heavily it relies on the use of pointers, compared with other languages, and the relatively permissive view of what you can do with them.

DECLARING POINTERS

Of course, just like other variables, you have to declare

pointers before you can use them. Pointer declarations look much like other declarations: but don't be misled. When pointers are declared, the keyword at the beginning (c int, char and so on) declares the type of variable that the pointer will point to.

The pointer itself is not of that type, it is of type pointer to that type. A given pointer only points to one particular type, not to all possible types.

Here's the declaration of an array and a pointer:

```
int ar[5], *ip;
```

We now have an array and a pointer:

ar [0]	ar [1]	ar [2]	ar [3]	ar [4]
ip				

Fig. An Array and a Pointer

The * in front of ip in the declaration shows that it is a pointer, not an ordinary variable. It is of type pointer to int, and can only be used to refer to variables of type int. It's still uninitialized, so to do anything useful with it, it has to be made to point to something.

You can't just stick some integer value into it, because integer values have the type int, not pointer to int, which is what we want. (In any case, what would it mean if this fragment were valid:

```
ip = 6;
```

What would ip be pointing to? In fact it could be construed to have a number of meanings, but the simple fact is that, in C, that sort of thing is just wrong.)

Here is the right way to initialize a pointer:

```
int ar[5], *ip;
ip = &ar[3];
```

In that example, the pointer is made to point to the member of the array ar whose index is 3, i.e. the fourth member. This is important. You can assign values to pointers just like ordinary variables; the difference is simply in what the value means. The values of the variables that we have now are shown in Figure

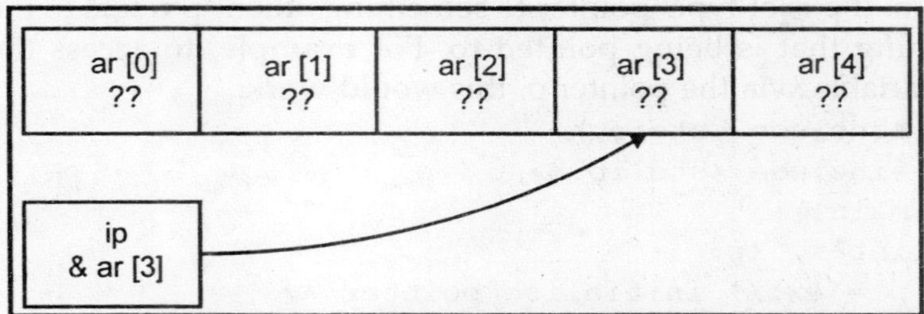

Fig. Array and Initialized Pointer

You can see that the variable ip has the value of the expression &ar[3]. The arrow indicates that, when used as a pointer, ip points to the variable ar[3].

What is this new unary &? It is usually described as the 'address-of' operator, since on many systems the pointer will hold the store address of the thing that it points to. If you understand what addresses are, then you will probably have more trouble than those who don't: thinking about pointers as if they were addresses generally leads to grief. What seems a perfectly reasonable address manipulation on processor X can almost always be shown to be impossible on manufacturer Y's washing machine controller which uses 17-bit addressing when it's on the spin cycle, and reverses the order of odd and even bits when it's out of bleach.

Admittedly, it's unlikely that *anyone* could get C to work an an architecture like that. But you should see some of the ones it *does* work on; they aren't much better.

We will continue to use the term 'address of' though, because to invent a different one would be even worse.

Applying the & operator to an operand returns a pointer to the operand:

```
int i;
float f;
/* '&i' would be of type pointer to int */
/* '&f' would be of type pointer to float */
```

In each case the pointer would point to the object named in the expression.

A pointer is only useful if there's some way of getting at the thing that it points to; C uses the unary * operator for this job. If p is of type 'pointer to something', then *p refers to the thing that is being pointed to. For example, to access the variable xvia the pointer p, this would work:

```
#include <stdio.h>
#include <stdlib.h>
main(){
int x, *p;
p = &x;/* initialise pointer */
*p = 0;/* set x to zero */
printf("x is %d\n", x);
printf("*p is %d\n", *p);
*p += 1;/* increment what p points to */
printf("x is %d\n", x);
(*p)++;/* increment what p points to */
printf("x is %d\n", x);
exit(EXIT_SUCCESS);
}
```

The precedence of (*p)++ deserves some thought. It will be given more later, but for the moment let's work out what happens. The brackets ensure that the * applies to p, so what we have is 'post-increment the thing pointed to by p'. Looking at Table 2.9, it turns out that ++ and * have equal precedence, but they associate right to left; in other words, without the brackets, the implied operation would have been *(p++), whatever that would mean. Later on you'll be more used to it—for the moment, we'll be careful with brackets to show the way that those expressions work.

So, provided that a pointer holds the address of something, the notation *pointeris equivalent to giving the name of the something directly. What benefit do we get from all this? Well, straight away it gets round the call-by-value restriction of functions. Imagine a function that has to return, say, two integers representing a month and a day within that month. The function has some (unspecified) way of determining these values; the hard thing to do is to return two separate values.

Here's a way that it can be done:

```
#include <stdio.h>
```

```
#include <stdlib.h>
void
date(int *, int *);/* declare the function */
main(){
int month, day;
date (&day, &month);
printf("day is %d, month is %d\n", day, month);
exit(EXIT_SUCCESS);
}
void
date(int *day_p, int *month_p){
int day_ret, month_ret;
/*
* At this point, calculate the day and month
* values in day_ret and month_ret respectively.
*/
*day_p = day_ret;
*month_p = month_ret;
}
```

Notice carefully the advance declaration of date showing that it takes two arguments of type 'pointer to int'. It returns void, because the values are passed back via the pointers, not the usual return value. The main function passes pointers as arguments to date, which first uses the internal variables day_ret andmonth_ret for its calculations, then takes those values and assigns them to the places pointed to by its arguments.

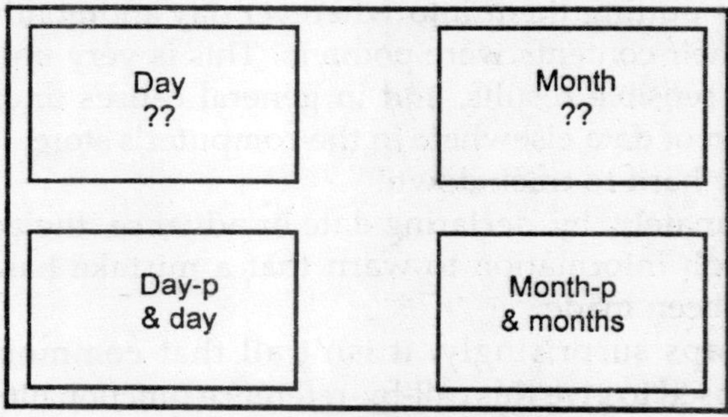

Fig. Just as Date is Called

The arguments have been passed to date, but in main, day and month are uninitialized. When date reaches the return statement, the situation is as shown in Figure (assuming that the values for day and month are 12 and 5 respectively).

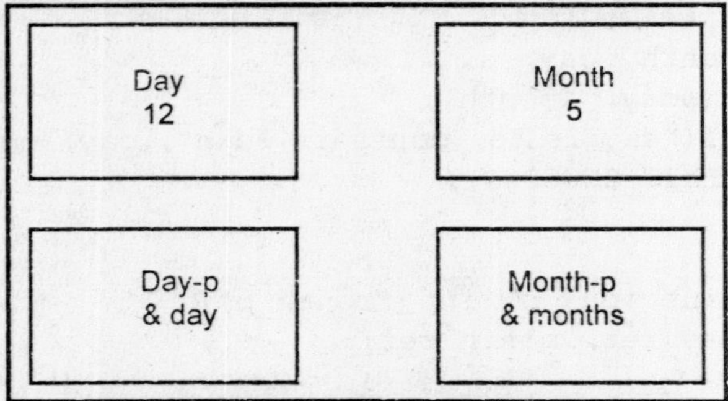

Fig. Just as date is about to Return

One of the great benefits introduced by the new Standard is that it allows the types of the arguments to date to be declared in advance. A great favourite (and disastrous) mistake in C is to forget that a function expects pointers as its arguments, and to pass something else instead. Imagine what would have happened if the call of date above had read date(day, month); and no previous declaration of date had been visible.

The compiler would not have known that date expects pointers as arguments, so it would pass the intvalues of day and month as the arguments. On a large number of computers, pointers and integers can be passed in the same way, so the function would execute, then pass back its return values by putting them into wherever day andmonth would point if their contents were pointers. This is very unlikely to give any sensible results, and in general causes unexpected corruption of data elsewhere in the computer's store. It can be extremely hard to track down!

Fortunately, by declaring date in advance, the compiler has enough information to warn that a mistake has almost certainly been made.

Perhaps surprisingly, it isn't all that common to see pointers used to give this call-by-reference functionality. In the majority of cases, call-by-value and a single return value are adequate. What is *much* more common is to use pointers to 'walk' along arrays.

ARRAYS AND POINTERS ELEMENTS

Array elements are just like other variables: they have addresses.

```
int ar[20], *ip;
ip = &ar[5];
*ip = 0;/* equivalent to ar[5] = 0; */
```

The address of ar[5] is put into ip, then the place pointed to has zero assigned to it. By itself, this isn't particularly exciting. What *is* interesting is the way that pointer arithmetic works. Although it's simple, it's one of the cornerstones of C.

Adding an integral value to a pointer results in another pointer of the same type. Adding *n* gives a pointer which points n elements further along an array than the original pointer did. Since *n* can be negative, subtraction is obviously possible too.

In the example above, a statement of the form:

```
*(ip+1) = 0;
```

would set ar[6] to zero, and so on. Again, this is not obviously any improvement on 'ordinary' ways of accessing an array, but the following is

```
int ar[20], *ip;
for(ip = &ar[0]; ip < &ar[20]; ip++)
*ip = 0;
```

That example is a classic fragment of C. A pointer is set to point to the start of an array, then, while it still points inside the array, array elements are accessed one by one, the pointer incrementing between each one. The Standard endorses existing practice by guaranteeing that it's permissible to use the *address* ofar[20] even though no such element exists. This allows you to use it for checks in loops like the one above. The guarantee only extends to one element beyond the end of an array and no further.

Why is the example better than indexing? Well, most arrays are accessed sequentially. Very few programming examples actually make use of the 'random access' feature of arrays. If you do just want sequential access, using a pointer can give a worthwhile improvement in speed. In terms of the underlying address arithmetic, on most architectures it takes one multiplication and one addition to access a one-dimensional array through a subscript. Pointers require no arithmetic at all—they nearly always hold the store address of the object that they refer to. In the example above, the only arithmetic that has to be done is in the forloop, where one comparison and one addition are done each time round the loop.

The equivalent, using indexes, would be this:

```
int ar[20], i;
for(i = 0; i < 20; i++)
ar[i] = 0;
```

The same amount of arithmetic occurs in the loop statement, but an extra address calculation has to be performed for every array access.

Efficiency is not normally an important issue, but here it can be. Loops often get traversed a substantial number of times, and every microsecond saved in a big loop can matter. It isn't always easy for even a smart compiler to recognize that this is the sort of code that could be 'pointerized' behind the scenes, and to convert from indexing (what the programmer wrote) to actually use a pointer in the generated code.

To be honest, C doesn't really 'understand' array indexing, except in declarations. As far as the compiler is concerned, an expression like x[n] is translated into*(x+n) and use made of the fact that an array name is converted into a pointer to the array's first element whenever the name occurs in an expression. That's why, amongst other things, array elements count from zero: if x is an array name, then in an expression, x is equivalent to &x[0], i.e. a pointer to the first element of the array. So, since *(&x[0]) uses the pointer to get to x[0], *(&x[0] + 5) is the same as *(x + 5) which is the same as x[5]. A curiosity springs out of all this. Ifx[5] is translated into *(x + 5), and the expression x + 5 gives the same result as 5 + x (it does), then 5[x] should give the identical result to x[5]

If you don't believe that, here is a programme that compiles and runs successfully:

```
#include <stdio.h>
#include <stdlib.h>
#define ARSZ 20
main(){
int ar[ARSZ], i;
for(i = 0; i < ARSZ; i++){
ar[i] = i;
i[ar]++;
printf("ar[%d] now = %d\n", i, ar[i]);
}
printf("15[ar] = %d\n", 15[ar]);
exit(EXIT_SUCCESS);
}
```

QUALIFIED TYPES

If you are confident that you have got a good grasp of the basic declaration and use of pointers we can continue. If not, it's important to go back over the previous material and make sure that there is nothing in it that you still find obscure; although what comes next looks more complicated than it really is, there's no need to make it worse by starting unprepared.

The Standard introduces two things called *type qualifiers,* neither of which were in Old C. They can be applied to any declared type to modify its behaviour—hence the term 'qualifier'—and although one of them can be ignored for the moment (the one named volatile), the other, const, cannot.

If a declaration is prefixed with the keyword const, then the thing that is declared is announced to the world as being constant. You must not attempt to modify (change the value of) const objects, or you get undefined behaviour. Unless you have used some very dirty tricks, the compiler will know that the thing you are trying to modify is constant, so it can warn you. There are two benefits in being able to declare things to be const.

- It documents the fact that the thing is unmodifiable

and the compiler helps to check. This is especially reassuring in the case of functions which take pointers as arguments. If the declaration of a function shows that the arguments are pointers to constant objects, then you know that the function is not allowed to change them through the pointers.

- If the compiler knows that things are constant, it can often do increased amounts of optimization or generate better code.

Of course, constants are not much use unless you can assign an initial value to them. We won't go into the rules about initialization here for the moment just note that any declaration can also assign the value of a constant expression to the thing being declared.

Here are some example declarations involving const:

```
const int x = 1;/* x is constant */
const float f = 3.5;/* f is constant */
const char y[10];/* y is an array of 10 const
ints */
/* don't think about initializing it yet! */
```

What is more interesting is that pointers can have this qualifier applied in two ways: either to the thing that it points to (pointer to const), or to the pointer itself (constant pointer).

Here are examples of that:

```
int i;/* i is an ordinary int */
const int ci = 1;/* ci is a constant int */
int *pi;/* pi is a pointer to an int */
const int *pci;/* pc is a pointer to a constant
int */
/* and now the more complicated stuff */
/* cpi is a constant pointer to an int */
int *const cpi = &i;
/* cpci is a constant pointer to an constant
int */
const int *const cpci = &ci;
```

The first declaration (of i) is unsurprising. Next, the declaration of ci shows that it is a constant integer, and therefore may not be modified. If we didn't initialize it, it would be pretty well useless. It isn't hard to understand what a pointer to an integer and a pointer to a constant integer do—but note that they are different types of pointer now and can't be freely intermixed. You can change the values of both pi and pci (so that they point to other things); you can change the value of the thing that pi points to (it's not a constant integer), but you are only allowed to inspect the value of the thing that pcipoints to because that is a constant.

The last two declarations are the most complicated. If the pointers themselves are constant, then you are not allowed to make them point somewhere else—so they need to be initialized, just like ci. Independent of the const or other status of the pointer itself, naturally the thing that it points to can also be const or non-const, with the appropriate constraints on what you can do with it.

A final piece of clarification: what constitutes a qualified type? In the example, ciwas clearly of a qualified type, but pci was not, since the pointer was not qualified, only the thing that it points to. The only things that had qualified type in that list were: ci, cpi, and cpci.

Although the declarations do take some mental gymnastics to understand, it just takes a little time to get used to seeing them, after which you will find that they seem quite natural. The complications come later when we have to explain whether or not you are allowed to (say) compare an ordinary pointer with a constant pointer, and if so, what does it mean? Most of those rules are 'obvious' but they do have to be stated.

POINTER ARITHMETIC

Although a more rigorous description of pointer arithmetic is given later, we'll start with an approximate version that will do for the moment.

Not only can you add an integral value to a pointer, but you can also compare or subtract two pointers of the same type. They must both point into the same array, or the result is undefined. The difference between two pointers is defined to be the number of array elements separating them; the type of this difference is implementation defined and will be one of short, int, or long. This next example shows how the difference can be calculated and used, but before you read it, you need to know an important point.

In an expression the name of an array is converted to a pointer to the first element of the array. The only places where that is not true are when an array name is used in conjunction with sizeof, when a string is used to initialize an array or when the array name is the subject of the address-of operator (unary &). We haven't seen any of those cases yet, they will be discussed later.

Here's the example:

```
#include <stdio.h>
#include <stdlib.h>
#define ARSZ 10
main(){
float fa[ARSZ], *fp1, *fp2;
fp1 = fp2 = fa;/* address of first element */
while(fp2 != &fa[ARSZ]){
printf("Difference: %d\n", (int)(fp2-fp1));
fp2++;
}
exit(EXIT_SUCCESS);
}
```

The pointer fp2 is stepped along the array, and the difference between its current and original values is printed. To make sure that printf isn't handed the wrong type of argument, the difference between the two pointers is forced to be of typeint by using the cast (int). That allows for machines where the difference between two pointers is specified to be long.

Unfortunately, if the difference does happen to be long and the array is enormous, the last example may give the wrong answers. This is a safe version, using a cast to force a long value to be passed:

```
#include <stdio.h>
#define ARSZ 10
main(){
float fa[ARSZ], *fp1, *fp2;
fp1 = fp2 = fa;/* address of first element */
```

```
while(fp2 != &fa[ARSZ]){
printf("Difference: %ld\n", (long)(fp2-fp1));
fp2++;
}
return(0);
}
```

VOID, NULL AND DUBIOUS POINTERS

C is careful to keep track of the type of each pointer and will not in general allow you to use pointers of different types in the same expression. A pointer to char is a different type of pointer from a pointer to int (say) and you cannot assign one to the other, compare them, substitute one for the other as an argument to a function.... in fact they may even be stored differently in memory and even be of different lengths.

Pointers of different types are not the same. There are no implicit conversions from one to the other (unlike the arithmetic types).

There are a few occasions when you *do* want to be able to sidestep some of those restrictions, so what can you do?

The solution is to use the special type, introduced for this purpose, of 'pointer tovoid'. This is one of the Standard's invented features: before, it was tacitly assumed that 'pointer to char' was adequate for the task. This has been a reasonably successful assumption, but was a rather untidy thing to do; the new solution is both safer and less misleading. There isn't any other use for a pointer of that type—void * can't actually point to anything—so it improves readability. A pointer of type void * can have the value of any other pointer assigned to and can, conversely, be assigned to any other pointer. This must be used with great care, because you can end up in some heinous situations. We'll see it being used safely later with the malloc library function.

You may also on occasion want a pointer that is guaranteed not to point to any object—the so-called *null pointer*. It's common practice in C to write routines that return pointers. If, for some reason, they can't return a valid pointer (perhaps in case of an error), then they will indicate failure by returning a null pointer instead. An example could be a table lookup routine, which returns a pointer to the object searched for if it is in the table, or a null pointer if it is not.

How do you write a null pointer? There are two ways of doing it and both of them are equivalent: either an integral constant with the value of 0 or that value converted to type void * by using a cast. Both versions are called the *null pointer constant*. If you assign a null pointer constant to any other pointer, or compare it for equality with any other pointer, then it is first converted the type of that other pointer (neatly solving any problems about type compatibility) and will not appear to have a value that is equal to a pointer to any object in the programme.

The only values that can be assigned to pointers apart from 0 are the values of other pointers of the same type. However, one of the things that makes C a useful replacement for assembly language is that it allows you to do the sort of things that most other languages prevent.

Try this:

```
int *ip;
ip = (int *)6;
*ip = 0xFF;
```

What does that do? The pointer has been initialized to the value of 6 (notice the cast to turn an integer 6 into a pointer). This is a highly machine-specific operation, and the bit pattern that ends up in the pointer is quite possibly nothing like the machine representation of 6. After the initialization, hexadecimal FF is written into wherever the pointer is pointing. The int at location 6 has had 0xFFwritten into it— subject to whatever 'location 6' means on this particular machine.

It may or may not make sense to do that sort of thing; C gives you the power to express it, it's up to you to get it right. As always, it's possible to do things like this by accident, too, and to be ***very*** surprised by the results.

CHARACTER HANDLING

C is widely used for character and string handling applications. This is odd, in some ways, because the language doesn't really have any built-in string handling features. If you're used to languages that know about string handling, you will almost certainly find C tedious to begin with.

The standard library contains lots of functions to help with string processing but the fact remains that it still feels like hard work. To compare two strings you have to call a function instead of using an equality operator. There is a bright side to this, though. It means that the language isn't burdened by having to support string processing directly, which helps to keep it small and less cluttered. What's more, once you get your string handling programs working in C, they do tend to run very quickly.

Character handling in C is done by declaring arrays (or allocating them dynamically) and moving characters in and out of them 'by hand'. Here is an example of a programme which reads text a line at a time from its standard input. If the line consists of the string of characters stop, it stops; otherwise it prints the length of the line. It uses a technique which is invariably used in C programs; it reads the characters into an array and indicates the end of them with an extra character whose value is explicitly 0 (zero). It uses the library strcmp function to compare two strings.

```
#include <stdio.h>
#include <stdlib.h>
#include <string.h>
#define LINELNG 100/* max. length of input line
*/
main(){
char in_line[LINELNG];
char *cp;
int c;
cp = in_line;
while((c = getc(stdin)) != EOF){
if(cp == &in_line[LINELNG-1] || c == '\n'){
/*
* Insert end-of-line marker
*/
*cp = 0;
```

```
if(strcmp(in_line, "stop") == 0)
exit(EXIT_SUCCESS);
else
printf("line was %d characters long\n",
(int)cp-in_line);
cp = in_line;
}
else
*cp++ = c;
}
exit(EXIT_SUCCESS);
}
```

Once more, the example illustrates some interesting methods used widely in C programs. By far the most important is the way that strings are represented and manipulated.

Here is a possible implementation of strcmp, which compares two strings for equality and returns zero if they are the same. The library function actually does a bit more than that, but the added complication can be ignored for the moment. Notice the use of const in the argument declarations. This shows that the function will not modify the contents of the strings, but just inspects them. The definitions of the standard library functions make extensive use of this technique.

```
/*
* Compare two strings for equality.
* Return 'false' if they are.
*/
int
str_eq(const char *s1, const char *s2){
while(*s1 == *s2){
/*
* At end of string return 0.
*/
if(*s1 == 0)
return(0);
s1++; s2++;
}
```

```
/* Difference detected! */
return(1);
}
```

STRINGS

Every C programmer 'knows' what a string is. It is an array of char variables, with the last character in the string followed by a null. 'But I thought a string was something in double quote marks', you cry. You are right, too. In C, a sequence like this,

```
"a string"
```

is really a character array. It's the only example in C where you can declare something at the point of its use.

Be warned: in Old C, strings were stored just like any other character array, and were modifiable. Now, the Standard states that although they are are arrays ofchar, (not const char), attempting to modify them results in undefined behaviour.

Whenever a string in quotes is seen, it has two effects: it provides a declaration and a substitute for a name. It makes a hidden declaration of a char array, whose contents are initialized to the character values in the string, followed by a character whose integer value is zero. The array has no name. So, apart from the name being present, we have a situation like this:

```
char secret[9];
secret[0] = 'a';
secret[1] = ' ';
secret[2] = 's';
secret[3] = 't';
secret[4] = 'r';
secret[5] = 'i';
secret[6] = 'n';
secret[7] = 'g';
secret[8] = 0;
```

an array of characters, terminated by zero, with character values in it. But when it's declared using the string notation, it hasn't got a name.

How can we use it?

Whenever C sees a quoted string, the presence of the string itself serves as the name of the hidden array—not only is the string an implicit sort of declaration, it is as if an array name had been given. Now, we all remember that the name of an array is equivalent to giving the address of its first element, so what is the type of this?

```
"a string"
```

It's a pointer of course: a pointer to the first element of the hidden unnamed array, which is of type char, so the pointer is of type 'pointer to char'. The situation is shown in Figure.

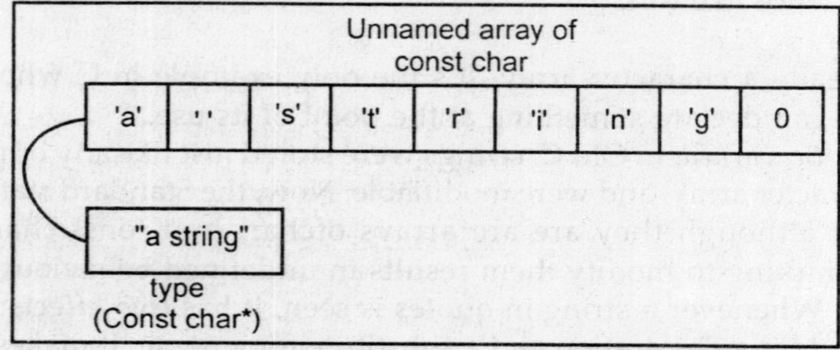

Fig. Effect of using a String

For proof of that, look at the following programme:

```
#include <stdio.h>
#include <stdlib.h>
main(){
int i;
char *cp;
cp = "a string";
while(*cp != 0){
putchar(*cp);
cp++;
}
putchar('\n');
for(i = 0; i < 8; i++)
putchar("a string"[i]);
putchar('\n');
exit(EXIT_SUCCESS);
}
```

The first loop sets a pointer to the start of the array, then walks along until it finds the zero at the end. The second one 'knows' about the length of the string and is less useful as a result. Notice how the first one is independent of the length—that is a most important point to remember.

It's the way that strings are handled in C almost without exception; it's certainly the format that all of the library string manipulation functions expect. The zero at the end allows string processing routines to find out that they have reached the end of the string—look back now to the example function str_eq. The function takes two character pointers as arguments (so a string would be acceptable as one or both arguments). It compares them for equality by checking that the strings are character-for-character the same. If they are the same at any point, then it checks to make sure it hasn't reached the end of them both with if(*s1 == 0): if it has, then it returns 0 to show that they were equal. The test could just as easily have been on *s2, it wouldn't have made any difference. Otherwise a difference has been detected, so it returns 1 to indicate failure.

In the example, strcmp is called with two arguments which look quite different. One is a character array, the other is a string. In fact they're the same thing—a character array terminated by zero (the programme is careful to put a zero in the first 'empty' element of in_line), and a string in quotes—which is a character array terminated by a zero. Their use as arguments to strcmp results in character pointers being passed, for the reasons explained to the point of tedium above.

POINTERS AND INCREMENT OPERATORS

We said that we'd eventually revisit expressions like,

```
(*p)++;
```

and now it's time. Pointers are used so often to walk down arrays that it just seems natural to use the ++ and — operators on them.

Here we write zeros into an array:

```
#define ARLEN 10
int ar[ARLEN], *ip;
```

```
ip = ar;
while(ip < &ar[ARLEN])
*(ip++) = 0;
```

The pointer ip is set to the start of the array. While it remains inside the array, the place that it points to has zero written into it, then the increment takes effect and the pointer is stepped one element along the array. The postfix form of ++ is particularly useful here.

This is very common stuff indeed. In most programs you'll find pointers and increment operators used together like that, not just once or twice, but on almost every line (or so it seems while you find them difficult). What is happening, and what combinations can we get? Well, the * means indirection, and ++ or — mean increment; either pre- or post-increment. The combinations can be pre- or post-increment of either the pointer or the thing it points to, depending on where the brackets are put.

Table gives a list:

Table. Pointer Notation

++(*p)	pre-increment thing pointed to
(*p)++	post-increment thing pointed to
*(p++)	access via pointer, post-increment pointer
*(++p)	access via pointer which has already been incremented

The expressions in the list above can usually be understood after a bit of head-scratching. Now, given that the precedence of *, ++ and — is the same in all three cases and that they associate right to left, can you work out what happens if the brackets are removed? Table shows that there's only one case where the brackets have to be there.

With parentheses Without, if possible,

Table. More pointer notation

++(*p)	++*p
(*p)++	(*p)++
*(p++)	*p++
*(++p)	*++p

The usual reaction to that horrible sight is to decide that you don't care that the parentheses can be removed; you will *always* use them in your code. That's all very well but the problem is that most C programmers have learnt the important precedence rules (or at least learnt the table above) and *they* very rarely put the parentheses in. Like them, we don't—so if you want to be able to read the rest of the examples, you had better learn to read those expressions with or without parentheses. It'll be worth the effort in the end.

UNTYPED POINTERS

In certain cases it's essential to be able to convert pointers from one type to another. This is always done with the aid of casts, in expressions like the one below:

```
(type *) expression
```

The *expression* is converted into 'pointer to *type*', regardless of the expression's previous type. This is only supposed to be done if you're sure that you know what you're trying to do. It is not a good idea to do much of it until you have got plenty of experience. Furthermore, do *not* assume that the cast simply suppresses diagnostics of the 'mismatched pointer' sort from your compiler. On several architectures it is necessary to calculate new values when pointer types are changed.

There are also some occasions when you will want to use a 'generic' pointer. The most common example is the malloc library function, which is used to allocate storage for objects that haven't been declared. It is used by telling it how much storage is wanted—enough for a float, or an array of int, or whatever. It passes back a pointer to enough storage, which it allocates in its own mysterious way from a pool of free storage (the way that it does this is its own business). That pointer is then cast into the right type—for example if a float needs 4 bytes of free store, this is the flavour of what you would write:

```
float *fp;
fp = (float *)malloc(4);
```

Malloc finds 4 bytes of store, then the address of that piece of storage is cast into pointer-to-float and assigned to the pointer. What type should malloc be declared to have? The type must be able to represent every known value of every type of pointer; there is no guarantee that any of the basic types in C can hold such a value.

The solution is to use the void * type that we've already talked about. Here is the last example with a declaration of malloc:

```
void *malloc();
float *fp;
fp = (float *)malloc(4);
```

The rules for assignment of pointers show that there is no need to use a cast on the return value from malloc, but it is often done in practice.

Obviously there needs to be a way to find out what value the argument to mallocshould be: it will be different on different machines, so you can't just use a constant like 4. That is what the sizeof operator is for.

SIZEOF AND STORAGE ALLOCATION

The sizeof operator returns the size in bytes of its operand. Whether the result ofsizeof is unsigned int or unsigned long is implementation defined—which is why the declaration of malloc above ducked the issue by omitting any parameter information; normally you would use the stdlib.h header file to declare malloccorrectly. Here is the last example done portably:

```
#include <stdlib.h>/* declares malloc() */
float *fp;
fp = (float *)malloc(sizeof(float));
```

The operand of sizeof only has to be parenthesized if it's a type name, as it was in the example. If you are using the name of a data object instead, then the parentheses can be omitted, but they rarely are.

```
#include <stdlib.h>
int *ip, ar[100];
ip = (int *)malloc(sizeof ar);
```

In the last example, the array ar is an array of 100 ints; after the call to malloc(assuming that it was successful), ip will point to a region of store that can also be treated as an array of 100 ints.

The fundamental unit of storage in C is the char, and by definition sizeof(char) is equal to 1, so you could allocate space for an array of ten chars with malloc(10) while to allocate room for an array of ten ints, you would have to use malloc(sizeof(int[10]))

If malloc can't find enough free space to satisfy a request it returns a null pointer to indicate failure. For historical reasons, the stdio.h header file contains a defined constant called NULL which is traditionally used to check the return value frommalloc and some other library functions. An explicit 0 or (void *) 0 could equally well be used.

The example is done first using fixed size arrays, then another version uses malloc and allocates space for the strings at run time. Unfortunately, the array of pointers is still fixed in size: a better solution would use a linked list or similar data structure to store the pointers and would have no fixed arrays at all. At the moment, we haven't seen how to do that.

The overall structure is this:

```
while(number of strings read < MAXSTRING
&& input still remains){
read next string;
}
sort array of pointers;
print array of pointers;
exit;
```

A number of functions are used to implement this programme:

```
char *next_string(char *destination)
```

Read a line of characters terminated by '\n' from the program's input. The first MAXLEN-1 characters are written into the array pointed to by destination.

If the first character read is EOF, return a null pointer, otherwise return the address of the start of the string (destination). On return, destination always points to a null-terminated string.

```
void sort_arr(const char *p_array[])
```

P_array[] is an array of pointers to characters. The array can be arbitrarily long; its end is indicated by the first element containing a null pointer.

Sort_arr sorts the pointers so that the pointers point to strings which are in alphabetical order when the array is traversed in index order.

`void print_arr(const char *p_array[])`

Like sort_arr, but prints the strings in index order.

It will help to understand the examples if you remember that in an expression, an array's name is converted to the address of its first element. Similarly, for a two-dimensional array (such as strings below), then the expression strings[1] [2] has type char, but strings[1] has type 'array of char' which is therefore converted to the address of the first element: it is equivalent to &strings[1][0].

```
#include <stdio.h>
#include <stdlib.h>
#include <string.h>
#define MAXSTRING 50/* max no. of strings */
#define MAXLEN 80/* max length. of strings */
void print_arr(const char *p_array[]);
void sort_arr(const char *p_array[]);
char *next_string(char *destination);
main(){
/* leave room for null at end */
char *p_array[MAXSTRING+1];
/* storage for strings */
char strings[MAXSTRING][MAXLEN];
/* count of strings read */
int nstrings;
nstrings = 0;
while(nstrings < MAXSTRING &&
next_string(strings[nstrings]) != 0){
p_array[nstrings] = strings[nstrings];
nstrings++;
}
/* terminate p_array */
p_array[nstrings] = 0;
```

```
sort_arr(p_array);
print_arr(p_array);
exit(EXIT_SUCCESS);
}
void print_arr(const char *p_array[]){
int index;
for(index = 0; p_array[index] != 0; index++)
printf("%s\n", p_array[index]);
}
void sort_arr(const char *p_array[]){
int comp_val, low_index, hi_index;
const char *tmp;
for(low_index = 0;
p_array[low_index] != 0 &&
p_array[low_index+1] != 0;
low_index++){
for(hi_index = low_index+1;
p_array[hi_index] != 0;
hi_index++){
comp_val=strcmp(p_array[hi_index],
p_array[low_index]);
if(comp_val >= 0)
continue;
/* swap strings */
tmp = p_array[hi_index];
p_array[hi_index] = p_array[low_index];
p_array[low_index] = tmp;
}
}
}
char *next_string(char *destination){
char *cp;
int c;
cp = destination;
while((c = getchar()) != '\n' && c != EOF){
if(cp-destination < MAXLEN-1)
*cp++ = c;
}
```

```
*cp = 0;
if(c == EOF && cp == destination)
return(0);
return(destination);
}
```

It is no accident that next_string returns a pointer. We can now dispense with the strings array by getting next_string to allocate its own storage.

```
#include <stdio.h>
#include <stdlib.h>
#include <string.h>
#define MAXSTRING 50/* max no. of strings */
#define MAXLEN 80/* max length. of strings */
void print_arr(const char *p_array[]);
void sort_arr(const char *p_array[]);
char *next_string(void);
main(){
char *p_array[MAXSTRING+1];
int nstrings;
nstrings = 0;
while(nstrings < MAXSTRING &&
(p_array[nstrings] = next_string()) != 0){
nstrings++;
}
/* terminate p_array */
p_array[nstrings] = 0;
sort_arr(p_array);
print_arr(p_array);
exit(EXIT_SUCCESS);
}
void print_arr(const char *p_array[]){
int index;
for(index = 0; p_array[index] != 0; index++)
printf("%s\n", p_array[index]);
}
void sort_arr(const char *p_array[]){
int comp_val, low_index, hi_index;
const char *tmp;
```

```
for(low_index = 0;
p_array[low_index] != 0 &&
p_array[low_index+1] != 0;
low_index++){
for(hi_index = low_index+1;
p_array[hi_index] != 0;
hi_index++){
comp_val=strcmp(p_array[hi_index],
p_array[low_index]);
if(comp_val >= 0)
continue;
/* swap strings */
tmp = p_array[hi_index];
p_array[hi_index] = p_array[low_index];
p_array[low_index] = tmp;
}
}
}
char *next_string(void){
char *cp, *destination;
int c;
destination = (char *)malloc(MAXLEN);
if(destination != 0){
cp = destination;
while((c = getchar()) != '\n' && c != EOF){
if(cp-destination < MAXLEN-1)
*cp++ = c;
}
*cp = 0;
if(c == EOF && cp == destination)
return(0);
}
return(destination);
}
```

Finally, for the extremely brave, here is the whole thing with even p_arrayallocated using malloc. Further, most of the array indexing is rewritten to use pointer notation. If you are feeling queasy, skip this example. It is hard. One word of explanation: char **p means a pointer to a pointer to a character. Many C programmers find this hard to deal with.

```
#include <stdio.h>
#include <stdlib.hi>
#include <string.h>
#define MAXSTRING 50/* max no. of strings */
#define MAXLEN 80/* max length. of strings */
void print_arr(const char **p_array);
void sort_arr(const char **p_array);
char *next_string(void);
main(){
char **p_array;
int nstrings;/* count of strings read */
p_array = (char **)malloc(
sizeof(char *[MAXSTRING+1]));
if(p_array == 0){
printf("No memory\n");
exit(EXIT_FAILURE);
}
nstrings = 0;
while(nstrings < MAXSTRING &&
(p_array[nstrings] = next_string()) != 0){
nstrings++;
}
/* terminate p_array */
p_array[nstrings] = 0;
sort_arr(p_array);
print_arr(p_array);
exit(EXIT_SUCCESS);
}
void print_arr(const char **p_array){
while(*p_array)
printf("%s\n", *p_array++);
}
void sort_arr(const char **p_array){
const char **lo_p, **hi_p, *tmp;
for(lo_p = p_array;
*lo_p != 0 && *(lo_p+1) != 0;
```

```
lo_p++){
for(hi_p = lo_p+1; *hi_p != 0; hi_p++){
if(strcmp(*hi_p, *lo_p) >= 0)
continue;
/* swap strings */
tmp = *hi_p;
*hi_p = *lo_p;
*lo_p = tmp;
}
}
}
char *next_string(void){
char *cp, *destination;
int c;
destination = (char *)malloc(MAXLEN);
if(destination != 0){
cp = destination;
while((c = getchar()) != '\n' && c != EOF){
if(cp-destination < MAXLEN-1)
*cp++ = c;
}
*cp = 0;
if(c == EOF && cp == destination)
return(0);
}
return(destination);
}
```

To further illustrate the use of malloc, another example programme follows which can cope with arbitrarily long strings. It simply reads strings from its standard input, looking for a newline character to mark the end of the string, then prints the string on its standard output. It stops when it detects end-of-file. The characters are put into an array, the end of the string being indicated (as always) by a zero. The newline is not stored, but used to detect when a full line of input should be printed on the output. The programme doesn't know how long the string will be, so it starts by allocating ten characters—enough for a short string.

If the string is more than ten characters long, malloc is called to allocate room for the current string plus ten more characters. The current characters are copied into the new space, the old storage previously allocated is released and the programme continues using the new storage.

To release storage allocated by malloc, the library function free is used. If you don't release storage when it isn't needed any more, it just hangs around taking up space. Using free allows it to be 'given away', or at least re-used later.

The programme reports errors by using fprintf, a close cousin of printf. The only difference between them is that fprintf takes an additional first argument which indicates where its output should go. There are two constants of the right type for this purpose defined in stdio.h. Using stdout indicates that the program's standard output is to be used; stderr refers to the program's standard error stream. On some systems both may be the same, but other systems do make the distinction.

```
#include <stdio.h>
#include <stdlib.h>
#include <string.h>
#define GROW_BY 10/* string grows by 10 chars
*/
main(){
char *str_p, *next_p, *tmp_p;
int ch, need, chars_read;
if(GROW_BY < 2){
fprintf(stderr,
"Growth constant too small\n");
exit(EXIT_FAILURE);
}
str_p = (char *)malloc(GROW_BY);
if(str_p == NULL){
fprintf(stderr,"No initial store\n");
exit(EXIT_FAILURE);
}
next_p = str_p;
chars_read = 0;
while((ch = getchar()) != EOF){
```

```
/*
* Completely restart at each new line.
* There will always be room for the
* terminating zero in the string,
* because of the check further down,
* unless GROW_BY is less than 2,
* and that has already been checked.
*/
if(ch == '\n'){
/* indicate end of line */
*next_p = 0;
printf("%s\n", str_p);
free(str_p);
chars_read = 0;
str_p = (char *)malloc(GROW_BY);
if(str_p == NULL){
fprintf(stderr,"No initial store\n");
exit(EXIT_FAILURE);
}
next_p = str_p;
continue;
}
/*
* Have we reached the end of the current
* allocation ?
*/
if(chars_read == GROW_BY-1){
*next_p = 0;/* mark end of string */
/*
* use pointer subtraction
* to find length of
* current string.
*/
need = next_p - str_p +1;
tmp_p = (char *)malloc(need+GROW_BY);
if(tmp_p == NULL){
fprintf(stderr,"No more store\n");
exit(EXIT_FAILURE);
```

```
}
/*
* Copy the string using library.
*/
strcpy(tmp_p, str_p);
free(str_p);
str_p = tmp_p;
/*
* and reset next_p, character count
*/
next_p = str_p + need-1;
chars_read = 0;
}
/*
* Put character at end of current string.
*/
*next_p++ = ch;
chars_read++;
}
/*
* EOF - but do unprinted characters exist?
*/
if(str_p - next_p){
*next_p = 0;
fprintf(stderr,"Incomplete last line\n");
printf("%s\n", str_p);
}
exit(EXIT_SUCCESS);
}
```

That may not be a particularly realistic example of how to handle arbitrarily long strings—for one thing, the maximum storage demand is *twice* the amount needed for the longest string—but it does actually work. It also costs rather a lot in terms of copying around. Both problems could be reduced by using the library reallocfunction instead.

A more sophisticated method might use a linked list, implemented with the use of*structures,* as described in the next chapter. That would have its drawbacks too though, because then the standard library routines wouldn't work for a different method of storing strings.

WHAT SIZEOF CAN'T DO

One common mistake made by beginners is shown below:

```
#include <stdio.h>
#include <stdlib.h>
const char arr[] = "hello";
const char *cp = arr;
main(){
printf("Size of arr %lu\n", (unsigned long)
sizeof(arr));
printf("Size of *cp %lu\n", (unsigned long)
sizeof(*cp));
exit(EXIT_SUCCESS);
}
```

The numbers printed will ***not*** be the same. The first will, correctly, identify the size of arr as 6; five characters followed by a null. The second one will always, on every system, print 1. That's because the type of *cp is const char, which can only have a size of 1, whereas the type of arr is different: array of const char. The confusion arises because this is the one place that the use of an array is not converted into a pointer first. It is never possible, using sizeof, to find out how long an array a pointer points to; you ***must*** have a genuine array name instead.

TYPE OF SIZEOF

Now comes the question of just what this does:

sizeof (sizeof (anything legal))

That is to say, what type does the result of sizeof have? The answer is that it is implementation defined, and will be either unsigned long or unsigned int, depending on your implementation. There are two safe things to do: either always cast the return value to unsigned long, as the examples have done, or to use the defined type size_t provided in the <stddef.h> header file.

For example:

```
#include <stddef.h>
```

```
#include <stdio.h>
#include <stdlib.h>
main(){
size_t sz;
sz = sizeof(sz);
printf("size of sizeof is %lu\n",
(unsigned long)sz);
exit(EXIT_SUCCESS);
}
```

POINTERS TO FUNCTIONS

A useful technique is the ability to have pointers to functions. Their declaration is easy: write the declaration as it would be for the function, say

```
int func(int a, float b);
```

and simply put brackets around the name and a * in front of it: that declares the pointer. Because of precedence, if you don't parenthesize the name, you declare a function returning a pointer:

```
/* function returning pointer to int */
int *func(int a, float b);
/* pointer to function returning int */
int (*func)(int a, float b);
```

Once you've got the pointer, you can assign the address of the right sort of function just by using its name: like an array, a function name is turned into an address when it's used in an expression.

You can call the function using one of two forms:

```
(*func)(1,2);
/* or */
func(1,2);
```

The second form has been newly blessed by the Standard.

Here's a simple example.

```
#include <stdio.h>
#include <stdlib.h>
void func(int);
main(){
void (*fp)(int);
```

```
fp = func;
(*fp)(1);
fp(2);
exit(EXIT_SUCCESS);
}
void
func(int arg){
printf("%d\n", arg);
}
```

Example: If you like writing finite state machines, you might like to know that you can have an array of pointers to functions, with declaration and use like this:

```
void (*fparr[])(int, float) = {
/* initializers */
};
/* then call one */
fparr[5](1, 3.4);
```

EXPRESSIONS INVOLVING POINTERS

Because of the introduction of qualified types and of the notion of incomplete types, together with the use of void *, there are now some complicated rules about how you can mix pointers and what arithmetic with pointers really permits you to do. Most people will survive quite well without ever learning this explicitly, because a lot of it is 'obvious', but we will include it here in case you do want to know. For the final word in accuracy, obviously you will want to see what the Standard says. What follows is our interpretation in (hopefully) plainer English.

You don't yet know the Standard means when it talks about *objects* or *incomplete types*. So far we have tended to use the term loosely, but properly speaking an object is a piece of data storage whose contents is to be interpreted as a value. A function is not an object. An incomplete type is one whose name and type are mostly known, but whose size hasn't yet been determined. You can get these in two ways:

- By declaring an array but omitting information about its size: int x[];. In that case, there must be additional information given later in a definition for the array. The type remains incomplete until the later definition.

- By declaring a *structure* or *union* but not defining its contents. The contents must be defined in a later declaration. The type remains incomplete until the later declaration.

CONVERSIONS

Pointers to void can be freely converted backwards and forwards with pointers to any object or incomplete type. Converting a pointer to an object or an incomplete type to void * and then back gives a value which is equal to the original one:

```
int i;
int *ip;
void *vp;
ip = &i;
vp = ip;
ip = vp;
if(ip != &i)
printf("Compiler error\n");
```

An unqualified pointer type may be converted to a qualified pointer type, but the reverse is not true. The two values will be equal:

```
int i;
int *ip;
const int *cpi;
ip = &i;
cpi = ip;/* permitted */
if(cpi != ip)
printf("Compiler error\n");
ip = cpi;/* not permitted */
```

A null pointer constant (see earlier) will not be equal to a pointer to any object or function.

ARITHMETIC

Expressions can add (or subtract, which is equivalent to adding negative values) integral values to the value of a pointer to any object type. The result has the type of the pointer and if *n* is added, then the result points *n* array elements away from the pointer. The most common use is repeatedly to add 1 to a pointer to step it from the start to the end of an array, but addition or subtraction of values other than one is possible.

Two pointers to *compatible types* whether or not qualified may be subtracted. The result has the type ptrdiff_t, which is defined in the header file <stddef.h>. Both pointers must point into the same array, or one past the end of the array, otherwise the behaviour is undefined. The value of the result is the number of array elements that separate the two pointers. E.g.:

```
int x[100];
int *pi, *cpi = &x[99];/* cpi points to the
last element of x */
pi = x;
if((cpi - pi) != 99)
printf("Error\n");
pi = cpi;
pi++;/* increment past end of x */
if((pi - cpi) != 1)
printf("Error\n");
```

RELATIONAL EXPRESSIONS

These allow us to compare pointers with each other. You can only compare:

- Pointers to compatible object types with each other
- Pointers to compatible incomplete types with each other

It does not matter if the types that are pointed to are qualified or unqualified. If two pointers compare equal to each other then they point to the same thing, whether it is an object or the non-existent element off the end of an array (see arithmetic, above). If two pointers point to the same thing, then they compare equal to each other. The relational operators >, <= and so on all give the result that you would expect if the pointers point into the same array: if one pointer compares less than another, then it points nearer to the front of the array.

A null pointer constant can be assigned to a pointer; that

pointer will then compare equal to the null pointer constant (which is pretty obvious). A null pointer constant or a null pointer will not compare equal to a pointer that points to anything which actually exists.

ASSIGNMENT

You can use pointers with the assignment operators if the following conditions are met:

- The left-hand operand is a pointer and the right-hand operand is a null pointer constant.
- One operand is a pointer to an object or incomplete type; the other is a pointer to void (whether qualified or not).
- Both of the operands are pointers to compatible types

In the last two cases, the type pointed to by the left-hand side must have at least the same qualifiers as the type pointed to by the right-hand side (possibly more). So, you can assign a pointer to int to a pointer to const int (more qualifiers on the left than the right) but you cannot assign a pointer to const int to a pointer toint. If you think about it, it makes sense. The += and -= operators can involve pointers as long as the left-hand side is a pointer to an object and the right-hand side is an integral expression. The arithmetic rules above describe what happens.

ARRAYS, OPERATOR AND FUNCTION

We have already emphasized that in most cases, the name of an array is converted into the address of its first element; one notable exception being when it is the operand of sizeof, which is essential if the stuff to do with malloc is to work. Another case is when an array name is the operand of the & address-of operator. Here, it is converted into the *address of the whole array*. What's the difference? Even if you think that addresses would be in some way 'the same', the critical difference is that they have different types. For an array of n elements of type T, then the address of the first element has type 'pointer to T'; the address of the whole array has type 'pointer to array of *n* elements of type T'; clearly very different.

Here's an example of it:

```
int ar[10];
int *ip;
int (*ar10i)[10];/* pointer to array of 10 ints
*/
ip = ar;/* address of first element */
ip = &ar[0];/* address of first element */
ar10i = &ar;/* address of whole array */
```

Where do pointers to arrays matter? Not often, in truth, although of course we know that declarations that look like multidimensional arrays are really arrays of arrays. Here is an example which uses that fact, but you'll have to work out what it does for yourself. It is *not* common to do this sort of thing in practice:

```
int ar2d[5][4];
int (*ar4i)[4];/* pointer to array of 4 ints */
for(ar4i= ar2d; ar4i < &(ar2d[5]); ar4i++)
(*ar4i)[2] = 0;/* ar2d[n][2] = 0 */
```

More important than addresses of arrays is what happens when you declare a function that takes an array as an argument. Because of the 'conversion to the address of its first element' rule, even if you do try to pass an array to a function by giving its name as an argument, you actually end up passing a pointer to its first element. The usual rule really does apply in this case! But what if you declare that the function *does* have an argument whose type is 'array of something'—like this:

```
void f(int ar[10]);
```

What happens? The answer may suprise you slightly. The compiler looks at that and says to itself 'Ho ho. That's going to be a pointer when the function is called' and then rewrites the parameter type to be a pointer. As a result, all three of these declarations are identical:

```
void f(int ar[10]);
void f(int *ar);
void f(int ar[]);/* since the size of the array
is irrelevant! */
```

Chapter 14

Libraries

INTRODUCTION

There is no doubt that the Standard Committee's decision to define a set of library routines will prove to be a huge benefit to users of C. Previously there were *no*standard, accepted, definitions of library routines to provide support for the language. As a result, portability suffered seriously.

The library routines do not have to be present; they will only be present in a *hosted environment*—typically the case for applications programmers. Writers of embedded systems and the writers of the hosted environment libraries will not have the libraries present. They are using 'raw' C, in a *freestanding environment*, and this chapter will not be of much interest to them. The descriptions (except for this introduction) are not meant to be read as a whole chapter, but as individual pieces. The material included here is meant more for information and convenient reference than as a full tutorial introduction. It would take a full book by itself to do real justice to the libraries.

HEADERS AND STANDARD TYPES

A number of types and macros are used widely by the library functions. Where necessary, they are defined in the appropriate #include file for that function. The header will also declare appropriate types and prototypes for the library functions. Some important points should be noted here:

- All external identifiers and macro names declared in any of the library headers are reserved. They must not be used, or redefined, for any other purpose. In some cases they may be 'magic'—their names may be known to the compiler and cause it to use special methods to implement them.

- All identifiers that begin with an underscore are reserved.
- Headers may be included in any order, and more than once, but must be included outside of any external declaration or definition and before any use of the functions or macros defined inside them.
- Giving a 'bad value' to a function—say a null pointer, or a value outside the range of values expected by the function—results in undefined behaviour unless otherwise stated.

The Standard headers are:

```
<assert.h> <locale.h> <stddef.h>
<ctype.h> <math.h> <stdio.h>
<errno.h> <setjmp.h> <stdlib.h>
<float.h> <signal.h> <string.h>
<limits.h> <stdarg.h> <time.h>
```

A last general point is that many of the library routines may be implemented as macros, provided that there will be no problems to do with side-effects (asChapter 7 describes). The Standard guarantees that, if a function *is* normally implemented as a macro, there will also be a true function provided to do the same job.

To use the real function, either undefine the macro name with #undef, or enclose its name in parentheses, which ensures that it won't be treated as a macro:

```
some function("Might be a macro\n");
(some function)("Can't be a macro\n");
```

CHARACTER SET AND CULTURAL DEPENDENCIES

The Committee has introduced features that attempt to cater for the use of C in environments which are not based on the character set of US ASCII and where there are cultural dependencies such as the use of comma or full stop to indicate the decimal point. Facilities have been provided for setting a program's idea of its *locale*, which is used to control the behaviour of the library functions.

Providing full support for different native languages and customs is a difficult and poorly understood task; the facilities provided by the C library are only a first step on the road to a full solution.

In several places the 'C locale' is referred to. This is the only locale defined by the Standard and effectively provides support for the way that Old C worked. Other locale settings may provide different behaviour in implementation-defined ways.

THE <STDDEF.H> HEADER

There are a small number of types and macros, found in <stddef.h>, which are widely used in other headers. They are described in the following paragraphs.

Subtracting one pointer from another gives a result whose type differs between different implementations. To allow safe use of the difference, the type is defined in <stddef.h> to be ptrdiff_t. Similarly, you can use size_t to store the result ofsizeof.

For reasons which still escape us, there is an 'implementation defined null pointer constant' defined in <stddef.h> called NULL. Since the language explicitly defines the integer constant 0 to be the value which can be assigned to, and compared with, a null pointer, this would seem to be unnecessary. However, it is *very*common practice among experienced C programmers to write this sort of thing:

```
#include <stdio.h>
#include <stddef.h>
FILE *fp;
if((fp = fopen("somefile", "r")) != NULL){
/* and so on */
```

There is also a macro called offsetof which can be used to find the offset, in bytes, of a structure member. The offset is the distance between the member and the start of the structure.

It would be used like this:

```
#include <stdio.h>
```

```
#include <stdlib.h>
#include <stddef.h>
main(){
size_t distance;
struct x{
int a, b, c;
}s_tr;
distance = offsetof(s_tr, c);
printf("Offset of x.c is %lu bytes\n",
(unsigned long)distance);
exit(EXIT_SUCCESS);
}
```

Example: The expression s_tr.c must be capable of evaluation as an address constant. If the member whose offset you want is a bitfield, then you're out of luck; offsetof has undefined behaviour in that case.

Note carefully the way that a size_t has to be cast to the longest possible unsigned type to ensure that not only is the argument to printf of the type that it expects (%luis the format string for unsigned long), but also no precision is lost. This is all because the type of size_t is not known to the programmer.

The last item declared in <stddef.h> is wchar_t, an integral type large enough to hold a wide character from any supported extended character sets.

THE <ERRNO.H> HEADER

This header defines errno along with the macros EDOM and ERANGE, which expand to nonzero integral constant expressions; their form is additionally guaranteed to be acceptable to #if directives. The latter two are used by the mathematical functions to report which kind of errors they encountered and are more fully described later.

Errno is provided to tell you when library functions have detected an error. It is not necessarily, as it used to be, an external variable, but is now a modifiable lvalue that has type int. It is set to zero at programme start-up, but from then on never reset unless explicitly assigned to; in particular, the library routines never reset it. If an error occurs in a library routine, errno is set to a particular value to indicate what went wrong, and the routine returns a value (often "1) to indicate that it failed.

The usual use is like this:

```
#include <stdio.h>
#include <stddef.h>
#include <errno.h>
errno = 0;
if(some_library_function(arguments) < 0){
/* error processing code... */
/* may use value of errno directly */
```

The implementation of errno is not known to the programmer, so don't try to do anything other than reset it or inspect its value. It isn't guaranteed to have an address, for example. What's more, you should only check errno if the particular library function in use documents its effect on errno. Other library functions are free to set it to arbitrary values after a call unless their description explicitly states what they do with it.

DIAGNOSTICS

While you are debugging programs, it is often useful to check that the value of an expression is the one that you expected. The assert function provides such a diagnostic aid.

In order to use assert you must first include the header file <assert.h>.

The function is defined as,

```
#include <assert.h>
void assert(int expression)
```

If the expression evaluates to zero (i.e. false) then assert will write a message about the failing expression, including the name of the source file, the line at which the assertion was made and the expression itself. After this, the abort function is called, which will halt the programme.

```
assert(1 == 2);
/* Might result in */
Assertion failed: 1 == 2, file silly.c, line 15
```

Assert is actually defined as a macro, not as a real function.

In order to disable assertions when a programme is found to work satisfactorily, defining the name NDEBUG *before* including <assert.h> will disable assertions totally. You should beware of side effects that the expression may have: when assertions are turned off with NDEBUG, the expression is *not* evaluated. Thus the following example will behave unexpectedly when debugging is turned off with the #define NDEBUG.

```
#define NDEBUG
#include <assert.h>
void
func(void)
{
int c;
assert((c = getchar()) != EOF);
putchar(c);
}
```

CHARACTER HANDLING

There are a variety of functions provided for testing and mapping characters. The testing functions, which are described first, allow you to test if a character is of a particular type, such as alphabetic, upper or lower case, numeric, a control character, a punctuation mark, printable or not and so on.

The character testing functions return an integer, either zero if the character supplied is not of the category specified, or non-zero if it was. The functions all take an integer argument, which should either be an int, the value of which should be representable as unsigned char, or the integer constant EOF, as returned from functions such as getchar(). The behaviour is undefined if it is not.

These functions depend on the program's locale setting.

A *printing character* is a member of an implementation defined character set. Each printing character occupies one printing position. A *control character* is a member of an implementation defined character set, each of which is not a printing character. If the 7-bit ASCII character set is used, the printing characters are ᵗhose that lie between space (0x20) and tilde (0x7e), the control characters are those between NUL (0x0) and US (0x1f), and the character DEL (0x7f).

The following is a summary of all the character testing functions. The header<ctype.h> must be included before any of them is used.

`isalnum(int c)`

True if c is alphabetic or a digit; specifically (isalpha(c) || isdigit (c)).

`isalpha(int c)`

True if (isupper(c)||islower(c)).

Also true for an implementation-defined set of characters which do not return true results from any of iscntrl, isdigit, ispunct or isspace. In the C locale, this extra set of characters is empty.

`iscntrl(int c)`

True if c is a control character.

`isdigit(int c)`

True if c is a decimal digit.

`isgraph(int c)`

True if c is any printing character except space.

`islower(int c)`

True if c is a lower case alphabetic letter. Also true for an implementation defined set of characters which do not return true results from any ofiscntrl, isdigit, ispunct or isspace. In the C locale, this extra set of characters is empty.

`isprint(int c)`

True if c is a printing character (including space).

`ispunct(int c)`

True if c is any printing character that is neither a space nor a character which would return true from isalnum.

`isspace(int c)`

True if c is either a white space character (one of ' ' '\f' '\n' '\r' '\t' '\v') or, in other than the C locale, characters which would not return true from isalnum

`isupper(int c)`

True if c is an upper case alphabetic character.

Also true for an implementation-defined set of characters which do not return true results from any of iscntrl, isdigit, ispunct or isspace. In the C locale, this extra set of characters is empty.

```
isxdigit(int c)
```

True if c is a valid hexadecimal digit.

Two additional functions map characters from one set into another. The functiontolower will, if given a upper case character as its argument, return the lower case equivalent.

For example,

```
tolower('A') == 'a'
```

If tolower is given any character other than an upper case letter, it will return that character.

The converse function toupper maps lower case alphabetic letters onto their upper case equivalent.

For each, the conversion is only performed if there *is* a corresponding character in the alternate case. In some locales, not all upper case characters have lower case equivalents, and vice versa.

LOCALIZATION

This is where the program's idea of its current locale can be controlled. The header file <locale.h> declares the setlocale and localeconv functions and a number of macros:

LC_ALL
LC_COLLATE
LC_CTYPE
LC_MONETARY
LC_NUMERIC
LC_TIME

all of which expand to integral constant expressions and are used as values of thecategory argument to setlocale (other names may also be defined: they will all start with LC_X where X is an upper case letter), and the type

```
struct lconv
```

which is used for storing information about the formatting of numeric values. For members of type char, CHAR_MAX is used to indicate that the value is not available in the current locale.

```
lconv contains at least the following members:
```

`char *decimal_point`

The character used for the decimal point in formatted non-monetary values."." in the C locale.

`char *thousands_sep`

The character used for separating groups of digits to the left of the decimal point in formatted non-monetary values. "" in the C locale.

`char *grouping`

Defines the number of digits in each group when formatting non-monetary values. The elements are interpreted as follows: A value of CHAR_MAXindicates that no further grouping is to be performed; 0 indicates that the previous element should be repeated for the remaining digits; if any other character is used, its integer value represents the number of digits that comprise the current group (the next character in the sequence is interpreted before grouping). "" in the C locale. As an example, "\3"specifies that digits should be grouped in threes; the terminating null in the string signifies that the \3 repeats.

`char *int_curr_symbol`

The first three characters are used to hold the alphabetic international currency symbol for the current locale, the fourth character is used to separate the international currency symbol from the monetary quantity. "" in the C locale.

`char *currency_symbol`

The currency symbol for the current locale. "" in the C locale.

`char *mon_decimal_point`

The character used as the decimal point when formatting monetary values."" in the C locale.

`char *mon_thousands_sep`

The digit group separator for formatted monetary values. "" in the C locale.

`char *mon_grouping`

Defines the number of digits in each group when formatting monetary values. Its elements are interpreted as those for grouping. "" in the C locale.

`char *positive_sign`

The string used to signify a non-negative monetary value. "" in the C locale.

`char *negative_sign`

The string used to signify a negative monetary value. "" in the C locale.

`char int_frac_digits`

The number of digits to be displayed after the decimal point in an internationally formatted monetary value. CHAR_MAX in the C locale.

`char frac_digits`

The number of digits to be displayed after the decimal point in a non-internationally formatted monetary value. CHAR_MAX in the C locale.

`char p_cs_precedes`

A value of 1 indicates that the currency_symbol should precede the value when formatting a non-negative monetary quantity; a value of 0 indicates that it should follow. CHAR_MAX in the C locale.

`char p_sep_by_space`

A value of 1 indicates that the currency symbol is separated by a space from the value when formatting a non-negative monetary quantity; 0 indicates no space. CHAR_MAX in the C locale.

`char n_cs_precedes`

As p_cs_precedes for negative monetary values. CHAR_MAX in the C locale.

`char n_sep_by_space`

As p_sep_by_space for negative monetary values. CHAR_MAX in the C locale.

`char p_sign_posn`

Index